# ESPIONAGE

A Reference Handbook

Other Titles in ABC-CLIO's
# CONTEMPORARY
# WORLD ISSUES
Series

*Capital Punishment, Second Edition*, Michael Kronenwetter
*Courts and Trials*, Christopher E. Smith
*Media and Politics in America*, Guido H. Stempel III
*Nuclear Weapons and Nonproliferation*, Sarah J. Diehl and James
    Clay Moltz
*Police Misconduct in America*, Dean J. Champion
*The Religious Right, Second Edition*, Glenn H. Utter and John W.
    Storey
*U.S. National Security*, Cynthia Watson
*War Crimes and Justice*, Howard Ball
*Women in Prison*, Cyndi Banks
*World Population*, Geoffrey Gilbert

Books in the Contemporary World Issues series address vital issues in today's society such as terrorism, sexual harassment, homelessness, AIDS, gambling, animal rights, and air pollution. Written by professional writers, scholars, and nonacademic experts, these books are authoritative, clearly written, up-to-date, and objective. They provide a good starting point for research by high school and college students, scholars, and general readers as well as by legislators, businesspeople, activists, and others.

Each book, carefully organized and easy to use, contains an overview of the subject; a detailed chronology; biographical sketches; facts and data and/or documents and other primary-source material; a directory of organizations and agencies; annotated lists of print and nonprint resources; a glossary; and an index.

Readers of books in the Contemporary World Issues series will find the information they need in order to better understand the social, political, environmental, and economic issues facing the world today.

# ESPIONAGE

## A Reference Handbook

Glenn Hastedt

**CONTEMPORARY WORLD ISSUES**

**ABC-CLIO**

Santa Barbara, California
Denver, Colorado
Oxford, England

Library of Congress Cataloging-in-Publication Data

Hastedt, Glenn.
   Espionage : a reference handbook / Glenn Hastedt.—1st ed.
      p. cm.—(Contemporary world issues)
Summary: Explores the role that espionage plays in world politics today, discussing how it has changed over time, profiling famous spies, and pointing out the key role that advanced warning plays in national security. Includes bibliographical references and index.
   ISBN 1-57607-950-3 (alk. paper); ISBN 1-57607-951-1 (e-book)
   1.  Espionage—History—20th century. 2.  Espionage—History. 3. Spies—History—20th century. [1. Espionage. 2. Spies. 3. Intelligence service.] I. Title. II. Series.

JF1525.I6H36  2003
327.12—dc21

                                                                      2003009680


07   06   05   04   03   9   8   7   6   5   4   3   2   1

This book is also available on the World Wide Web as an e-book. Visit abc-clio.com for details.

ABC-CLIO, Inc.
130 Cremona Drive, P.O. Box 1911
Santa Barbara, California 93116-1911

This book is printed on acid-free paper ∞.
Manufactured in the United States of America

*To Cathy, Sarah, and Matthew*

# Contents

# Preface and Acknowledgments

Espionage and its inevitable partner, counterespionage, are central to the pursuit of a state's national security. This is true regardless of whether the state is large or small, rich or poor, democratic or authoritarian, new or old. Without intelligence about the plans and capabilities of others, and the ability to protect one's own plans and capabilities from being discovered, a state's foreign policy will be ineffective and ultimately doomed to failure. For all of its importance, however, most of us know very little about espionage. It receives far less attention than covert action or intelligence analysis in academic literature, and it appears in the popular literature irregularly and most frequently as a journalistic account of an exposed spy's life history that is written in a "whodunit" fashion that pits the spy against the spy catcher. Although spies and spy catchers are the central players in the game of espionage, in a democracy there is a third key actor: the overseers whose task it is to make sure that laws are obeyed and citizens' rights are protected. More often than not they come onto the scene only after transgressions have been committed or intelligence failures revealed.

This reference handbook introduces interested readers to the field of espionage and provides a road map of where to go next to gain additional insight. It presumes no special knowledge, only an interest in the subject. Increased knowledge about espionage is especially important today in the world after 9/11. Anxieties about the ability to protect American national security have been raised as new threats and enemies appear. Espionage and counterespionage are emerging as central policy tools to address these national security concerns. An enlightened public discussion of American national security policy in the coming years requires that we obtain a better understanding of the potentials and pitfalls of espionage.

Chapter 1 provides an overview of espionage in the United States going back to the American Revolution. In addition to providing a historical context for understanding the present, the chapter also introduces key themes and people in American espionage. Chapter 2 surveys the major academic and policy debates surrounding the conduct of espionage and counterespionage. It is organized around ten major themes and issues and provides readers with the "big picture" of espionage policy. Chapter 3 places espionage in a comparative and global context. The operation of the British, Chinese, Russian, and Israeli intelligence agencies are detailed as they relate to espionage. Case studies of important espionage events are presented for each. Chapter 4 presents biographical sketches of important figures in espionage who have been introduced in previous chapters. Here an effort is made to summarize key events in their lives and their roles either as spies, spy catchers, or spy overseers. Chapter 5 presents a selection of key U.S. government espionage documents. They provide an overview of the legal and institutional environment in which the spies and spy catchers have operated in the United States. The documents are organized into three sections: organizational procedures and authorities to act, laws, and evidence of domestic spying. Chapter 6 presents a brief chronology of key espionage events and chapter 7 provides an annotated bibliography of print and nonprint resources on espionage.

I would like to thank Alicia Merritt and Gina Zondorak at ABC-CLIO for all of their hard work and efforts on this project. At James Madison Uniersity I would like to thank Gordon Miller, Political Science Liaison Librarian, for his help on this project. Over the years, Gordon has given untiringly of his time to the faculty and students in the political science department and at JMU in aiding and simplifying their research efforts.

# 1

# Espionage in the United States

Espionage is the act of secretly collecting information. Americans more commonly refer to it as spying. Though in the United States people tend to associate spying with the Cold War, it is an age-old activity. By necessity espionage occurs out of sight; only occasionally does it burst out of the shadows and into the open. However, even then a full picture rarely emerges. People find bits and pieces of evidence that point to an explanation for why an act of espionage occurred or how it was discovered, but important questions frequently remain unanswered long after the fact. This chapter will present a historical overview of espionage involving the United States.

Two points are worth noting in advance. First, this is a history told more in terms of the activities of individuals than of organizations, because it is only relatively recently that large intelligence bureaucracies have become prominent features of the national security landscape. Second, the history of espionage entails telling more than one story. Two play at the "spy game"; there are spies and spy catchers.

## The American Revolution

For most observers the history of American espionage begins after World War II when the United States abandoned its staunch isolationist outlook on world affairs and entered into the Cold War with the Soviet Union. A closer look reveals that a much

1

longer legacy exists, though. Several notable cases of espionage occurred during the period surrounding the American Revolution. For example, after the Boston Tea Party a group of some thirty Americans formed the Revere Gang or Mechanics to secretly gather information about British troop movements. It was their information that provided warning to the Minutemen about the pending British advance on Lexington.

In 1776 with his retreating forces threatened by superior British firepower, General George Washington enlisted the services of Nathan Hale to spy on the British. Hale is best remembered for his famous last words, "I only regret that I have but one life to lose for my country" (Corson 1977, 490). Hale joined the Continental army in 1775 and agreed to be a spy only after his commanding officer had twice failed to obtain a volunteer as requested by Washington. Hale posed as a Loyalist schoolteacher and traveled on Long Island gathering information and drawing pictures of enemy fortifications. He did not fare well as a spy; his mission only lasted from September 1 to 22, 1776. He was captured while attempting to return to Washington's forces and was executed without a trial the following day.

The Continental army made good use of information obtained by spies on several occasions. Washington's famous crossing of the Delaware River on Christmas night 1776 was made possible by information supplied by a Trenton butcher who had customers among the British forces. General Horatio Gates's successful campaign against British General John Burgoyne, which led to the capture of Saratoga, was aided by an American spy posing as a tailor in Burgoyne's camp.

Two notable spy rings were organized and run by the Continental army during the Revolutionary War. One spy ring operated in Philadelphia from September 1777 to June 1778. Organized by Major John Clark, it provided Washington's forces at Valley Forge with information about British General Howe's capabilities and movements. This information is credited with having prevented the destruction of Washington's forces at least three times. A second spy ring, the Culper Net, operated in the New York City and Long Island area. Characterized as the most successful spy operation of the Revolutionary War, it was organized at Washington's request by Major Benjamin Tallmadge. Consisting of a network of farmers, barmaids, merchants, fishermen, domestics, and clerks, the Culper Net played a key role in exposing General Benedict Arnold as a British spy.

Benedict Arnold was a "walk-in": rather than being recruited as a spy he volunteered his services to the British. Arnold had a checkered military and personal career before offering to become a spy. He had developed a reputation for being an aggressive and spirited military officer for the colonies but at the same time repeatedly found himself the subject of investigations by the Continental Congress for corruption and abuse of power. Arnold apparently approached British General Henry Clinton in May 1779, claiming he had become disillusioned with the revolutionary cause. In July he quoted 10,000 pounds as the price of his services. The British asked for information about the American defenses at West Point in return for this payment. By August, Arnold had succeeded in being placed in command of this mission. His British handler, John Andre, was captured with incriminating documents on the way to a meeting with Arnold. With his treason disclosed, Arnold fled to New York to be with Clinton. For the remainder of the war he would serve in the British army, leading campaigns in Virginia and Connecticut.

Arnold was not the only British spy during the American Revolution. Dr. Benjamin Church, the director of hospitals for the Continental Congress and a member of the Massachusetts Congress, was a spy for British General Gage. General Howe captured Philadelphia in September 1777 with the help of information provided by a spy. And, in Paris, the British relied upon information secretly provided to them by Benjamin Franklin's personal secretary while Franklin was trying to negotiate an alliance with France against the British. The danger posed by spies was recognized by all concerned. On the American side of the war, Committees of Safety were established to provide secure means of communication, crack British codes, and run security checks on all members of revolutionary groups (Ameringer 1990).

Finally, it should be noted that the colonists and the British were not the only ones running spies in this country during the Revolution. Using Havana as a base, Spain sent agents to the rebelling colonies disguised as merchants. One agent, Juan de Miralles, not only provided information to Spain about political and military events during the Revolutionary War but also made contact with American officials in hopes of bringing Spain into the war on the colonists' side in exchange for the return of Florida to Spain.

# The Early Republic

The first decades of the American Republic saw espionage move from a wartime setting to a peacetime one. The transition brought out a theme that would be repeated time and again in the history of American espionage. The public's attention became riveted on the dangers posed by domestic spies who came from groups outside the mainstream of American society. Caught up in a battle for their political survival, the Federalists depicted immigrants as spies and supported the passage of the Alien and Sedition Acts of 1798. These laws were directed largely at French and Irish immigrants who had emerged as strong supporters of Thomas Jefferson and his Republican Party. The split between the Federalists led by Alexander Hamilton and John Adams and the Republicans led by Thomas Jefferson represented the beginnings of the American party system. The Federalists drew their political strength from wealthy merchants and landowners. These groups could easily be outnumbered in time by newly arriving immigrants. The three alien laws extended the period required to obtain citizenship from five to fourteen years, permitted detention of aliens without cause, and allowed the U.S. president to expel aliens.

The clandestine collection of information to further national security interests continued at a measured pace up until the Civil War. One area to which it made a significant contribution was the exploration of the trans–Mississippi West. In 1832, for example, Captain Benjamin Bonneville took a leave from the War Department to pose as a fur trapper and explore the continental United States all the way to the Pacific Ocean. Decades earlier, Captain Meriwether Lewis and Lieutenant William Clark had undertaken their famous expedition to the Pacific. The trip was officially described as a commercial expedition, but President Thomas Jefferson also entrusted Lewis and Clark with the task of bringing back basic intelligence about the region, including the economic and military activities of the Indians they encountered along the way.

Two wars punctuated this time period; espionage played a minimal role in each. The War of 1812 saw no organized American efforts directed at secretly collecting information about the British; American intelligence was as unprepared for war as the rest of the country. The United States possessed little intelligence of merit on the state of British forces in Canada and little basic intelligence about Canada itself. The most notable espionage activities during the War of 1812 were carried out by pirates who were allied with the United States. They reported on British naval movements throughout the Gulf coast and West Indies. This general lack of American intelligence preparedness stood in contrast to British capabilities. The British had continued their intelligence collection efforts in the United States after the American Revolution.

Organized spying also played only a minor role in the Mexican War. In part this was due to the absence of any concrete war plans. Without such plans military intelligence could not be effectively tasked to collect information. Also, General Zachary Taylor simply did not value intelligence. During the war, intelligence was collected on an ad hoc basis, with American military officials relying upon non-Americans to conduct espionage. Bands of outlaws were recruited at a base pay of $2 per day. Although their loyalty was suspect, as many as 200 such bandits were recruited (Ameringer 1990).

# The Civil War

American espionage in the Civil War continued to focus on the actions of individuals rather than organizations. For the North, the first leading force in intelligence work was Allan Pinkerton, who founded the Pinkerton Detective Service in 1850. Pinkerton was hired by President Abraham Lincoln to evaluate the state of the North's security, and he later joined General George McClellan's staff. Not surprisingly given his background, Pinkerton was far more successful at counterespionage than he was at producing analytical intelligence for McClellan. One of his most successful spy catching efforts was the arrest of Rose O'Neal Greenhow, a Confederate agent in Washington, D.C., whose spy ring Pinkerton infiltrated. Her information sources included antislavery Northern senators, foreign diplomats, bankers, doctors, and housewives. The North also had its spies. One of the most successful was Elizabeth Van Lew, who lived in Richmond, Virginia. One of her agents was a servant in the home of Jefferson Davis, president of the Confederacy, and her home often served as temporary quarters for visiting military officers.

Also notable in the history of Civil War espionage were the actions of Lafayette Baker. He engaged in espionage behind the

Confederate lines in the first year of the war. When his true intentions became suspect by Confederate officials, he fled to Washington, D.C., where he was put in charge of a new Secret Service Bureau. By all accounts Baker was an intolerant individual who abused his newfound power. In his hunt for enemy spies he adopted brutal interrogation techniques and built a large network of informers and secret agents. Thousands of suspected Confederate spies were arrested and sent to prison by Baker. In defending his actions Baker asserted that "my duties are hard to define . . . [they] are to obey the Secretary of War in looking after the interests of the Government, arresting disloyal persons, . . . and other duties which I cannot enumerate" (Corson 1977, 540). Baker's outlook on spy catching as an activity carried out according to rules of war rather than peace, and his sense of commitment to a set of values that transcended democratic procedures, foreshadowed the outlook of future generations of American spy catchers.

Perhaps more so than with any other conflict in the United States's past, the American Civil War has been engulfed in an espionage mythology that makes it difficult to distinguish fact from fiction in assessing the impact made by spies and spy catchers. For example, on the spy side, both the efforts of Pinkerton and Greenhow have been reinterpreted. Pinkerton is generally condemned for his constant overstatement of Confederate troop strength, suggesting not only a failure in analysis but also in espionage and data collection. When Lee's army numbered 80,000, Pinkerton placed it at 200,000. It is now suggested that Pinkerton's estimates may in fact have been tailored to the needs of General McClellan, who displayed a consistent unwillingness to engage Confederate forces. In modern parlance this would be referred to as producing "intelligence to please," and though it represents a failing of intelligence, it is not a failing of espionage. At the other extreme, it is now argued that Greenhow's contributions have been overrated. She is credited with having provided Confederate forces with key information on Union strategy prior to the First Battle of Bull Run. Historians now doubt that was the case because the timing of events would have required her to know the details of these plans before the Union army had formulated them. Regarding the spy catchers, both Pinkerton and Baker referred to their organizations as "the Secret Service" (as this book did above), but in reality neither of their spy catching organizations had official bureaucratic titles. The

U.S. Secret Service was not created until 1865, after the Civil War, without the help of either Pinkerton or Baker (Fishel 1996).

The establishment of the Secret Service actually had little to do with espionage. It was established in 1865 with the assigned mission of suppressing the spread of counterfeit currency. It was for this reason that the Secret Service organizationally was placed in the Treasury Department. By the end of the Civil War, somewhere between one-third and one-half of currency circulating in the United States was counterfeit. Two years later, its mission was expanded to include "detecting persons perpetuating frauds against the government." Under this mandate the Secret Service has investigated the Ku Klux Klan, land-fraud schemes, and the Teapot Dome oil scandal. This broadened mission statement also provides the grounds for engaging in counterespionage activities. Following the assassination of President William McKinley in 1901, the Secret Service was also tasked with the responsibility of protecting the president. Protection of the White House first took place during the Civil War when the "Bucket Brigade," composed of members of the 150th Regiment of the Pennsylvania Volunteers and members of the Washington police force, had this responsibility. A White House police force was established in 1922 by President Warren Harding. It was placed under the supervision of the Secret Service in 1930.

# World War I and the Interwar Years

Espionage from World War I through the interwar years began to take on a permanent organizational form, but the activities of individuals continued to be crucial to its historical development. One such individual was Major General Ralph H. Van Deman. Overcoming the anti-intelligence bias of Army Chief of Staff General Hugh Scott, Van Deman successfully lobbied for the creation of a Military Intelligence Section during World War I. In rejecting the need for a special intelligence unit with the military, Scott shared the prevailing organizational wisdom that intelligence was not central to success on the battlefield. Scott went so far as to assert that since the British and French military had intelligence units, there was no need for an independent American capability. The United States, he affirmed, could simply ask for that intelligence to be given to it. William Corson suggests that in challenging this denigration of the value of intelligence, Van Deman was acting much as Martin Luther did in challenging the teachings of the Catholic Church (Corson 1977, 48). After the war it would become the Military Intelligence Division. Van Deman's view of intelligence included information gathering, espionage, and counterespionage activities. His success in creating an organizational basis for combining these different aspects of intelligence into a coherent whole has earned Van Deman the title "Father of American Military Intelligence" (Corson 1977, 53). Van Deman also saw the intelligence problem in all of its dimensions as one transcending the dividing line between foreign and domestic policy.

This view of intelligence, and especially of espionage, became a defining feature of the interwar period. In 1917 the attorney general encouraged the organization of private volunteer citizen groups to uncover disloyalty. Singled out for high praise in the report was the American Protective League (APL). In search of traitors and spies, the APL infiltrated anarchist groups and leftist labor groups such as the International Workers of the World. Once these perceived threats had been squelched, the APL directed its attention to draft evaders.

Once the war ended a concern for countering foreign espionage remained. This fear exploded onto the political scene with the Red Scare of 1919–1920. Attorney General A. Mitchell Palmer announced that the United States was being consumed by a "blaze of revolution." He placed J. Edgar Hoover in charge of a newly created General Intelligence Division within the Bureau of Investigation with orders to compile a listing of radical organizations and individuals. Palmer's raids of January 2, 1920, resulted in the arrest of practically every leader of the American Communist Party or allied labor organization. Often carried out without warrants, these raids resulted in many innocent people being arrested and also resulted in a public outcry over their excesses.

One technological espionage achievement of note occurred during World War I. In 1917 in anticipation of beginning a policy of unrestricted submarine warfare in the Atlantic, Germany secretly contacted Mexico with an offer of alliance. American vessels approaching Great Britain would be targeted as part of this policy, and it was expected that the United States might be provoked into war. Mexico was offered the return of territory it had lost in the Mexican War for entering into an alliance with Germany. British authorities intercepted the message as it was relayed from the German embassy in the United States to the one Mexico. The British passed the document on to American military intelligence. The release of this Zimmermann Telegram by the Wilson administration fueled anti-German and pro-war sentiments in the United States. The content of the Zimmermann Telegram was also released in such a fashion as to protect the fact that the British had broken the German code. They key accomplishment in producing the Zimmermann telegram was breaking the German code. Breaking the German code was the result of a marriage of intelligence analysis and technology since the encoding of messages is entrusted to machines that generate the codes, and these machines must be duplicated if the code is to be cracked. The success was also made possible in large part by the fact that the British had severed most undersea cables, thus forcing the Germans to send messages through cables that passed through British territory or by wireless methods. This permitted the British to have almost unfettered access to German communications, providing them with a large database to use in attacking the German code.

# World War II

Espionage and counterespionage moved forward in three directions during World War II. One involved creating the Office of Strategic Services (OSS). In 1941 President Franklin Roosevelt put in place the forerunner of the OSS when he created the post of Coordinator of Information (COI) and tabbed William "Wild Bill" Donovan for the position. He authorized Donovan to collect and analyze information and gave him the informal authority to engage in espionage. Once the United States entered World War II, Roosevelt expanded on the COI and through an executive order established the OSS. It was formally charged with collecting and analyzing information and carrying out special duties. This marriage of intelligence analysis, covert operations, and espionage provided a rough blueprint for the Central Intelligence Agency (CIA) that came into existence after the war (Dunlop 1982).

Although Roosevelt officially created the OSS and Donovan had lobbied for its establishment, the OSS actually was created with a great deal of covert help from Great Britain. The British recognized that success in World War II would depend heavily on close cooperation between the two governments. A major impediment standing in the way of such cooperation was the absence of any centralized institutions within the United States for prosecuting the war effort. One need lay in the area of military coordination. The British possessed a centralized military command structure, but the United States did not. To address this void, Roosevelt established the Joint Chiefs of Staff that brought together army, army air force, and navy officers. A second gap existed in the area of intelligence gathering and covert operations. Again, the British possessed such organizations, but the United States did not. Intelligence, such that it existed, was divided among several different organizations. Creating a central intelligence organization in the United States was further complicated by the American de-emphasis of intelligence that has already been noted. These considerations led the British to employ a clandestine strategy to accomplish the goal of creating an American central intelligence organization.

The guiding British force behind the creation of the OSS was Sir William Stephenson, who was a chief British espionage agent in New York. Stephenson had initially hoped to work with the FBI and J. Edgar Hoover, but that relationship did not develop largely due to Hoover's intransigence. Stephenson then identified Donovan as the person he would work with to promote the British vision of a central intelligence organization in the United States. Donovan was experienced in intelligence but lacked official standing in the Roosevelt administration. Roosevelt's personal intelligence envoy to Europe, there Donovan met Stephenson who helped him form his views on intelligence.

Donovan created two branches within the OSS to carry out espionage-related tasks. The Secret Intelligence Branch (SI) conducted espionage. Stations were set up in Sweden, Switzerland, Turkey, Portugal, Spain, and Vichy France. General Douglas MacArthur succeeded in keeping the OSS out of Asia, where he was the commanding military officer and jealously guarded his dominance in the Pacific war theater. Likewise, J. Edgar Hoover, now head of the Federal Bureau of Investigation, was able to keep the OSS out of Latin America, an area it claimed exclusive jurisdiction over. The FBI was established in President Theodore Roosevelt's administration in 1908 by Attorney General Charles Bonaparte as a force of Special Agents. Their creation is best understood in the context of the Progressive movement of the times that sought to replace a government of special favors and political payoffs with one rooted in professionalism, expertise, and efficiency. These agents and their support staff became the

Bureau of Investigation in 1909. By law, the OSS was not to operate inside the United States. The Spanish OSS station ran more
than 1,000 agents into France in addition to carrying out espionage in neutral Spain. One of the most successful SI station
chiefs was Allen Dulles who would become a future head of the
Central Intelligence Agency. One of Dulles's agents was Fritz
Kobel who worked in the German foreign office and delivered
more than 1,600 diplomatic cables. Spy catching was the province of the Counterespionage (X-2) Branch. Accounts suggest
that the OSS station in Sweden ran double agents that resulted
in the neutralization of over 150 German agents (Karalekas
1977).

The second direction in which espionage made great advances
involved the use of technology as a means of spying on the
enemy. Logically, breakthroughs in cryptanalysis, the breaking of
codes and ciphers, followed breakthroughs in the technology that
governments used to communicate with their diplomats, military
officers, and spies that were stationed abroad. The first great figure in American cryptanalysis was Herbert Yardley, who was
recruited by Van Deman to join his Military Intelligence Division.
After World War I Yardley set up an operation in New York to
break the codes used by foreign governments. An agreement with
Western Union and one with Postal Telegraph gave him illegal
access to these communications. Yardley's Black Chamber, as his
operation came to be known, succeeded in breaking the codes of
Argentina, China, Cuba, Great Britain, France, Germany, Japan,
and others before it was shut down in 1929 because, according to
Secretary of State Henry Stimson, "gentlemen do not read each
other's mail."

The value of reading each other's mail became apparent during World War II as the United States and its Allies experienced
two great triumphs in cryptanalysis. The first involved the war
with Japan. Codenamed MAGIC, this effort allowed the United
States to read key diplomatic traffic between the government of
Japan and its embassies. Tightly held within Washington policy-
making circles, the information provided by MAGIC did not prevent the Pearl Harbor attack. Once the Unites States entered the
war, MAGIC was expanded to include Japanese naval codes.
Information provided by MAGIC to Admiral Chester Nimitz
proved to be invaluable in defeating the Japanese navy at the battle of Midway. The second cryptanalytic triumph was realized by

the British, who successfully solved one of Germany's key cipher machines. Codenamed ULTRA, it provided the Allies with key information regarding German land, sea, and air campaigns in Europe and North Africa (Kahn 1967).

The third direction in which espionage moved forward involved increased counterespionage activities inside the United States. During 1942 the FBI uncovered three major espionage rings. One involved a group of eight saboteurs recruited and led by George John Dasch. His handler was Lieutenant Walter Kappe of German intelligence. One group of four landed on Long Island on June 13, 1942, and the other landed in Florida on June 17. They were to bring the war onto American soil and thereby demoralize and intimidate the United States. By June 27 all eight saboteurs were under arrest before they could carry out any part of their mission. One was sentenced to life imprisonment, one was sentenced to thirty years, and six received a death penalty that was carried out within days.

The second espionage ring was uncovered by the FBI that month. On June 10, 1942, three individuals were indicted for conspiracy to violate the Espionage Act. At the center of this conspiracy was Count Anastase Andreievitch Vonsiatsky, the self-proclaimed führer of American fascism. Evidence indicates that at no time did these three individuals actually make contact with German agents or pass intelligence to them. Vonsiatsky received a five-year prison term and was fined $5,000.

The third espionage ring involved thirty-three members and was headed by Frederick Joubert Duquesne. On January 2, 1942, the members of this ring were sentenced to a total of more than 300 years in prison. Duquesne was a naturalized American citizen born in South Africa. Much of the information that he obtained and tried to pass on to Germany involved industrial and technological matters; he acquired the information through correspondence with American business concerns in which he pretended to be a student. The key to uncovering the espionage ring was William Sebold, a German-born naturalized American citizen. On a trip to Germany Sebold was approached by Nazi intelligence and was asked to spy against the United States. Sebold quickly informed American authorities of this, and he agreed to serve as a double agent.

# The Cold War

## America on the Defense

The OSS was disbanded with the end of World War II and its various functions distributed among existing intelligence agencies spread through the foreign affairs agencies and military bureaucracy. It was not until 1947 that the Central Intelligence Agency (CIA) was established. It should be stressed, however, that this centralization of intelligence was incomplete in may respects. Although the head of the CIA, the Director of Central Intelligence (DCI), was also the head of the intelligence community, he possessed only limited budgetary powers over other bureaucracies. Furthermore, different agencies took different approaches to intelligence issues. For the CIA, counterespionage involved protecting secrets. For the FBI, it entailed catching spies so they could be prosecuted for violating the law. This difference in perspective would become a major source of friction between the two agencies throughout the Cold War.

All of the historical trends outlined to this point accelerated as the Cold War era unfolded. Quantum leaps were made in the area of espionage through technological means. The launching point for many of these efforts was the 1954 report of the Killian Committee. Charged with suggesting ways for monitoring Soviet military capabilities, this committee recommended the development of a high-speed plane equipped with a high-definition camera. Seventeen months after government approval was given, the U-2 was operational, and nine months later the first U-2 flight was taking pictures of targets in the Soviet Union. U-2 flights ended after the May 1960 downing of the plane piloted by Francis Gary Powers. At first the United States denied Soviet accusations that it was spying, but President Dwight Eisenhower was forced to acknowledge U.S. actions after the Soviets captured Powers. The accompanying diplomatic fallout caused the collapse of a scheduled summit meeting between Eisenhower and Soviet leader Nikita Khrushchev in Paris. The Francis Gary Powers incident also heightened ongoing interest in space surveillance as an alternative to overhead reconnaissance. Responsibility for managing satellite reconnaissance was given to the National Reconnaissance Office (NRO). Created in 1960 by an executive order, it remains one of the most secret U.S. intelligence organizations. Its existence was not even acknowledged until 1973 (Andrew 1995).

A second area of technological espionage centered on the acquisition of signals intelligence. The lead intelligence organization here was the National Security Agency (NSA). Secretly created in 1952, its existence was not officially acknowledged until 1957. Signals intelligence (SIGINT) involves several different types of activities. One form of signals intelligence involves eavesdropping on secure conversations between diplomats, military officials, and political leaders. A second form involves intercepting data being relayed by weapons during tests or spy satellites. Finally, it can refer to electronic emissions given off by weapons and tracking systems. One of the most successful SIGINT satellites was Rhyolite. Its primary mission was intercepting telemetry from Soviet missile tests. It was also capable of simultaneously transmitting 11,000 two-way telephone conversations. The Rhyolite program was compromised in 1975 when Christopher Boyce and Andrew Lee provided the Soviet Union with information about its technological capabilities. In 1995 the CIA released SIGINT intercepts from project VENONA. Project VENONA was set up secretly in February 1943 by the U.S. Army Signals Intelligence Service, the predecessor of the National Security Agency. Its mission was to intercept and analyze Soviet diplomatic communications. The SIGINT intercepts played a central role in identifying Julius and Ethel Rosenberg, Klaus Fuchs, and Alger Hiss as Soviet spies. Along with others (more than 100 individuals, according to one informant), they constituted a Soviet "atom spy" ring that penetrated the Manhattan Project and passed secret information about the atomic bomb to the Soviets (Romerstein and Breindel 2000).

Spy catching efforts continued to be directed both at foreign threats to U.S. security and at suspected domestic threats. The most famous spy catchers of the Cold War were James Angleton, J. Edgar Hoover, and Senator Joseph McCarthy. McCarthyism burst onto the U.S. political scene on February 9, 1950. On that date in Wheeling, West Virginia, Senator McCarthy gave a speech in which he claimed to have a list of 205 names "that were known to the secretary of state as being members of the communist party and who nevertheless are still working and shaping policy in the State Department." McCarthy's charges were never documented, but his speech set off a nationwide search for communists and communist sympathizers within the government and in positions of influence throughout American society. The most politically charged investigation was into the activities of former State

Department employee Alger Hiss. Two weeks before McCarthy's speech, Hiss had been convicted of perjury for having denied that he passed secret material to Whittaker Chambers, a communist agent.

In 1953 McCarthy became chair of the Permanent Subcommittee on Investigations of Government Operations. He demanded positive loyalty oaths from State Department personnel and ran background checks on them that involved the use of lie detectors and phone taps. Almost 200 individuals were identified as security risks and were fired as a result of these investigations. In 1954 McCarthy turned his attention on the U.S. Army. McCarthy's attack on the army proved to be his undoing, as a coalition of political forces soon mobilized against him.

The Rosenberg and Hiss cases provide two powerful stories that illustrate just how differently espionage can be uncovered. The Rosenberg case involved spying during World War II that resulted in atomic secrets being passed on to the Soviet Union from the Los Alamos Laboratories, where work on the American atomic bomb was being conducted. The trial and execution of the Rosenbergs were politically charged events that brought forward protests from around the world as both Rosenbergs maintained their innocence. The first piece of evidence in the case surfaced in 1944–1945 when the FBI intercepted coded messages between the Soviet consulate in New York City and Soviet intelligence in Russia. Because the FBI lacked the ability to break the code, nothing came of this intercept for some two years. In 1947, however, with the help of the Army Security Agency, the FBI was able to break the code, and it discovered the first evidence of an atomic spy ring. The intercepted messages indicated that the Soviet Union had managed to penetrate the British contingent of the Manhattan Project. Armed with this information, a mole hunt began that culminated in the 1949 arrest of Klaus Fuchs. The intercepted communications also pointed to the existence of a courier, whom the FBI came to suspect was Harry Gold. Fuchs confirmed their suspicions, and Gold was arrested and pled guilty. Gold then began to cooperate with the FBI and identified David Greenglass as a Soviet spy at Los Alamos. Greenglass was then arrested and began cooperating with the FBI in hopes of receiving a more lenient sentence. Greenglass identified his sister and her husband, Ethel and Julius Rosenberg, as having recruited him as a Soviet spy. Greenglass, Ethel and Julius Rosenberg, and Morton Sobell, a fourth member of the atomic spy ring, were tried together and found guilty in March–April 1951. It was primarily on the basis of Greenglass's testimony that the Rosenbergs were convicted. Greenglass received a fifteen-year prison sentence. Sobell was sentenced to thirty years' imprisonment. Ethel and Julius Rosenberg were sentenced to death. Gold received a thirty-year prison sentence. Fuchs was arrested in Great Britain in 1950 and sentenced to prison. He remained in prison until 1959 when he was released and went to East Germany.

The Hiss case evolved quite differently. Hiss was accused of spying by Whittaker Chambers. Chambers, then an editor of *Time* and himself a former communist spy, had sought for some time to convince government officials that the State Department had been penetrated by a spy ring in the 1930s. He finally succeeded in finding a sympathetic audience in 1948 when he testified before the House Un-American Activities Committee and accused Hiss of being a communist. Hiss denied the charge, and in the public and private exchanges that followed, Chambers also alleged that Hiss had engaged in spying, and by implication now acknowledged that he, too, had spied. The most sensational and damning evidence against Hiss consisted of microfilms of papers that Chambers argued Hiss had given him. They were hidden for safekeeping in hollowed-out pumpkins on Chambers's farm. Hiss continued to maintain his innocence throughout the affair. Because of the statute of limitations, his trial focused on the charge of perjury. He was convicted of two counts and served forty-four months in prison. Chambers escaped punishment of any kind in spite of the fact that he virtually confessed to spying. He went on to enjoy a long career in journalism and commented frequently on the political scene in the United States.

In both the Rosenberg and Hiss cases the principal evidence used to convict them of being spies was the testimony of an acknowledged spy. Each trial also saw corroborating evidence produced. In neither case were the defendants caught in the act of spying. In the Rosenberg case the chain of accusations and evidence was lengthy. In the Hiss case it consisted of the testimony of one individual whose story changed over time and had internal inconsistencies. In the public dimension both cases also occurred against a backdrop of communist Cold War victories and domestic political attempts to lay blame for these developments.

A key ally of the House Un-American Activities Committee in its search for communist spies was J. Edgar Hoover, who can properly be identified as the first expert on domestic communism. He rose to the position of director of the Federal Bureau of Investigation by virtue of his prosecution of anarchists, communists, and radicals during and after World War I. In the 1930s his undercover investigations led to the arrest of key American Nazi officials. Hoover's key counterespionage initiative in the Cold War era was the Counterintelligence Program (COINTELPRO). Originally targeting the American Communist Party and designed to carry out "dirty tricks" as much as it was to gather intelligence on espionage activities, COINTELPRO's operations were expanded to include leftist groups such as the Black Panthers. All totaled, between 1955 and 1975 the FBI conducted 740,000 investigations into subversive matters and 190,000 investigations into extremist matters (Donner 1981).

The FBI was not alone in carrying out investigations of Americans for possible security violations. In 1967 the CIA began Operation CHAOS. It was designed to determine the extent to which foreign governments and organizations were directing the behavior of groups within the United States. Antiwar protest groups were a particular concern. Over the course of five years Operation CHAOS created 13,000 files and a computerized index list of more than 300,000 people and organizations.

Most of the CIA's interest in counterespionage, however, was directed inward to its own operations. James Angleton was head of the CIA's counterintelligence operation. For a decade he was at the center of a raging controversy within the CIA over the extent to which it was penetrated by Soviet spies. Angleton's principal source of information was Anatoliy Golitsyn, who was a walk-in defector to the United States in 1961 when he literally appeared unannounced at the doorstep of the CIA station chief in Helsinki. Walk-ins, those who volunteer their services as a spy without any prior inducement from another intelligence service, are one type of spy. Most commonly, spies are recruited by intelligence services after a careful appraisal both of the potential information they have to offer and the likelihood that they will be receptive to such a proposal. The offer of money, appeals to an ideology or cause, and blackmail are among the most frequently employed recruitment tools. Golitsyn contended that the KGB had deeply penetrated most Western intelligence agencies, including the CIA. Although many doubted Golitsyn, Angleton was a firm believer in the accuracy of his information. During the ensuing counterintelligence investigation, no one was above suspicion. Possible spies were dismissed or isolated within the CIA, and for a time the Soviet bloc division was cut off from sensitive information. No mole was found, but the CIA was wracked with self-doubt, something Golitsyn's detractors claimed was one of his true goals (Martin 1980).

However, spies did exist in the United States's national security bureaucracy. This chapter will use the cases of Philip (Robert) Hanssen, the Johnny Walker family spy ring, and Aldrich Ames to illustrate the nature of the Cold War spy game. Respectively, they were Soviet spies in the FBI, U.S. Navy, and CIA.

### Philip (Robert) Hanssen

In February 2001, Philip (Robert) Hanssen, a twenty-seven-year FBI veteran who specialized in counterintelligence, was arrested and charged with having spied for Russia since 1985. (Hanssen, as a double agent, used both the names Philip and Robert.) He was the third FBI agent ever charged with espionage. The 109-page affidavit released at the time and the indictment that followed in May asserted that Hanssen had received some $600,000 in cash and diamonds along with $800,000 escrowed in Russian bank accounts for his efforts. Included among the charges leveled at Hanssen were fourteen that were punishable by death. Specific charges against Hanssen included the following: in 1986 he told Soviet officials that the United States was exploiting a weakness in Soviet satellites to intercept transmissions. In 1988 he told them about limitations in National Security Agency eavesdropping technology that helped the Soviets protect their secrets. That same year he also provided them with top secret documents detailing an FBI list of defectors and recruits and a secret CIA study of KGB recruitment. Hanssen was also charged with betraying the identities of American intelligence sources operating secretly in Russia. The most important of these was Russian Army General Dimitri Polyakov, who was subsequently executed for treason. Hanssen turned over twenty-six computer disks and more than 6,000 pages of documents to Soviet officials. In 1989 he gave the Russians information about how the United States planned to "ensure the continuity of the government in case of a Soviet military attack." He informed his Soviet contacts about the existence of a secret tunnel that lay beneath the Soviet embassy in Washington that was being used for electronic spying.

Hanssen was excellently placed to spy on the United States intelligence system. From 1987 to 1990 he was deputy chief of the FBI's Soviet Analytical Unit. He also served as a key supervisor in a mid-1980s FBI domestic spying program that monitored the activities of Americans thought to be Soviet spies. The principal targets of these investigations were Americans involved in peace protests and antinuclear activities. From 1995 until January 2001 Hanssen was on assignment from the FBI to the State Department's Office of Foreign Missions, which was responsible for monitoring foreign diplomats. In that position Hanssen handled requests from FBI counterterrorism officials about diplomats in the United States from Libya, Syria, Iran, and other countries believed to be sponsoring international terrorism.

The damage done by Hanssen's spying is not easy to calculate. Not all of this information was equally valuable. The tunnel beneath the Soviet embassy, for example, was troubled by engineering problems, so some U.S. government officials doubt that any important information was ever obtained from it; also, the tunnel had not been used for spying for many years. On the other hand, Hanssen's information was directly linked to the executions of KGB officers Sergey Motorin and Valeriy Martynov. Both of these KGB officers were American spies, and their deaths reduced the flow of information to the United States. Hanssen also gave the Soviets key information that compromised the investigation into the actions of Felix Bloch, a State Department official who was under investigation for spying in the late 1980s.

Hanssen was arrested right after being videotaped leaving a garbage bag of secret documents for his Russian controllers at a dead drop site (a site whose location had been previously agreed upon by coded communications). It was not an accident that Hanssen was able to operate as a spy for as long as he did. In part, he was helped by FBI standard operating procedures. Unlike the CIA, which requires random lie detector tests of its employees, the FBI has no such requirement. Hanssen also succeeded due to the great lengths he took to protect his identity. He refused to meet with his Russian controllers because he knew they would be under surveillance. Instead, information was exchanged using dead drops, in which codes were employed to establish the locations and dates of information exchanges. He refused to accept KGB radio transmitters that could be used for arranging contact, because they would immediately implicate him as a spy should they be discovered. He frequently searched the FBI's electronic case file to determine whether it contained any references to him. It is clear that over time Hanssen developed a strong psychological bond with his Russian controllers. This type of relationship is typical in espionage cases in which the spy leads a vulnerable and solitary existence. In correspondence, he and his contacts frequently addressed each other as "friend."

Much remains unclear about the Hanssen case. A key issue is why it took so long for the FBI to determine that Hanssen was a spy. Part of the answer appears to lie in the reluctance of spy catching agencies to believe that one of their own could be a spy and in the low level of cooperation and trust that exists among the members of the intelligence community. The FBI was convinced that the source of the intelligence leak was within the CIA and had actually identified Brian Kelly as the spy. Unfortunately, it could not find any information that proved that Kelly was spying. In the end the FBI turned to the Russians for help. It contacted a retired KGB official and set up a meeting. To their astonishment, the KGB official had removed Hanssen's case file from KGB headquarters upon retiring. The FBI paid $7 million for the file and agreed to bring the KGB official's family to the United States for protection. Included in the file was a tape recording that contained Hanssen's voice and some material that contained his fingerprints (Wise 2002).

Hanssen pled guilty to spying as part of a deal to avoid the death penalty. This type of plea bargain agreement is not unusual in spy cases. From the prosecution's point of view, accumulating evidence against a spy is a time-consuming process, and there is little incentive to make it public. Doing so risks revealing sensitive sources of information and investigative techniques. It is partly for this reason that, once detected, spies are often allowed to continue in their places. Far more can be gained by following their activities and hoping that it leads to other spies than by arresting them and putting an end to their spying. The scale of espionage in which Hanssen engaged and the damage done to U.S. national security interests precluded him from being left in his position. For the spy, a plea bargain often provides the only escape from the death penalty. What the spy can offer in return for a reduced sentence is his or her cooperation in helping government officials construct a complete picture of their activities.

Hanssen's capture set in motion a chain reaction in the spy game between Russia and the United States. Russian authorities launched an aggressive investigation to determine who may have tipped off American authorities about Hanssen. Speculation at the time of this writing centered on Sergei Tretyakov, who served under diplomatic cover as a member of Russia's mission to the United Nations. Tretyakov defected to the United States in October 2000 around the time when U.S. authorities got hold of the KGB case file that ultimately led them to Hanssen. One month after Hanssen was arrested, President George W. Bush expelled fifty-two Russian diplomats in retaliation. Four were suspected spies, who were given ten days to leave. Another forty-six were given until July 1 to leave, and two others who had already left were forbidden from returning to the United States. The next day, Russia ordered four American diplomats to leave within days, and another forty-six were ordered to leave by the summer (Havill 2001).

## The Johnny Walker Family

The second Cold War spy case discussed in this chapter involves the activities of the Johnny Walker family spy ring. Shortly after 3:30 A.M. on May 20, 1985, FBI agents arrested John Walker at a Ramada Inn in Rockville, Maryland. At 11:30 the next morning FBI agents confronted Jerry Whitworth in California. At about 9:00 that evening, they confronted Arthur Walker, John's brother, at his home in Norfolk, Virginia. That same day Seaman Michael Walker, John's son, was placed into custody aboard the aircraft carrier USS *Nimitz*. The arrests of these men would bring to an end the operation of what some considered the most successful Soviet spy ring of the Cold War.

John Walker was the head of the spy ring. He began spying for the Soviet Union in 1968, apparently out of boredom and depression over the state of his marriage and of his career as a communications watch officer on the Norfolk staff of the commander of submarine forces in the Atlantic. He was the classic "walk-in" spy, appearing at the Soviet embassy in January of that year and announcing that he wished to speak with someone from security. To prove his seriousness and value to the Soviets, Walker brought with him the key lists (lists of the formulas necessary to break codes) for the past thirty days to the KL-47 cipher machine.

The heart of a cipher machine is a mathematical formula that is used to transform a plain-text message into an encrypted one. The logic is so sophisticated that there is no one-to-one correspondence between a real letter and the letter that appears in the encrypted text. That is, no single letter will represent the letter *o* throughout the encrypted text. To further ensure the security of the communication system, a key is required to read the encrypted message. The key is a single-use card that is used to engage the cipher machine. In essence it sets the starting point for the mathematical formula. Keys are changed every twenty-four hours. The KGB recognized the potential value of the information Walker was peddling. Walker told them he could also provide complete data for the KRW-37 cipher system (the primary system used to communicate with U.S. submarines and naval forces in Europe) and other cipher machines. Additionally, he said he could provide copies of secret messages sent to submarines and ships in the Atlantic. For his efforts Walker wanted to be paid $1,000 per week. The meeting ended with Walker receiving $2,000 or $3,000 (it is unknown what amount he received because Walker simply did not remember what amount it was) and instructions for a meeting in February.

In February Walker flew to Washington National Airport from Norfolk to meet with a KGB officer. Without even inspecting the material Walker delivered, the Soviets gave him $5,000. They also informed him that this would be the last face-to-face meeting he would have with them. From then on, dead drops would be used, and he was given an elaborate signaling system that required him to go to six different locations before dropping off his material. Every few weeks Walker returned to the Washington, D.C., area to deliver information. The volume and quality of the information apparently overwhelmed the Soviets, who soon instructed Walker to only make deliveries once every few months.

For the next two years, Walker provided the Soviet Union with information that, for all practical purposes, allowed them to read all messages to and from American submarines and supporting ships. In 1970 Walker was transferred by the navy to San Diego. With this transfer the quality of his information deteriorated. The quality of information improved, however, with his next transfer, which was to the USS *Niagara Falls*, a supply ship. This was an ideal platform from which to conduct espionage, as it had to communicate with a wide range of naval vessels and therefore had access to the codes used by all of them. Walker was the naval officer responsible for guarding all cryptographic material. Two or three times per year Walker dropped material off to his Soviet controllers. Especially valuable to the Soviets was information about the operational plans for the Atlantic fleet as well as the radio frequencies they would use to communicate.

The KGB did not want Walker to recruit other spies but did ask him to identify potential spies. Acting against KGB instructions, Walker recruited Jerry Whitworth and began his own spy ring. The two first met in February 1971. Whitworth was working in a communications training laboratory, and Walker was his supervisor. They parted ways and did not meet again until Walker made contact with him in 1974. By then, Walker had been given orders transferring him from the USS *Niagara Falls*. Walker feared he would loose access to the cryptographic data he was giving the Russians. With the promise of money (Walker promised perhaps a couple thousand dollars a month) he convinced Whitworth to reenlist in the navy, obtain a position in communications, and deliver information to him. Whitworth accepted Walker's offer and began supplying him with information. In July 1978 Whitworth received $24,000 from Walker for his efforts. In a stunning turn of events, Whitworth was then transferred to the *Niagara Falls*, where he took up duty as the Communications Materials Systems custodian, Walker's old job. In September Whitworth made what he described as the most significant single delivery of his spy career: he provided the Soviet Union with the complete diagrams for several cipher machines along with keys for ships deployed in the Pacific. In May 1980 he received a payment of $100,000 from Walker. In June the payment was $120,000, and in September it was $60,000. In each case Walker reserved a similar amount for himself. Around this time Whitworth began expressing doubts about continuing as a spy. Walker now recruited his son, Michael, into his spy ring in order to replace Whitworth in case he quit. Walker's concerns about Whitworth quitting were proven to be well founded: in October 1983 Whitworth retired from the navy with no warning. In April John Walker gave Michael $1,000 for material he stole. Michael joined the navy in December 1982. He began a tour of duty aboard the USS *Nimitz* in January 1984 where he stole documents for his father. In October Michael was transferred to the Operations Administrations Office where he obtained access for the first time to secret information. Though he continued to gather information until his arrest, this would be the only payment he would receive. Arthur Walker, John's brother, was also recruited into the spy ring.

Walker's activities as a spy and spy master went unnoticed for more than fifteen years although signs abounded that the U.S. communication system has been compromised. The problem was that these separate warning signs were never brought together at a single place or before a single individual who could see an emerging pattern. It was a phone call from Barbara Walker, by then John's ex-wife, to the FBI on November 17, 1984, that marked the beginning of the end for the Walker spy ring. Barbara Walker had known about Walker's spying since 1968, almost from the beginning. She was supported and prompted into making the phone call by their daughter, Laura, whom Walker had also tried to recruit as a spy in 1982. Barbara's phone call led to her being interviewed by FBI officials but little else. Eventually, though, the FBI acted on the information. After six weeks of electronic surveillance that produced no leads, FBI agents received a break when, on May 17, 1985, Walker indicated that he could not attend the funeral of a relative he was particularly close to. Physical surveillance of Walker on May 19 led the FBI from Norfolk to the Washington, D.C., area where Walker attempted to drop information to his Soviet handlers. That drop was intercepted by the FBI, and early the next morning Walker was arrested.

In the final analysis, the FBI's case against Whitworth was based largely on circumstantial evidence. The information confiscated from Walker when he was captured was stolen from the FBI by his son, so the key to a conviction lay in getting John Walker to testify against Whitworth. Walker agreed to testify against Whitworth in hopes of getting a reduced sentence for his son. Whitworth's trial began on March 6, 1986, and ended on July 24. Found guilty by the jury, Whitworth was sentenced to 365 years in prison and fined $410,000. Michael Walker was sentenced to twenty-five years in prison (Barron 1987).

### Aldrich Ames

The third Cold War case of espionage involves the activities of Aldrich Ames. His spying activities for the Soviet Union are widely considered to be the single most damaging breach of security in the CIA's history, costing at least ten agents their lives and compromising more than fifty-five intelligence operations over nearly a decade.

On the morning of February 21, 1994, Aldrich Ames received an unexpected phone call asking him to come to CIA headquarters where he worked. Ames was set to depart for Moscow the next day to represent the CIA in a meeting with the Russian Federal Security Service, one of the successor intelligence organizations to the KGB following the fall of the Soviet Union. Ames drove away from his $540,000 home in his $40,000 Jaguar. About one and one-half blocks from his house, Ames's car was stopped and surrounded by FBI agents, who placed him under arrest for violating U.S. espionage statutes. Simultaneously, they surrounded his home and arrested his wife, Rosario, for espionage.

Ames began working in the CIA's Directorate of Operations in 1968. His first overseas posting came in 1969 with his assignment to Ankara, Turkey. His job was to recruit communist intelligence officials and diplomats as spies. He did not excel in this capacity. His performance evaluation states that Ames was "unsuited for field work and should spend the remainder of his career at Headquarters." Ames returned to Washington, D.C., in 1972. In the first of many surprising turns of events Ames was promoted in 1976 to serve in New York in the CIA's Foreign Resources Division office, which was in charge of operations against foreign targets. Ames's next posting took him to Mexico City, where he stayed from 1981 until 1983. As in Ankara, he was supposed to recruit Soviet diplomats as spies. Once again he received low performance evaluations. On the personal side, Ames's life was entering a turbulent period. His marriage was failing and he was becoming a heavy drinker, something noted in his performance evaluations.

Instead of his career stalling, as one might expect given his poor performance evaluations, Ames's next assignment was a prized position. He became head of the Soviet branch of the counterintelligence group at CIA headquarters. In this capacity he had access to highly secret information regarding CIA operations against Soviet intelligence agencies outside of the Soviet Union, and he supervised CIA assets inside the Soviet Union. One of the most important duties Ames was responsible for in his new position was to identify possible Soviet spies, or moles, within the CIA. Ames was appointed to this position on the recommendation of someone who had supervised him in New York. His poor performance evaluation in Mexico City was not given great weight, and his drinking problem was unknown to those who selected him and approved his appointment, despite the fact that his drinking problem was recorded in his evaluation. (The failure of officials in one part of the CIA to inquire about information held by other sections is a reoccurring theme in the literature on the intelligence community.)

In September 1984 Nancy Ames filed for divorce. The settlement left Aldrich Ames, who was now living with Rosario Casas Dupuy, facing what he perceived to be a significant debt that embarrassed him. It was to escape this debt that Ames later claimed he turned to espionage. On April 16, 1985, Ames walked into the Soviet embassy and presented the guard with a letter addressed to the resident KGB officer. The letter Ames gave to embassy officials provided the Soviet Union with the descriptions of two CIA moles operating within the Soviet embassy. Along with those names, he provided the Soviets with information that established his identity as chief of the Soviet counterintelligence branch of the CIA. In return, Ames sought to be paid $50,000. Realizing that he would have been observed entering the Soviet embassy, Ames reported his visit to the Soviet embassy to the CIA. To his superiors, he explained it as part of an effort to recruit the embassy's First Secretary Sergei Chuvakhin as a spy.

On May 15 Ames was contacted by the KGB and told he would be paid his $50,000. The transaction took place two days later. Ames later claimed that this was to have been a onetime act of espionage, but in mid-June Ames provided the Soviet Union with the identities of virtually all of the Soviet agents working for the CIA and other intelligence services. He did so without prompting from the Soviets and without demanding payment. Ames simply walked out of CIA headquarters with between five and seven pounds of cable traffic and other secret documents. The KGB responded by indicating to Ames that it had put away $2 million for him.

Among those whose files came across Ames's desk were Lt. Col. Valeriy Martynov, a KGB officer who began spying for the United States in 1982; KGB Major Sergey Motorin; and General Dimitri Polyakov of Soviet military intelligence. All three were betrayed by Ames and were executed by the Soviets. Polyakov had spied for the United States for twenty years and provided important information on Soviet strategic missiles, chemical and biological warfare programs, and nuclear strategy. Near the end of his tour of duty in his post, Ames helped debrief Soviet defector Vitaly Yurchenko in August–September 1985. A senior KGB official, Yurchenko was a walk-in defector who provided information about two KGB penetrations into the U.S. intelligence community. One operative was a CIA officer, Edward Lee

Howard; the other, Ronald Pelton, worked for the National Security Agency (NSA). Ames reported all of the information given by Yurchenko to his KGB handlers. The CIA had known for two years that Howard was a spy but had not informed the FBI. He had been allowed to resign from the agency and now lived in Santa Fe, New Mexico. Now aware of his activities, the FBI confronted Howard, who eluded them and fled to Russia. Pelton was caught after six months of intensive investigation. In a twist that still causes a debate among intelligence officials, Yurchenko defected back to the Soviet Union in November 1985.

From CIA headquarters, Ames's next assignment took him to Rome in 1986, where he served as Soviet branch chief. Before leaving for Rome, Ames took and passed a polygraph test. He was specifically asked if he had any unauthorized contact with foreign intelligence officials or had disclosed classified information. A CIA report describes his performance in Rome in these terms: "he once again began to drink heavily . . . did little work, sometimes slept at his desk in the afternoon, rarely initiated developmental activity, and often fell behind in accounting." In Rome, Ames followed procedures he had initiated at CIA headquarters in spying for the Soviet Union. He simply walked out of the embassy with secret material and literally gave shopping bags full of secret material to his handlers in return for cash payments that ranged from $20,000 to $50,000. So large were these payments that Ames deposited almost $1 million into two Swiss bank accounts during his tour of duty. Near the end of his time in Rome, Ames's Soviet handlers provided him with a list of information they wanted once he returned to CIA headquarters. Included were the identities of CIA moles operating within Soviet intelligence services and possible Soviet spy recruits within the CIA. They also provided him with pictures of land in the Soviet Union where his retirement *dacha* (a small summer house) would be built. KGB payments continued to flow to Ames following his return from Rome. In addition to his Swiss bank accounts in Zurich, he had deposits in banks in Geneva, Bogota, and Rome as well as eight investment accounts. In 1991 Ames deposited $91,100 into his accounts. The following year he deposited $187,000. All totaled, between 1985 and 1993 Rosario and Aldrich Ames (they married in 1984) spent almost $1.4 million. By contrast, Ames's yearly salary with the CIA was $69,843.

It did not take long for the Soviets to act on Ames's information. As the CIA report into the Ames affair observes, "in 1985 and

1986, it became increasingly clear to officials within the CIA that the Agency was faced with a major CI problem. A significant number of CIA Soviet sources began to be compromised, recalled to the Soviet Union, and, in many cases, executed" (Permanent Select Committee on Intelligence, House of Representatives 1994, 14). It is still uncertain how many agents were compromised. Published numbers run from some twenty agents up to nearly fifty. Ames placed the number at twenty-five. At least ten are now presumed to have been executed. The speed with which CIA sources were disappearing was unusual. Under normal operating procedures the KGB would not have moved so quickly on Ames's information for fear of drawing attention to him. The decision to proceed appears to have been taken at the highest levels of the Soviet system and reflects the dominance of political concerns in the decision-making process.

The CIA was slow to react for several reasons. At first, the losses of personnel were attributed to Edward Lee Howard. In some instances this was correct: Howard's information had alerted the KGB to several CIA penetrations. However, by late 1985 it became clear that Howard did not possess information concerning all of the CIA spies now being compromised. Attention then shifted to the possibility that the losses were due to bad luck, faulty practices and handling by CIA officers, or an electronic penetration of CIA property or communications. It was with great reluctance that still another possibility was embraced: the CIA had been penetrated by a Soviet agent.

The CIA authorized a mole hunt in October 1986 when it set up a Special Task Force. For about two years it focused on the possibility of a communications breach. The FBI began its own probe that month. The FBI probe ended in 1987. The CIA investigation continued but at a reduced pace. The KGB also began a concerted program of disinformation designed to protect Ames by sending the investigation down false paths and dead ends. Attention first began to center on Ames in late 1989 when a CIA employee reported that Ames was living beyond his means. An investigation into Ames's finances discovered that he and Rosario had paid cash for a $540,000 home upon their return from Rome. It would be December 1990, however, before a formal request was made that Ames be the subject of an investigation and a polygraph test administered. The information produced in this investigation was not shared with those conducting the polygraph test. Ames passed the lie detector test.

In April 1991 a joint CIA-FBI investigation was launched in search of uncovering the Soviet mole. By August the CIA-FBI team had identified 198 CIA employees with access to all of the compromised cases. Twenty-nine individuals were identified as leading suspects, with Ames numbered among them. A major breakthrough occurred in late 1992 when investigators were able to match dates of Ames's meetings with Soviet officials with large bank deposits on his part. The joint investigative team issued its report in March 1993. It concluded that the CIA had been penetrated. The FBI formally opened an investigation that month. In May it opened a case file on Ames, and he was placed under surveillance. In June a wiretap was placed on his home phone, and his CIA office was searched. There they found 144 secret documents and ten top secret documents, many of which were unrelated to his work. It was not until September, however, that the FBI obtained conclusive proof that Ames was spying for the Soviet Union. In his trash they found a Post-It note containing the draft of a message to his Soviet handler regarding an upcoming meeting. A surreptitious entry into his home that involved copying computer files produced more proof that Ames was an active spy. Throughout the remainder of 1993 the FBI kept its distance from Ames, hoping to catch him in the act. Unable to accomplish this goal, they determined not to allow Ames to escape and flee the country as Howard had done. The day before he was scheduled to leave for Moscow as part of a CIA team that would confer on international narcotics trafficking with Russian internal security officials, Ames was arrested.

A few months later, on April 28, 1994, Ames pled guilty to espionage. Rosario did not have access to secret material and was charged with being part of conspiracy to commit espionage. At first she denied any knowledge of Ames's spying activities but later recanted. In return for cooperating with U.S. officials, Ames received a life sentence with no possibility of parole, and Rosario received a five-year sentence. In 1999 Ames unsuccessfully sought to have his sentence reduced, saying he was surprised by the extent of the espionage activities attributed to him. He claimed his arrest was a way of putting off responsibility for intelligence failures and compromises for which he was not truly responsible (Wise 1995).

## The United States on the Offensive

The Soviet Union did not have a monopoly on espionage during the Cold War. A full accounting of espionage during these four decades also requires recounting American efforts to spy on the Soviet Union. The most important American spy of the Cold War was KGB Colonel Oleg Penkovsky (his story will be more fully recounted in chapter 3), but he was neither the first nor the last American spy of note. The most important American spy in the 1950s was "Major B." He was a walk-in who recruited himself in Vienna on January 1, 1953, by handing a letter to an American embassy official. Major B served in Soviet military intelligence (GRU). He claimed he was motivated by ideological considerations, but later it became clear that he was also involved in an extramarital affair and needed money. Major B met with his CIA handler once or twice per month for up to eight or nine hours at a time. He was arrested in September 1959 shortly after he was recalled to Moscow from Vienna. His case officer was arrested in October after an emergency meeting was arranged, and Major B was executed shortly after that. Major B provided technical information on conventional weapons and Soviet tanks, detailed orders of battle plans, and Soviet tactical missile systems.

In the mid 1970s another GRU officer approached the United States in Algeria and offered his services as a spy. Colonel Anatoli Filatov spied for the United Sates for fourteen months, providing the American government with military and political secrets. He continued to spy for the United States for about a year after his transfer to Moscow. He was caught at a dead drop leaving material for his CIA contact. He was sentenced to death, but his sentence was commuted to fifteen years in prison as part of a spy exchange in which two KGB agents captured in the United States were sent to the Soviet Union. A second and controversial spy in the 1970s was Alexsadr Ogorodnik. Depending upon what account is accepted, he either was an ideologically motivated walk-in or was entrapped in a compromising sexual relationship and blackmailed. Recruited in Colombia, he began spying for the CIA in 1974. He was later transferred back to Moscow and served in the Foreign Ministry's Global Affairs Department, where he had access to secret documents containing Soviet evaluations of international events and trends. It is unclear how much information Ogorodnik had passed to the Americans by the time he came under suspicion of espionage, and whether or not he was being used to pass inflammatory documents to the United States. All accounts agree that he eventually committed suicide.

The most publicized spy penetration in the 1980s involved A. G. Tolkachev, who was a staff member of one of Moscow's research institutes. He was caught in the act of passing secret defense material to a CIA official who was serving undercover as the second secretary of the American embassy. He was arrested in June 1985 and executed. Tolkachev's case is linked to Edward Hunt. Hunt was a CIA official who was being trained to be Tolkachev's case officer in Moscow. He had been dismissed from the CIA for failing a lie detector test that pointed to drug use and petty theft. A Soviet spy, Hunt tipped the KGB off to Tolkachev and then fled the United States. Tolkachev is credited with having provided the United States with key information about Soviet military aviation programs involving stealth technology and electronic guidance systems (Richelson 1987).

With World War II over and the Cold War beginning to heat up, the realization gripped American officials that they had little intelligence information on the Soviet Union. Gaps in their knowledge extended down to the most basic features such as the distribution and state of repair of road and railroad systems and the location of bridges, factories, and airports. Information from diplomats and military attachés in the American embassy was of little value due to the secrecy of Soviet society and the travel and living restrictions placed on these individuals by Soviet authorities. As the United States tried to fill in the missing pieces, the initial source of their information was refugees and prisoners of war. By 1948 these sources of information were drying up, and the CIA faced the challenge of replacing them. The fear of war over Berlin gave an urgency to the search for new sources of information. The former German capital was a highly contested prize in the early years of the Cold War. Divided into East and West occupation zones, deep within Soviet-controlled East Germany, Berlin was the site of U.S.-Soviet confrontations in 1948, 1958, and 1961. Soviet control over all of Berlin would have given the Soviet Union a significant psychological and political edge in the Cold War competition in Europe by calling into question the American commitment to defend its allies.

The answer hit upon was to secretly drop agents by plane into the Soviet Union. The first mission took place on September 5, 1949. It took off from an airfield in the American zone of Germany and dropped two Ukrainian nationals into the Soviet

Union. In the tradition of the OSS, their mission was to collect information and to work with Ukranian resistance groups. Their primary intelligence charge was to provide early warning of a Soviet attack. For the next five years these intelligence drops became a key element of the American espionage program. Agents were recruited from among defectors, refugees, and Soviet citizens living in the West. Preparation for these missions was time-consuming. Proper documents had to be forged in order to legitimize these agents to the Soviet police and other officials. The individuals had to learn the details of their legends, or fictional lives, in the smallest detail. They had to learn key features of their new careers such as being able to correctly identify planes; learn how to send and receive secret radio messages as well as put together, repair, and dismantle a transceiver; and learn to take photographs with cameras that were disguised as cigarette lighters. In all, the training took ten months. One such agent whose career has been documented reported for thirteen months before going silent. He sent five radio messages and three letters containing secret writings. Secret writing was necessary, as it was common practice for both the U.S. and Soviet intelligence agencies to open mail going in and out of the Soviet Union. Agents often relied on letters rather than radios to transmit information so as not to call attention to themselves. Although this helped protect their identities, it also worked against providing early warning about an attack. U-2 overflights began two years after the last agent was dropped into the Soviet Union.

Beyond trying to penetrate the Soviet Union itself, the CIA and other American intelligence organizations have sought to penetrate the second and third circles of communist power. The second circle consisted of the Soviet's allies in Eastern Europe, China, and North Korea. The third circle consisted of the Soviet Union's Third World allies. Before the Berlin Wall went up in 1961, a common stratagem was to provide an agent with false documentation and a railway ticket into East Germany. From there, American spies could readily fan out into regions under Soviet domination and influence. A number of strategies were employed to recruit spies. One method was to place a job announcement in West Berlin newspapers and try and recruit those who applied. A second approach was to simply ask defectors and refugees if they knew of anyone who would be interested in spying. A third approach, and the least successful, was a cold call in which someone would be approached to act as a spy without any prior indication of a willingness to do so on their part. Reportedly, the agents who were recruited infiltrated high party offices, economic ministries, police and militia offices, and railway and postal services.

Throughout this process the Soviet Union engaged in a campaign of counterespionage to ferret out spies. They infiltrated refugee and émigré groups. These Soviet counterspies would identify Western spies and also serve as conduits for false information back to the West. Because of this, the value of intelligence produced by these spies and those who had previously been dropped into Soviet territory is considered to have been minimal compared to the amount of effort that went into these operations.

Following Stalin's death a thaw occurred in U.S.-Soviet relations that resulted in an influx of tourists into the Soviet Union and the freer movement of American citizens there. These tourists became a ready source of intelligence for the United States. They would be recruited and briefed on points of information that were of interest to the intelligence community. Tourists photographed such things as Intercontinental Ballistic Missile (ICBM) production facilities and deployment sites, the first Soviet nuclear submarine, and the construction of a missile test range. The CIA also began a major covert operation to obtain Soviet military equipment, operating specifications, training manuals, and related material. Their targets were not so much located inside the Soviet Union as they were in recipient states where security was lax and bribery easier. It is estimated that 90 percent of the Soviet military equipment in the hands of the Pentagon in the 1960s came from the CIA.

A principal target for penetration in third-circle countries was the Communist Party. Two methods were followed in recruiting someone to spy within the party. The first was by "seeding" a young person into a party cell and guiding his or her career upward. The second approach was to recruit an individual who already held a high-ranking position. Of the two approaches, the first was the easiest but often ended up being nonproductive because the person's career never developed as hoped for or the individual changed his or her mind. The information produced by spies in the third circle covered a wide variety of political matters. Khrushchev's de-Stalinization speech to the Twentieth Party Congress reportedly came to light this way, as did information about the Sino-Soviet split (Rositzke 1977).

# The Post–Cold War Period

Just as the onset of the Cold War did not mark the beginning of espionage by and against the United States, so its passing in 1989 did not mark the end of espionage. If anything, espionage in the post–Cold War era is a more complex phenomenon and therefore one more difficult to counter.

During the Cold War the United States concentrated its national security resources on one enemy: the Soviet Union. Likewise, it had to protect its secrets from only one enemy. The end of the Cold War reduced but did not eliminate the Russian security threat. At the same time it elevated the challenges and threats posed by other countries. As a consequence the United States faces a situation in which prudence suggests that it must seek to obtain information about the policies and capabilities of many countries and it must protect its own secrets from a larger number of countries.

In addition, the national security agenda of countries has expanded. Where once, questions of military capability and strategy sat atop this agenda and dominated all others, today one is as likely to find trade, monetary, scientific, and technology issues being contested at the highest levels of government. Just as espionage served to further the development of military policy in the Cold War, it has the potential for advancing state policy in these areas as well.

The simultaneous expansion of the national security agenda along with the expansion in the number of potential national security threats have resulted in a blurring of the line between friend and foe. Allies in some policy areas find themselves as competitors in others, with the result that espionage is now often directed at friends in these areas of competition. Spying on friends has always occurred; one particularly controversial episode of Israeli spying on the United States will be examined in chapter 3. Recent revelations suggest either that this form of espionage is on the rise or that states are devoting more resources to stopping it.

Evidence on the continued relevance of espionage surfaces regularly. In 1996 CIA officer Harold Nicholson was arrested and charged with spying for Russia. He pled guilty and is serving a twenty-three-year sentence. In 1997 Earl Pitts, a thirteen-year FBI agent, was charged with spying for Russia. The FBI was tipped off to his case by a Russian double agent. Pitts is serving a twenty-seven-year prison term. In 1998 David Boone, an analyst with the National Security Agency, was arrested for spying for Russia. Boone was a walk-in. Among the information he passed to the Russians was the list of Russian sites targeted by U.S. nuclear weapons. In 2000 Army Reserve Colonel George Trofimoff was arrested for spying for Russia for more than twenty-five years. He is the highest-ranking military officer ever charged with espionage.

On the subject of non-Russian hostile spying, in 2002 the Defense Intelligence Agency's senior Cuban analyst, Ana Belan Montes, pled guilty to spying for Cuba for more than sixteen years. In October 2002 she was sentenced to twenty-five years in prison. Montes began spying in 1992. She communicated with her Cuban handlers via shortwave radio or by pay phones at the National Zoo in Washington, D.C., using prepaid calling cards and a beeper system. By all accounts, Montes was only paid for her expenses and nothing more. In the courtroom she told the judge that she "obeyed my conscience rather than the law." In retaliation for Montes's actions, in November 2002 the United States expelled two Cuban diplomats and requested that two others also be sent home. The four officials were given ten days to leave.

Two years earlier Mariano Faget, a senior immigration official based in Miami, was charged with spying for Cuba. Faget received a light five-year prison sentence reflecting the value of the information he passed on. Also in 2002 a federal grand jury indicted Brian Regan, a retired air force master sergeant, with trying to spy for Iraq, Libya, and China. He wrote encrypted letters to leaders of Iraq and Libya, offering them American intelligence reports on their countries, satellite spy photographs, and related information. In March 2003 Regan accepted a surprise deal when he assented to a life sentence for engaging in espionage. Prosecutors had sought the death penalty, but the jury that convicted him ruled that he was ineligible for the death penalty. This same year the George W. Bush administration also expelled an Iraqi diplomat, who had been posted to the United Nations, for spying. The Iraqi ambassador to the United Nations protested by affirming that his staff were diplomats, not spies. This was the first time the United States had expelled an Iraqi diplomat since 1994. In the 1994 case the charge was not espionage but lobbying Congress to end UN economic sanctions.

In April 2003 yet another spy case broke into public view. Katrina Leung, a prominent Republican Party campaign contributor in California, was arrested as a Chinese double agent. She had been employed under the cover position of PARLOR MAID by the intelligence community to transmit tainted intelligence to China. The FBI paid her $1.7 million for these efforts. Unknown to the U.S. intelligence community, Leung was working for the Chinese government. In its initial damage assessment the FBI concluded that all Chinese counterintelligence operations since 1991 had to be considered as compromised. She was aided in her spy efforts on behalf of China by a twenty-year-long affair with FBI agent James Smith and another lengthy affair with another agent. In 1991 the FBI alerted Smith that Leung could be a double agent.

Cases of friendly spying have also emerged. In 1988, one year before the fall of the Berlin Wall and the symbolic end of the Cold War, Douglas Tsou was arrested for spying for Taiwan. He had worked for the FBI for six years as a translator. In 1998 German counterintelligence reported a CIA attempt to recruit a German government official for espionage. French officials have also complained about American electronic espionage activities directed against their country. Perhaps proving the point, the United States uncovered evidence that French authorities had tried to bribe Brazilian officials into awarding a communications contract to a French firm. After the United States protested, Brazil awarded the contract to an American firm.

Advances in technology have not stopped, and the game of spy and counterspy continues apace in this country. In 1999, for example, India knew when American spy satellites would be over their nuclear testing facilities and took countermeasures to ensure that their development of a nuclear weapon would go undetected. And although satellite technology remains very much an area in which the advanced industrial states of the North hold a comparative advantage over all others, the burgeoning commercial satellite industry is making satellite technology available to all.

President George W. Bush's first foreign policy crisis involved the downing of a spy plane over China on March 31, 2001. A U.S. Navy surveillance plane collided with a Chinese fighter pilot who had been "playing tag" with it in international airspace over the South China Sea. The American plane and crew landed safely in China. China demanded an apology for the incident and called for the pilot to be executed. The United States refused and demanded the return of its plane and crew; however, the Chinese pilot was executed. The crisis ended peacefully, but not until the U.S. aircraft had been subjected to careful analysis by Chinese authorities.

Spy satellites also remain very much an important part of the United States's espionage arsenal, especially in war or in preparations for war. Published accounts suggest that Keyhole and Lacrosse satellites (the former produces digital pictures; the latter, radar images) flew over Baghdad nineteen times in the first eighteen hours of the land war against Iraq during the Persian Gulf War. More recently, in Afghanistan as part of the war against terrorism, the United States made use of Predator drone aircraft that provided long-range coverage. The Keyhole and Lacrosse satellites were over their Iraqi targets for only a few minutes at a time, but the Predator could provide twenty-four-hour coverage. Some suggest that perhaps the most significant long-term post–Cold War development in the technology area was the decision of the Clinton administration to approve the export of advanced encryption software. This will greatly complicate the task of trying to intercept and break enemy codes and ciphers.

Lastly, there is no evidence that those engaged in American counterespionage efforts will not continue to look upon non-mainstream domestic groups with suspicion in the post–Cold War era. The most notable case involves Wen Ho Lee. A physicist at Los Alamos, he was arrested in December 1999 on charges of spying for China. As part of his indictment Lee was accused of downloading classified information to a nonsecure computer. The government's handling of the case came under heavy criticism when an FBI agent admitted giving false testimony against Lee and when Asian-American groups argued that he was being singled out because of his Asian heritage. In the end, Lee pled guilty in September 2000 to one count of mishandling information, and the government dropped the other fifty-eight charges it had lodged against him (Stober and Hoffman 2001). Even with this result, in January 2001 President Clinton established a new counterintelligence board, bringing together the FBI, CIA, and Defense Department in an effort to be more proactive in conducting counterespionage. Known as CI-21, or Counterintelligence for the Twenty-First Century, it seeks to improve information sharing and place a heightened focus on economic espionage.

# Post–September 11, 2001

The events of September 11, 2001, were a transformational event for the United States's intelligence services. Both the FBI and CIA came under public and congressional criticism for their failure to anticipate and provide warning of the terrorist attacks on the Pentagon and World Trade Center. The last time their performance was the subject of such sustained and highly visible criticism was following the revelations of questionable covert action and illegal domestic espionage uncovered by the Church Committee in 1975. This was a Senate Select Committee that was established following revelations about illegal activity by the Nixon administration in its reelection bid that became known as the Watergate scandal and revelations about illegal CIA activity abroad. Senator Frank Church (D-Idaho) chaired the committee. Selected documents from the committee's hearings are included in the appendix. President George W. Bush resisted efforts by Congress to establish an independent bipartisan commission to study the performance of the intelligence community leading up to 9/11, but he ultimately relented in November 2002. If there had been any doubt, the politically charged nature of this inquiry quickly became apparent when Henry Kissinger, Bush's choice to head the commission, was forced to step down almost immediately due to charges of potential conflicts of interest with clients in his consulting firm and due to veiled critiques over the policies he had advocated as secretary of state and national security advisor in the Nixon and Ford administrations. The first Democratic choice for cochair, former Senator George Mitchell, also resigned. Kissinger and Mitchell were replaced by former New Jersey governor Thomas Keane and former congressman Lee Hamilton, respectively.

A joint congressional intelligence committee investigation into those 9/11 events provides insight into the initial analysis of what went wrong. It calls for disciplining those officials whose poor decisions or inaction contributed to the success of the terrorist attack, creating a cabinet-level intelligence czar to oversee the operation of the intelligence community, and it also calls for the creation of a separate domestic spy agency. Asserting that responsibility begins at the top, Senator Richard Shelby (R-Alabama), who sat on the intelligence committee, has called upon Director of Central Intelligence George Tenet to resign. In the report the FBI is criticized for its bureaucratic culture and cumbersome bureaucracy, which prevent it from adequately responding to national security threats. The FBI and CIA are also criticized for their failure to share information. To some observers this problem is not new. Mark Riebling (2002) traces it back to the Ames and Hanssen cases, in which the FBI and CIA engaged in a halting and unproductive cooperation that was marked by mutual suspicion and distrust.

The possibility of creating a new, independent domestic intelligence agency was also supported by an independent terrorism commission chaired by the former Republican governor of Virginia, James Gilmore III. FBI director Robert Mueller III gave a spirited defense of the FBI in December 2002. He rejected calls for separating domestic intelligence and law enforcement into two different organizations. He also claimed that the FBI was adapting to the post-9/11 world and that the FBI had thwarted almost 100 terrorist attacks since that date and helped capture some 3,000 terrorists worldwide.

The new emphasis on domestic spying and counterespionage that comes with this antiterrorist focus also raises some concerns. Some within the intelligence community are concerned that it will lead to a neglect of spy satellites. In place is a program to develop a new generation of spy satellites, the Future Imagery Architecture program. One estimate suggests that between $625 and $900 million is needed to get the program back on track so that new satellites will be operational when needed to replace the existing inventory of KH-11 Keyhole satellites. Others are concerned about possible violations of civil rights and liberties that might accompany an overzealous or excessive interpretation of the mandate given to those charged with domestic spying. Less than one week after Mueller defended the FBI, a coalition of Arab and Muslim groups brought a class action lawsuit against the Justice Department for its mass detention of immigrants from Muslim countries who registered with the Immigration and Naturalization Service (INS) as required by post-9/11 legislation. One estimate placed the number of detainees in Los Angeles at 1,000. Official INS figures placed it at less than 250.

As daunting as the counterespionage challenge facing the intelligence community is in the area of terrorism, it pales in scope when compared to the challenge of recruiting spies within these terrorist organizations. Operating in small cells, these groups are not easily penetrated. Walk-ins are highly valued but less likely to surface, or survive, in nonbureaucratic environments. There are also the issues of language and ethnicity. Not everyone can be a spy in a Muslim- or Arab-centered terrorist network. Indicative of the extent of the problem is the difficulty the intelligence community is having in hiring Arab linguists. The head of the FBI's language services estimates that it takes interviewing ten applicants for the FBI to find one acceptable linguist. She estimates that 65 percent fail the language test, 20 percent fail the polygraph, and 10 percent are eliminated for security reasons. Another FBI official commented: "kitchen Urdu is not the same as how to make a bomb Urdu."

The following chapter turns to the debate over the practice of espionage in the contemporary world. The chapter will examine how espionage relates to world politics, other elements of intelligence, the intelligence bureaucracy, and national security policy.

# Further Reading

A good place to start studying espionage in the United States is with historical overviews of the subject. Several very readable ones exist. They tend to be told from either a supportive or critical perspective, so more than one should be consulted in order to maintain objectivity. Among them are Christopher Felix, *A Short Course in the Secret War* (New York: Dell, 1988, second edition); G. J. A. O'Toole, *Honorable Treachery: A History of Intelligence, Espionage, and Covert Action from the American Revolution to the CIA* (New York: Atlantic Monthly Press, 1991); John Ranelagh, *The Agency: The Rise and Decline of the CIA* (New York: Touchstone, 1987); John Waller, *The Unseen War in Europe: Espionage and Conspiracy in the Second World War* (New York: Random House, 1966); John Prados, *Presidents' Secret Wars: CIA and Pentagon Covert Operations from World War II to Iranscam* (New York: William Morrow, 1986); and David Robarge, *Intelligence in the War for Independence* (Washington, DC: Center for the Study of Intelligence, 1997).

Given the prominence of the CIA in the study of espionage in the United States, it is also important to develop a good sense of this organization and its internal dynamics and history. Again, because of the highly charged nature of CIA activities over the years it is important to read more than one of these before making conclusions. Starting places include Ray Cline, *The CIA: Reality vs. Myth* (Washington, DC: Acropolis, 1982); Burton Hersh, *The Old Boys: The American Elite and the Origins of the CIA* (New York: Charles Scribner's Sons, 1992); Loch Johnson, *The Central Intelligence Agency: History and Documents* (New York: Oxford University Press, 1989); David Rudgers, *Creating the Secret State: The Origins of the Central Intelligence Agency, 1943–1947* (Lawrence: Kansas University Press,

2000); Thomas Troy, *Will Bill and Intrepid: Donovan, Stephenson, and the Origins of the CIA* (New Haven, CT: Yale University Press, 1966); Patrick McGarvey, *CIA: The Myth and the Madness* (Baltimore: Penguin, 1973); David Wise, *The Politics of Lying: Government Deception, Secrecy, and Power* (New York: Vintage, 1973); Morton Halperin et al., *The Lawless State: The Crimes of the U.S. Intelligence Agencies* (Baltimore: Penguin, 1976); and David Wise and Thomas Ross, *The Invisible Government* (New York: Vintage, 1964).

A valuable source of insight into the operation of the intelligence agencies comes from memoir-type accounts written by retired intelligence professionals or about them. As the intelligence organizations engage in activities that extend beyond espionage (and many are written by intelligence officials engaged in covert action), espionage is not always a prominent theme in the writings. Among the most popular of these accounts are Victor Marchetti and John Marks, *The CIA and the Cult of Intelligence* (New York: Dell, 1974); Frank Snepp, *Decent Interval: An Insider's Account of Saigon's Indecent End Told by the CIA's Chief Strategy Analyst in Vietnam* (New York: Vintage, 1977); David Atlee Phillips, *The Night Watch, 25 Years of Peculiar Service* (New York: Atheneum, 1977); William Colby, *Honorable Men: My Life in the CIA* (New York: Simon and Schuster, 1978); Tom Mangold, *Cold Warrior: James Jesus Angleton, the CIA's Master Spy Hunter* (New York: Simon and Schuster, 1991); Mary Bancroft, *Autobiography of a Spy* (New York: Morrow, 1983); and Thomas Powers, *The Man Who Kept Secrets: Richard Helms and the CIA* (New York: Pocket Books, 1979).

A number of good works are readily available on the technological dimension of espionage both as it relates to codebreaking and aerial surveillance. See James Bamford, *The Puzzle Palace: A Report on America's Most Secret Agency* (Boston: Houghton Mifflin, 1982); William Burrows, *Deep Black: Space Espionage and National Security* (New York: Random House, 1986); Dwayne Day et al., eds., *Eye in the Sky: The Story of Corona Spy Satellites* (Washington, DC: Smithsonian, 1998); Jeffrey Richelson, *America's Secret Eyes in Space: The History of U.S. Spy Satellites* (New York: Harper and Row, 1990); Peter Calvocoressi, *Top Secret Ultra* (New York: Ballantine, 1980); and Paul Lasher, *Spy Flights of the Cold War* (London: Sutton, 1996).

Finally, a number of treatments of individual cases of espionage against the United States are available. They include Robert Lindsey, *The Falcon and the Snowman: A True Story of Friendship and Espionage* (London: Jonathan Cape, 1980) [about Christopher Boyce and Andrew Lee]; Pete Early, *Confessions of a Spy: The Real Story of Aldrich Ames* (New York: G. P. Putnam's Sons, 1997); and William Blum, *I Pledge Allegiance* (New York: Simon and Schuster, 1987) [about the Walker spy ring].

# References

Ameringer, Charles. 1990. *U.S. Foreign Intelligence: The Secret Side of American History*. Lanham, MD: Lexington Books.

Andrew, Christopher. 1995. *For the President's Eyes Only: Secret Intelligence and the American Presidency from Washington to Bush*. New York: HarperCollins.

Barron, John. 1987. *Breaking the Ring: The Bizarre Case of the Walker Family Spy Ring*. Boston: Houghton Mifflin.

Corson, William. 1977. *The Armies of Ignorance: The Rise of the American Intelligence Empire*. New York: Dial.

Donner, Frank. 1981. *The Age of Surveillance: The Aims and Methods of America's Political Intelligence System*. New York: Vintage.

Dunlop, Richard. 1982. *Donovan: America's Master Spy*. Santa Monica, CA: Rand Corporation.

Fishel, Edwin C. 1996. *The Secret War for the Union: The Untold Story of Military Intelligence in the Civil War*. Boston: Houghton Mifflin.

Havill, Adrian. 2001. *The Spy Who Stayed Out in the Cold: The Secret Life of FBI Double Agent Robert Hanssen*. New York: St. Martin's.

Kahn, David. 1967. *The Codebreakers: The Story of Secret Writing*. New York: Macmillan.

Karalekas, Anne. 1977. *The History of the Central Intelligence Agency*. Laguna Hills, CA: Aegean Park.

Martin, David. 1980. *Wilderness of Mirrors*. New York: Ballantine.

Permanent Select Committee on Intelligence, United States House of Representatives. 1994. *Report of Investigation: The Aldrich Ames Espionage Case*. Washington, DC: U.S. Government Printing Office.

Richelson, Jeffrey. 1987. *American Espionage and the Soviet Target*. New York: Quill.

Riebling, Mark. 2002. *Wedge: From Pearl Harbor to 9/11: How the Secret War between the FBI and CIA Has Endangered National Security*. New York: Simon and Schuster.

Romerstein, Herbert, and Eric Breindel. 2000. *The VENONA Secrets: Exposing Soviet Espionage and America's Traitors*. Washington, DC: Regnery.

Rositzke, Henry. 1977. *CIA's Secret Operations: Espionage, Counterespionage, and Covert Action*. Boulder, CO: Westview.

Stober, Dan, and Ian Hoffman. 2001. *Convenient Spy: Wen Ho Lee and the Politics of Nuclear Espionage*. New York: Simon and Schuster.

Wise, David. 1995. *Nightmover: How Aldrich Ames Sold the CIA to the KGB for $4.6 Million.* New York: HarperCollins.

Wise, David. 2002. *Spy: The Inside Story of How the FBI's Robert Hanssen Betrayed America.* New York: Random House.

# 2

# Understanding the Contemporary Espionage Debate

Chapter 1 surveyed the history of espionage with a special focus on the American experience. This chapter will examine espionage in a global context in order to provide a comparative perspective from which to better judge the American experience. Here, the purpose is to place the history of espionage, and in particular its contemporary forms, in a conceptual context. This chapter will examine ten issues that go to the heart of questions concerning espionage and the dilemmas of counterespionage today.

## Spies and Spy Catchers

It was noted at the outset of this book that two people play the game of espionage. One is the spy; the other is the spy catcher. Spy novels, movies, and Cold War propaganda on both the American and Soviet sides have conspired to create a popular image of spies and of spy catchers that bears little resemblance to reality. Spies and spy catchers come from a variety of backgrounds, but it is not easy to find a James Bond among them.

Spies are motivated by a number of factors that are not unique to any country or historical period. One motivation to spy is blackmail. It is often associated with Soviet recruitment practice, but others practice it as well. Sexual preference or illicit

**45**

affairs are common fodder for blackmail. In pre–World War I Austria-Hungary the Russians blackmailed Alfred Redl, who was homosexual and was the head of the Austro-Hungarian Empire's counterespionage unit, into spying for them. He spied for Russia from 1902 to 1913. After World War II the Soviet Union recruited a number of spies in Europe by threatening to expose their fascist or Nazi backgrounds. Blackmail is also employed in trying to turn an exposed spy into a double agent. A second motivation for spying is money. In some cases the amounts may be large, but this is not necessarily the case. Often only small sums of money are sufficient to induce someone to spy or to keep him or her engaged as a spy. As has been shown in this book, paying spies large sums of money is often dangerous because it attracts attention to them. Often, spies will have most of their money placed in bank accounts that are beyond the view of their home governments. They will then draw upon this money during their retirements. A third motivational factor is ideology. Some spies are politically motivated; they believe in the cause they are working for and do not judge their actions as treasonous. The "isms" involved may be quite varied: communism, capitalism, ethnic nationalism, or patriotism are among the most prevalent. Finally, some spies are motivated by a complex set of psychological needs that combine ambition, power, and adventure.

In all likelihood, more than one set of motives is present in any given situation. It is up to the spy handler to understand his or her agent and manage him or her accordingly. Spies who work for money are likely to exaggerate their accomplishments or perhaps try to sell their services to a higher bidder. The ideological spy may loose sight of his or her immediate objective and overreach it, thereby risking exposure. The blackmailed spy may grow resentful, become unproductive, or come to present a security risk.

Counterespionage, or spy catching, is an endeavor beset by contradictory forces. It is defensive in nature yet offensive in outlook. Where covert action seeks to secretly bring about changes in policies on conditions abroad, spy catching is passive and defensive. It is designed to protect secrets. Yet to successfully protect secrets requires that spy catchers go on the offensive. They must actively be on the lookout for spies and take steps to frustrate them. In outlook, the spy catcher is part detective and part spy. Counterespionage requires an awareness of the motivations of spies, their standard operating procedures or tradecraft, and their targets. It requires care and stealth in order not to draw attention to oneself and alert the spy. The goal of the spy catcher is also marked by contradictions. On the one hand, the spy catcher seeks to capture the spy so that he or she may be punished and the spy catcher's secrets protected. On the other hand, the spy catcher is interested in leaving spies in place, observing their behavior in hopes of tracing their activity to other spies. Finally, the success of spy catching efforts depends simultaneously on close cooperation between intelligence services and on compartmentalization of effort. Close cooperation and trust is needed in order to ensure that information is passed quickly between those seeking to protect secrets and those engaged in covert action or the collection, analysis, and dissemination of information. But, distance and distrust (or at least a healthy skepticism) are also needed if spy catchers are to practice their craft effectively and the damage caused by spies is to be minimized.

# Espionage and the Nature of World Politics

There is disagreement on the fundamental nature of world politics. Realists see world politics as an arena in which states struggle to survive by acquiring and managing power. In their view the game of world politics is played with few rules. International law, pubic opinion, and the promises of other states count for little. Sovereignty is the key concept, and, by definition, this means that there exists no source of authority above the state. In the realist view, the only rules of world politics are those agreed upon by states and that states can enforce. Self-reliance and self-protection are the highest values.

Liberals view world politics through a neo-Wilsonian lens. They see the root causes of conflict as lying less in the basic nature of world politics as in flawed policies and flawed individuals. In particular, they reject policies that stress balancing power and zero-sum approaches to promoting security. Where realists tend to see promoting the national interest and promoting the global interest as incompatible goals, liberals see no inherent tension. Promoting democracy, building international institutions, linking people through free trade, and respecting fundamental human rights are viewed as providing a solid foundation for a successful foreign policy.

Realism and liberalism are not the only perspectives from which world politics can be studied. Many scholars also employ dependency theory, feminism, globalism, and postmodernism as the starting point for their studies. Regardless of which perspective is used, one of the fundamental problems that must be explained is why states cooperate. Again, realists and liberals tend to put forward different answers. Liberals stress the importance of absolute gains: states will cooperate as long as they improve their position in some absolute sense. Realists stress the importance of relative gains: states will only cooperate when they can improve their position relative to an adversary.

Agreement between the two positions does exist, however, at a more fundamental level. Both agree that a major obstacle to cooperation is uncertainty. It is uncertainty over what can be gained by cooperating. It is uncertainty over whether the other states can be trusted. It is uncertainty over what the motives are behind the actions of the other states. The starting point for overcoming uncertainty and increasing the predictability of the actions of other states is the acquisition of information about them. Espionage is a means of doing so, but given the deceit and potentially treasonous nature of the act, it is also one surrounded by ambivalence (Stein 1990).

International law recognizes the central role played by espionage in information gathering in times of war. As far back as the Declaration of Brussels of 1874, espionage has been considered to be a lawful means of warfare. Its unique nature has also been recognized. Spies, for example, need to be captured in the act of spying in order to be convicted. A spy who flees the country he or she was spying in and returns to his or her homeland is not considered to be a spy any longer. This is different from a criminal, who remains a criminal until captured. If captured in the act of spying, however, international law supports denying a spy certain rights and privileges that would otherwise be afforded to people charged with a crime. The peacetime status of espionage is less clear. Some international law scholars treat espionage as illegal in times of peace. It is seen as a violation of sovereignty and the political independence of states. Others see it as a morally, politically, and legally acceptable activity (Demerest 1996).

The distinction between wartime and peacetime espionage is losing its theoretical and practical importance. The formal declaration of war is becoming an anachronism. World War II was the last declared war the United States participated in. Korea,

Vietnam, the Persian Gulf War, peacekeeping operations in Kosovo and Lebanon, Grenada, and the war against terrorism have all been conducted without an official declaration of war. In operational terms the boundary between peace and war is also fading. During the Cold War the United States and Soviet Union considered themselves to be in a state of warfare short of actual combat but one that included military, political, and diplomatic competition and conflict. The foreign policies of many lesser states, especially those locked into rivalry wars such as those between India and Pakistan and Israel and its Arab neighbors, also do not make a distinction between war and peace. Nowhere is the boundary between war and peace more blurred and ill defined than in the case of terrorism. As the events of 9/11 reveal, successful antiterrorist policy making depends upon information, but the collection and analysis of information cannot wait until the terrorist act has taken place. It must precede it and take place during times of peace.

## Espionage and Surprise

On any given day there is little reason for policymakers to expect the unexpected when taking an inventory of the state of the world. Bureaucratic inertia, domestic political pressures, vested personal interests, and constraints imposed by other states and existing policies conspire to prevent much more than incremental change from taking place. The normal solution to a stubborn diplomatic or military problem is to undertake a new initiative. On close inspection, however, that new initiative is generally little more than a variation on an old theme.

But, surprise does happen. At 3:00 A.M. on June 22, 1941, 151 German divisions supported by some 3,500 tanks and 1,800 aircraft caught the world by surprise and crossed into the Soviet Union. In its first four weeks Operation BARBAROSSA swept across 400 miles and closed in on Moscow. By midsummer, German forces had conquered an area twice the size of France. The Japanese attack on Pearl Harbor on December 7, 1941, was equally spectacular in its results. The United States suffered the severe damage or loss of eight battleships, three light cruisers, four other ships, and 188 planes, and it suffered 3,435 casualties. On July 15, 1971, in less than ninety seconds, President Richard Nixon startled the world when he announced that he would soon make a visit to the People's Republic of China, bringing an end to more than two decades of diplomatic isolation and hostility between these two states (Betts 1982).

In and of itself, surprise is not important, though. As Hitler's invasion of Russia and the Japanese attack on Pearl Harbor illustrate, surprise, no matter how great, does not guarantee victory. Surprise is important when it invalidates the fundamental assumptions on which policies are based. In doing so, surprise acts as a power multiplier. It dramatically increases the amount of power possessed by the state carrying out the surprise. This is true irrespective of whether the power is military, diplomatic, technological, or economic in nature.

The power-multiplying impact of surprise is thus a constant danger that policymakers must guard against. Preventing surprise, however, is not an easy task, because the root causes of surprise are numerous. First, surprise can come about due to the deliberate actions of the enemy. At a minimum, states contemplating surprise will try to cloak their actions in secrecy. They will also engage in deception. Second, surprise may come about because of the decision-making processes of the enemy state. Indecision may make it difficult to identify an emerging pattern of behavior. Also, the attacking state always has the option of changing its plans, and in the process falsifying intelligence predictions of a pending attack.

A second set of obstacles to anticipating surprise is found in the normal ebb and flow of world events. Major lines of policy simply do not come in nice, neat packages. It is only with 20-20 hindsight that the correct interpretation of information is obvious. The most commonly cited impediments to correctly assessing a situation are the inherent ambiguity of information and noise. On the eve of Pearl Harbor the problem was not too little information but too much information. A great deal of information existed supporting all the wrong interpretations of the last-minute information being received. Where deception deliberately seeks to confuse an adversary, noise confuses the adversary simply by existing as extraneous information that intelligence services pick up. It is information that must be examined, evaluated, and dismissed in the search for signals of possible surprise.

A final set of obstacles to anticipating surprise is self-generated. Policymakers do not sit back and passively take in information. They interact with it, picking and choosing which pieces are relevant to their needs and which are not. One of the most important filters that determines what is seen is the immediate concerns that dominate the policymakers' agenda. Concerned only with military espionage, they may be blind to signs of economic espionage. Fearful of overseas terrorism, they may not pick up signs of domestic terrorist threats. Contingency plans may have the same blinding effect. Having spent considerable time and energy putting together a plan of action, the tendency is for it to color one's perceptions to the point where all future events are seen as being consistent with its fundamental assumptions. In a similar fashion, adherence to an ongoing line of action can blind policymakers to signs of a surprise. Selecting a course of action and building support for it is an expensive undertaking. Once adopted, personal and institutional prestige becomes attached to its success, and policymakers often find it difficult to accept information that suggests impending failure (Jervis 1976).

Espionage is an important means of trying to avert surprise. It offers policymakers a window through which to accurately gauge an adversary's true intentions and capabilities. It can negate deception and cut through noise. For these reasons espionage is unlikely ever to disappear. Though the risks of failure are great and the instances of failure may far outnumber the instances of success, policymakers will judge the effort worthwhile if even one Pearl Harbor or 9/11 can be averted. Espionage is not, however, a panacea or cure-all for the problem of surprise. It may yield a great amount of noise. We routinely see spies gathering more information then their handlers know what to do with. John Walker, it will be recalled, passed so much information to the Soviet Union that they reduced the frequency with which he passed secrets to them.

Espionage cannot overcome the self-generated blinders that prevent policymakers from seeing signs of surprise. If discovered, espionage may also become an instrument of deception by the target state, as it allows false and misleading information to be transmitted back to its adversary's intelligence services. The desire to do this is one reason that intelligence services are reluctant to expose a spy once he or she is identified. Their preference is to allow the spy to continue to engage in espionage in order to identify the entirety of the spy ring and to use the spy for their own purposes by feeding him or her false information.

# Espionage and the Intelligence Cycle

Espionage does not occur in isolation. It is part of a broader set of activities that are designed to inform policymakers about the world around them. Collectively these activities are referred to as the intelligence cycle. Successful intelligence estimating requires that all aspects of the intelligence cycle function effectively and that its individual parts interact in a productive fashion (CIA 1975).

The first step in the intelligence cycle is tasking. It is here that policymakers and senior intelligence officials determine what information they need to help them accomplish their missions and policy objectives. Without such guidance, intelligence agencies have no means of setting their collection priorities or targets. Personal and institutional definitions of national security threats and foreign policy goals will by default become the basis on which information is gathered.

The second step in the intelligence process is collection. It is here that espionage enters the intelligence cycle. It is one way of obtaining the information that was identified as important in the first stage. The intelligence community has a wide variety of collection strategies to choose from. A more basic choice is between open source information and secret information. Open source information is publicly available information. It may be obtained from a wide variety of sources including newspapers, the other media, government documents, databases, academic and professional journals, and the Internet.

Espionage is used to obtain secret information. A fundamental choice here is between technological espionage and classic human espionage. Technological espionage relies heavily upon satellites, planes, and electronic means to map the adversary's capabilities and intercept human communications. Human espionage seeks to directly acquire photographs, documents, and other materials of intelligence value by infiltrating key organizations.

The third step in the intelligence cycle is processing and evaluating the information obtained. Within the intelligence community a distinction is drawn between information and intelligence. Information is the raw material collected by overt and secret means that is provided to intelligence analysts. Information becomes intelligence only after it is evaluated and assessed. The evaluation of information involves two judgments. First, how reliable is the source? Second, how good is the information? As this suggests, spies who over time prove themselves to be reliable and provide good information are particularly valued.

The "goodness" of information can be established in several ways. It can be judged by the extent to which it fits with other information being collected and thus is part of a larger and internally consistent picture of the adversary. It is also judged by the extent to which other collection sources report the same information. Confidence about the value of the information under review increases as multiple sources report the same information. In order to boost confidence in the information they are working with, intelligence organizations will task multiple collection platforms (spies, satellites, military attachés, etc.) with obtaining the same information.

Processing information can be a complicated undertaking. In the area of technological espionage, intercepted messages must be decoded and translated, telemetry and signals intercepts must be displayed in a meaningful fashion, and photographic images must be produced. A key concern in classic human intelligence is protecting the spy. In the cases of John Walker, Philip (Robert) Hanssen, and Aldrich Ames, great care was given to protecting their identities through the use of code signals, periodic meetings that changed location, and dead drops. An important by-product of the need to protect the spy is that real-time crisis information will be difficult to obtain, as it places the spy at great risk of discovery.

Counterespionage enters the intelligence cycle at this point. By actively searching for spies and protecting one's own secrets, counterintelligence operations serve to increase the confidence of analysts and consumers in the information they are receiving. Paradoxically, counterespionage can also have the opposite effect. It can cripple intelligence analysis by calling the loyalty of everyone into doubt, and with it the information being provided. When the suspicions and doubts created by the conspiratorial mindset of counterespionage are left unchecked, a "wilderness of mirrors" is created from which there is no escape. Both the CIA under James Angleton and the British SIS in its search for the fifth man, to be discussed in the following section of this chapter, fell into this trap (Martin 1980).

The fourth stage in the intelligence cycle is analysis and production. Here the individual pieces of information that have been collected and assessed are now brought together. It is the job of analysts to determine their collective meaning and importance and to convey this intelligence to policymakers. Analysis can be both an individual and a group exercise, depending upon the nature of the issue being investigated. Intelligence estimates of enemy troop strength in Vietnam and the state of Soviet nuclear weapons programs routinely brought together officials from many intelligence organizations.

Finished intelligence, that which has been analyzed and assessed, is made available to policymakers in a number of forms. Current intelligence reports on day-to-day events provide policymakers with new developments and warnings about future developments. Intelligence estimates are reports that deal with specific problems. They are intended to help shape thinking about a problem by laying out its history, detailing what is known and unknown, and suggesting alternative futures. These reports may be produced on a regular basis, such as with the annual estimate on Soviet nuclear forces, or they may be commissioned on a onetime basis as new issues arise. A third type of finished intelligence is warnings intelligence. It focuses on urgent problems that may require action. Research intelligence provides in-depth background studies on a particular problem. Most commonly it either takes the form of basic background information or operational support information for the military. The final category of finished intelligence is scientific and technical intelligence. It generally focuses on the technical characteristics and performance capabilities of weapons systems.

The final stage in the intelligence cycle is a feedback stage in which policymakers respond to the intelligence they have received. In the process of doing so, they set in motion the first stage in which tasks and priorities are developed. When the intelligence cycle is working smoothly, such feedback occurs on an almost daily basis. One of the most important forms of current intelligence is the daily intelligence briefing given by the Central Intelligence Agency (CIA) to the president. The questions asked by the president, and his interest or disinterest in items in the briefing, are used by the CIA in organizing the next day's presentation.

One of the key questions that must be addressed in reaching a judgment on the future of espionage is: how central a role does it play in the intelligence cycle? If we in the modern world were to stop spying, what impact would that have on our ability to understand and anticipate the actions of adversaries? There is no clear-cut answer here. In some instances information might be obtained by alternative means that are less risky or morally compromising. It is also quite likely that some information considered vital can only be obtained through espionage. The impact of no longer engaging in espionage is also likely to be felt unevenly across the different reporting areas. Basic reports and background intelligence pieces might be least affected. The quality of warnings intelligence and estimates, however, might suffer greatly. Although there is no easy resolution of this matter, a starting point for thinking about how to make better use of espionage (or limit its use) is with intelligence tasking. Clearly stated and well-thought-out intelligence priorities and objectives might reduce the danger that espionage and other collection means will proceed with little oversight or purpose other than to collect everything possible.

## Espionage and the National Security Bureaucracy

The game of spy versus spy catcher is played by individuals. As such, personality counts for a great deal, both in the motivation of the spy and the ability of the spy catcher to see through the deception. It is impossible to read the accounts of John Walker, Philip (Robert) Hanssen, or Aldrich Ames (presented previously) or those of Jonathan Pollard and Oleg Penkovsky (presented in the following chapter) and not come away with a sense of how peculiar spies are. Just as important, however, for understanding the dynamics of espionage is its bureaucratic setting. The spy and spy catcher are supported by large organizations. Policymakers create organizations to address problems. The temptation is to view the organizations as neutral machines that respond in almost automatic fashion to external directives regarding goals, missions, tactics, and procedures, but only at the most general level is this imagery correct. It belies a more complex reality in which both competition between organizations and internal bureaucratic norms shape the behavior of organizations and their ability to achieve the purposes set for them.

Before examining the ways in which bureaucracy affects espionage, this chapter will briefly introduce some of the key organizational players. To simplify matters this chapter will only note those organizations that play active roles in the collection stage of the intelligence cycle, as the previous section has already noted that espionage enters the intelligence cycle in the collection stage.

The CIA is a major collector; two of its four directorates collect information. The Directorate of Operations is responsible for the clandestine collection of information. In an effort to facilitate cooperation with the military within the Directorate of Operations, there is an Office of Military Affairs. There is also a Counterintelligence Center and a Counterterrorism Center. The Directorate of Science and Technology provides support for the entire intelligence community in the areas of collecting, processing, and exploiting intelligence from open and secret sources of intelligence. In doing so it works closely with other non-CIA intelligence organizations such as the Foreign Broadcast Information Service and the National Photographic Interpretation Center. The other two directorates of the CIA are Administration and Intelligence. The latter is responsible for producing analysis and estimates.

Five units within the Department of Defense collect information. The National Security Agency collects, processes, and reports signals intelligence (SIGINT). The Defense Intelligence Agency oversees an all-source collection effort to ensure that current and future Department of Defense military requirements are met. The National Reconnaissance Office manages the government's spaceborne reconnaissance system. The Defense Airborne Reconnaissance Office operates the Defense Department's airborne reconnaissance program, including manned and unmanned aircraft and their ground processing stations. Finally, each of the military services maintains their own collection efforts within their areas of specialization.

Moving beyond these two main collectors of information, there are four other organizations. The State Department collects and transmits information through its diplomatic reports. The Treasury Department collects open source data on financial and monetary matters. The FBI has primary responsibility for counterintelligence and counterterrorism in the United States. In the course of carrying out these tasks the FBI will generate information that may be of value to other members of the intelligence community. Finally, the Department of Energy collects information regarding nuclear proliferation and related weapons development issues (Richelson 1985).

These organizations and others that are active in the production and dissemination of intelligence make up the U.S. intelligence community, which, however, is a community only in the loosest sense. The concept of community implies likeness and similarity; it suggests a group of organizations that share common goals and outlooks. More accurately, though, the members of the intelligence community constitute a federation of units that coexist and are jealous of maintaining their institutional autonomy. Within the U.S. intelligence community cooperation between the CIA and FBI on espionage matters has often been strained. This was especially true in the case of Edward Lee Howard, whom the CIA suspected of spying but about whom the CIA said nothing to the FBI until it was too late to stop him from fleeing to the Soviet Union. This has become an issue again in efforts to prevent terrorist attacks in the post-9/11 era as questions have been raised about internal information processing procedures and cooperation between these two institutions.

There is nothing abnormal about this conflict. Organization theorists note that specialization breeds parochialism as the lines on an organizational chart become lines of secrecy and loyalty. Hierarchy has a similar effect. Rank in an organization is a source of power and status. When hierarchy is combined with control over information, a situation results in which subordinates will often resist transmitting information to superiors that could be used to disparage their performance or upset comfortable routines. Because organizations are in competition with one another, the means selected to achieve policy objectives will be hotly contested. Organizations do not simply propose policy options; they lobby for the option that they are best able to implement or control. The CIA will not propose that the Defense Intelligence Agency collect certain data if it can do so. The FBI will not propose that the CIA be given the lead in counterespionage activity (Wilensky 1967).

The internal value system of intelligence organizations affects espionage and counterespionage in several important ways. First, there exists a kind of professional pecking order within intelligence agencies. Certain skills and career tracks are more highly valued than are others. Intelligence analysis is most favored, with covert action and counterintelligence being considered second rank.

Second, one finds a tendency for those inside an intelligence bureaucracy to adopt a protective and paternalistic attitude toward its members. Theirs is not a 9–5 job but a way of life, and one that requires a certain degree of separation from the rest of society. It also requires personal sacrifices of a magnitude that are seen as not being fully appreciated by those outside the secret world of intelligence. Background checks and lie detector tests are formal ways of screening candidates for membership into this fraternal order, but once admitted their loyalty and fitness for duty are rarely questioned. The discovery of Aldrich Ames was significantly delayed because the possibility that a spy might exist within the CIA was discounted. It was further hindered by the blocking effect that specialization had on information flow. An even more stunning case emerged in Great Britain, where Kim Philby and his spy ring went undetected in large part because their Cambridge credentials made them accepted members in intelligence circles (see the following chapter).

## Espionage and National Security Threats

When the Cold War ended with the disintegration of the Soviet Union and repudiation of communism, there were frequent references to a peace dividend, the idea that it would no longer be possible to reduce the high level of federal government spending. National security expenditures could be reduced because the threat to the United States had diminished significantly. The United States had emerged from the Cold War triumphant and was the only remaining superpower. The major target for advocates of a peace dividend was the military budget, but other elements of the national security and foreign policy bureaucracy were not immune from calls for downsizing. The State Department was forced to close embassies and consulates, and it underwent a major reorganization. The intelligence community found itself on the defensive for its failure to predict the end of the Cold War. There were even calls in the Senate for dismantling the CIA.

Because so much of the United States's espionage effort was targeted either directly or indirectly at Soviet targets, it is not surprising that many saw a diminished need for classical human espionage in the post–Cold War world. The prospect of a democratic Russia held the hope that whatever information might be needed could be obtained through open sources and that Russian compliance with arms control agreements and other cooperative measures could be verified through technical means and through increased transparency and the open exchange of information.

Proponents of espionage found it difficult to challenge the view that the scope of the Soviet threat to the United States had diminished greatly. Instead, they built their case on three different arguments. First, although the threat of deliberate Soviet military action against the United States had diminished, a different threat existed. The problem now was accidental war and the uncontrolled proliferation of Soviet nuclear weapons and related technologies. The root causes of these problems were found in the decay of the Soviet system. Organizational decay and political infighting had created a situation in which the Russian government lacked the capability to control its own military forces. The disintegration of the military had left many scientists in poverty, and many were reportedly willing to sell their services to the highest bidder.

A second line of argument held that although the United States was the sole remaining superpower, this condition could not last. The fundamental dynamics of world politics required that other world states move to balance the power of the United States. The emergence of challengers was inevitable, the espionage proponents warned. The prudent exercise of American power could delay this process but not prevent it from occurring. It was simply a matter of when and what state or states would be the challenger. Some expected a resurgence of Russian power. Others pointed to China as the most likely challenger. Japan and Germany were also identified as states that needed to be watched closely.

Finally, some argued that although the Russian threat had diminished, a new breed of security threats now faced the United States. Although in the Cold War and throughout American history foreign states had been the primary threat to American security, in the post–Cold War era nonstate actors would constitute the greatest threat. In the popular imagery employed to make this argument it was asserted that during the Cold War the United States had faced a dangerous dragon, and in the post–Cold War era it was being confronted by a legion of poisonous snakes. Two types of snakes were singled out as especially dangerous. The first type was international criminal groups and drug smugglers. The second type was international terrorist groups (Berkowitz and Goodman 1989).

From the point of view of intelligence collection, these new threats are extremely challenging. The sheer size of the Soviet military, diplomatic, and espionage operations provided American intelligence organizations with multiple points of entry, but this is not the case with these new threats. They require that espionage be directed at either individuals or small groups. Gaining access to these people and gaining their confidence will not be easily done. It will require time and the recruitment of new individuals into the spy game as well as the development of new competencies. Someone who has spied or run agents in the Soviet Union targeting Soviet diplomats is not necessarily qualified to operate in the Middle East, Africa, or Asia against a drug smuggler, terrorist cell, or ex-patriot Russian physicist.

Directing espionage against potential challengers to the United States's superpower status, such as China, is also fraught with danger. Without clearly articulated collection tasks and priorities it is quite possible that little information of value will be collected. Organizational routine and bureaucratic inertia could come to dominate the espionage effort. Moreover, there is a danger of setting in motion a self-fulfilling prophecy: if, or more accurately when, these new U.S. spies are caught, it is possible that the targeted state may respond by increasing its military power or taking steps to distance itself politically from the United States. These are the very events that are most undesirable.

## Economic Espionage

By definition espionage is not an activity that is directed solely at military targets. Espionage is a means of acquiring information that would otherwise be unavailable. One area of espionage that has begun to receive a great deal of attention is economic espionage. It is estimated that in the post–Cold War era the percentage of collection and analysis resources devoted to economic issues by the U.S. intelligence community has risen from 10 percent to 40 percent. Unlike most espionage directed at military targets, economic espionage is as likely to be carried out by an ally as it is an adversary. The top twelve states placing economic spies in the United States are China, Canada, France, India, Japan, Germany, South Korea, Russia, Taiwan, Great Britain, Israel, and Mexico (Johnson 2000).

Three broad styles of economic espionage against the United States have been identified. The first targets are present and former nationals who work for American companies. China, Taiwan, and South Korea are said to practice this type of economic espionage. The second type of economic espionage relies heavily on traditional forms of Cold War military-oriented techniques and practices such as bribery, theft, and wiretapping. France, Russia, and Israel are identified as the leading practitioners of this type of economic espionage. The third style of economic espionage is practiced by Japan. It relies upon networks of industry and private organizations to obtain desired information.

Insight into the type of information sought after in economic espionage comes from a U.S. government study of Israeli spying. The report identifies three primary types of information being targeted. They are information to strengthen Israel's industrial base; information that can be exchanged with others for profit; and information that can be used to strengthen Israeli political ties with other states, especially as they relate to arms and intelligence needs. In concrete terms this translates into an interest in technology related to artillery gun tubes, coating for missile reentry vehicles, avionics, missile telemetry, and aircraft communications systems (Fialka 1997).

The existence of a globalized economy means that economic espionage against American firms does not have to be carried out in the United States. Many of the most aggressive spy operations are run abroad, where communication security is more lax and surveillance less sophisticated. According to one estimate, about 40 percent of economic espionage cases occur in Asia and 30 percent occur in Western Europe. A Canadian study concluded that roughly 1/3 of a group of 500 companies operating there had experienced security problems.

For its part the United States has refused to spy on private companies. Instead it focuses its resources on uncovering unfair trading practices and providing support for U.S. trade negotiations. One of the most celebrated cases involved a 1994 incident in which the United States uncovered evidence of a French bribe of Brazilian officials that was intended to steer a communications contract to a French firm. The U.S. government intervened and Brazil awarded the contract to Raytheon. All that is referenced is the fact that the U.S. government approached Brazil and complained. A similar situation had developed earlier with a potential French contract in Saudi Arabia that was suddenly awarded to a U.S. firm after the American government complained to the Saudis about bribery being involved in the deal with the French.

This case highlights some of the difficult issues that must constantly be addressed in economic espionage and that separate economic espionage from military espionage. In cases of military espionage, the discovery of a spy does not necessarily lead to immediate action. The spy may be fed false information, and his or her network of agents and handlers will be mapped. It is also quite clear that it is national security concerns that are being protected in this sort of spy catching. But what of economic espionage? If espionage uncovers evidence that secrets are being stolen, that a company is being undermined from within, or that competitors hold an unfair advantage, what should be done? What is the government's responsibility to private firms? Who is economic counterespionage intended to protect: a firm, an industry, or the American economy? What should one do if economic espionage helps General Motors but harms Ford? Complicating matters even further is the question, what is an American firm in an era of globalization?

# Controlling Espionage

No one doubts the need for secrecy in the area of intelligence. No one doubts the need for control over intelligence. Espionage is not immune from the tension inherent in these competing imperatives. The enduring challenge of intelligence policy is to accomplish both objectives at the same time without sacrificing the effectiveness of either one.

The conventional starting place in thinking about control is passing laws and exercising legislative oversight. Each is problematic in the area of intelligence. Most of the rules governing intelligence agencies, such as the prohibition on assassinations, are found in executive orders and not in laws passed by Congress. Lawmakers have been reluctant to pass legislation detailing how espionage, counterespionage, covert action, and intelligence analysis should be conducted. Instead, Congress has treated these activities as executive functions best left to the discretion of the president. What Congress does insist upon is that it be informed and briefed by the intelligence community. Since the mid-1970s each house of Congress has had a standing intelligence committee for this purpose. Prior to that, the intelligence community briefed a variety of committees, and congressional oversight was haphazard. A key factor prompting the creation of these committees was a series of revelations that the CIA had been spying on American citizens (Johnson 1988).

Presidential control presents its own problems. Crowded agendas, limited time, and limited interest conspire to push intelligence to the background. Even presidents who are interested in intelligence matters may not be interested in the details of espionage operations. Because espionage operations involve deceit and treasonous activity, a case can be made that presidents should not know all the details of espionage operations. "Plausible denial" is a valued and time-honored phrase in intelligence work that allows policymakers to feign ignorance of operations gone wrong. The more intimately presidents or legislators are involved in espionage operations, the more difficult it is to assert such a claim. It will be shown in the next chapter that the close interaction of key Israeli officials ultimately made it impossible to sustain the argument that Jonathan Jay Pollard was part of a rogue operation in spying on the United States.

In addition to thinking about controlling espionage in terms of externally imposed restrictions and standards, one can approach it from the perspective of control being provided by the intelligence organizations themselves. This brings this discussion back to the subject of espionage and bureaucracy. It has already been asserted that the organizational culture within which espionage is carried out serves to protect its members and not to control their behavior.

To this, one can add a further complicating factor. Espionage involves deceit and treachery. In most Americans' everyday lives and in their dealings with friends, family, and coworkers, these are not traits people value or respect. Their inclination is to follow Secretary of State Henry Stimson's lead when he rejected American espionage on the grounds that it was ethically wrong to read other people's mail. A basis for morally imposed standards to control espionage would thus seem to exist. Working against this moral imperative are the reasons of state doctrine. This doctrine asserts that although certain actions are clearly indefensible in people's personal lives, they can be justified as necessary in the realm of foreign policy because the survival of the state is at stake. Espionage and counterespionage are easily justified from this value perspective.

To point out the difficulties with internal control over espionage, however, is not to assert that it is impossible. Military officers often find themselves in circumstances in which externally imposed controls are imprecise and distant and in which the moral basis for their decisions is far from clear. We rely upon their professionalism to guide them in their decision making. We also hold them accountable for their actions. The same logic can be applied to intelligence work. Just as is the case for military officers, intelligence professionals operate in a turbulent environment for which detailed rules of conduct cannot be written in advance or to cover all possibilities. Superiors rely upon the professionalism of intelligence officials to act in an appropriate manner when recruiting agents, countering foreign espionage efforts, or intercepting and handling secret information. The rough and tough image of intelligence work should not hide the reservoir of professionalism that exists within the intelligence community. It needs only to be recalled that much of the information wrongdoing that formed the heart of the Church Committee Report on abuses by the intelligence community (a portion of which is included in chapter 5) was provided by CIA intelligence officers in response to a call by Director of Central Intelligence William Colby for them to come forward with information of wrongdoing.

Within the CIA and the intelligence community a series of directives provide a baseline for exercising such professional judgment. Guidelines were issued in 1995 that instructed CIA case officers to balance human rights concerns and other criminal violations against the value of the intelligence the agent might provide in making a decision as to whether or not to recruit an individual. In 1975 Director of Central Intelligence George Bush issued guidelines restricting the recruitment of members of the clergy and the media. The CIA's use of the media and the clergy for intelligence operations had emerged as one of the major areas of concern in congressional investigations of questionable activity by the intelligence community. It was widely held by political commentators across the political spectrum that the integrity of a free press and the principle of separation of church and state had to be placed above suspicion.

The popular image of the CIA in the 1970s was that of a rogue elephant out of control engaging in covert operations and espionage with little regard to laws or the national interest. Investigations by the Church and Pike Committees showed this reputation to be unwarranted. The external and internal control mechanisms in place provide a forum for public debate and government supervision over espionage. It is important to recognize that this system of oversight may produce widely differing outcomes. In the mid 1990s the CIA came under criticism for having on its payroll several agents in Guatemala who had a record of human rights abuses. The CIA took steps such as instructing officers to weigh the human rights and criminal records of potential intelligence sources in their recruitment programs. After the September 11, 2001, terrorist attacks, Congress urged the CIA to reconsider its "dirty hands" prohibition and to take greater risks in recruiting agents that might possess valuable information (Hitz 2002).

## Counterespionage and National Security

Espionage makes counterespionage necessary. Counterespionage efforts can range from the passive protection of secrets to proactive efforts to ferret out spies and turn them into double agents. Counterespionage is police work and involves a different mindset than does intelligence. This is most evident when sufficient evidence exists to arrest a spy. Intelligence agencies prefer not to make that arrest, in hopes that surveillance will provide additional information about the spy and his or her level of penetration into the organization. The FBI, which has primary jurisdiction for counterespionage, would prefer that the arrest be made. Its record of success and failure is measured by the number of spies that are caught and successfully prosecuted. Both approaches to counterespionage make valid points, and thus the tension between counterespionage as police work and as intelligence work can never be fully reconciled. Further complicating matters is the reality that identifying and pursuing someone as a spy from the perspective of counterespionage as intelligence and counterespionage as police work proceed from different standards of evidence. The FBI must have sufficient evidence to make its case stand up in a court of law. The CIA can proceed with less-compelling evidence and with evidence that will remain secret if no arrest is made.

Most damaging to the conduct of counterespionage in the United States has been the repeated tendency for counterintelligence to be directed at domestic groups. Especially vulnerable have been ethnic groups and dissident political groups that hold views outside of the political mainstream. Two sets of factors combine to make members of these groups the target of counter-intelligence efforts. The first lies with the political insecurity of government leaders. These groups are viewed as political enemies that have to be defeated.

The second factor is more fundamental and transcends the identities of the individuals in office. It lies in the quest for absolute security (Chace and Carr 1988). Linked closely to the historical American sense of exceptionalism and separation from the world is the belief that proper policies can make the United States immune to foreign threats. Foreign policies of isolationism and unilateralism help to ensure that foreign governments cannot directly harm the United States either through war or entrapment. The danger remains, however, that hostile foreign powers could attack American national security indirectly by working from within, by using domestic American groups as proxies. Because this danger is general rather than specific it requires constant vigilance and surveillance. And it is only a short step from vigilance and surveillance to infiltration and manipulation.

Historically, legal, political, and bureaucratic measures have been taken to reduce this potential for abuse and excess in the conduct of counterespionage activities. On the legal front, the constitutional ban on unwarranted searches and seizures makes no exception for counterespionage operations. Politically it is hoped that congressional oversight powers will detect and limit excesses. Bureaucratically, an organizational division of labor exists in which the FBI has primary jurisdiction for counterespionage activities in the United States, and the CIA is prohibited from having domestic law enforcement, subpoena, or police powers. Neither collectively nor individually have these control mechanisms succeeded in totally preventing counterespionage abuses. In politically charged times the quest for absolute security has proven to be too strong and the shroud of secrecy surrounding espionage too blinding.

# Espionage and 9/11

Previously in this chapter, the changing nature of national security threats was noted. Up until the terrorist attacks on the World Trade Center and Pentagon on September 11, 2001, few citizens were involved in the debate over how best to protect American national security or where those threats emanated from. This has now changed, and the place of intelligence in American national security policy is very much debated. Much of this attention has been focused on the analytical challenge involved in detecting an impending terrorist attack (along with recriminations for why the attacks of September 11 were not more precisely foreseen). A concern for improved intelligence analysis leads one quickly to the field of espionage and counterespionage, for as was noted in the discussion of the intelligence cycle, espionage is one important tool used by the intelligence community in collecting the data on which to base its analysis, and counterespionage is a necessary activity to protect one's own secrets. The unique challenge that terrorism presents to espionage and counterespionage is twofold. First, the nongovernmental nature of the enemy requires the rethinking of penetration strategies and of who might be an enemy agent. Keeping track of possible Soviet agents and penetration targets in the United States during the Cold War was an immense task but one that is now dwarfed by the challenge presented by terrorist groups. Second, it is not just government or economic secrets that must be protected. Terrorists are interested in obtaining a much wider set of information, and much of it is publicly available.

Two major initiatives have been taken in the year following the September 11, 2001, terrorist attacks that potentially hold great significance for the conduct of espionage and counterespionage by American authorities. The first is the USA PATRIOT Act. The second is the establishment of the Department of Homeland Security.

Officially known as the Uniting and Strengthening America by Providing Appropriate Tools Required to Intercept and Obstruct Terrorism Act, the USA PATRIOT Act was adopted by Congress on October 25, 2001, and signed into law the following day by President George W. Bush. The USA PATRIOT Act, 342 pages in length, emerged as the Bush administration's immediate legislative response to the September 11, 2001, terrorist attacks on the World Trade Center and the Pentagon. Its intent is to provide law enforcement officials with an enhanced ability to investigate and prosecute terrorism. One of its provisions expands the definition of engagement in terrorist activity to include providing support for groups that the individual "knew or should have known were terrorist organizations." Rather than obtain a wiretap order, authorities will be able to use search warrants to read opened voice mail messages and electronic mail from Internet providers. The USA PATRIOT Act also expands the list of toxins that are classified as dangerous and requires background checks of scientists who work with them.

One of the most important sets of provisions in the USA PATRIOT Act affects the conduct of intelligence activities in the United States. Intelligence surveillance is not permitted when foreign intelligence is a "significant purpose" rather than "the purpose" of the undertaking. The act broadens the authority of the government to contract for terrorist information with individuals who were once placed off-limits because of human rights violations or other transgressions. It also contains a number of directives intended to promote intelligence sharing and cooperation among intelligence agencies. Included here is the prompt disclosure of information obtained in a criminal investigation and the establishment of a virtual translation center within the intelligence community, the center's purpose being to speed the rate of translation of information and its dissemination through the entire intelligence community.

Many of the provisions of the USA PATRIOT Act (some of which contain sunset provisions that take effect on December 31, 2005), as well as the speed with which the act was passed, concern many onlookers. The legislation was passed so quickly that there were no committee reports or votes taken, thus denying law enforcement officials and outside experts the opportunity to comment on the act's provisions. Furthermore, the absence of typical committee hearings deprived implementers and legal officials of insight into the congressional intent in passing the USA PATRIOT Act. Congress did not establish oversight procedures for measuring the effectiveness of these provisions and by which to judge the actions of those who were carrying them out. Finally, the sunset provisions written into many portions of the USA PATRIOT Act guarantee that Congress will have to return to these issues in 2005.

On November 25, 2002, President George W. Bush signed into law the bill creating the Department of Homeland Security. Bush encountered considerable opposition in the pre-November 2002 general election in his attempt to create the department. It was only with the Republican Party's victories in that election, which guaranteed a Republican Congress in 2003, that the bill was passed. The most significant stumbling block centered on civil service protections and bargaining rights of those who were slated to work in the new agency. Most Democrats supported a plan that would have required Bush to work closely with labor unions before changing the personnel system. The president wanted the agency itself to have the freedom to hire, fire, move, and discipline workers in the Department of Homeland Security. The impasse was broken when the election provided the Republican Party with a majority in the next Congress.

According to the legislation the Department of Homeland Security is to combine activities from twenty-two different federal agencies in order to better protect the United States from terrorism. It is envisioned that all agencies will be merged into the Department of Homeland Security by September 20, 2003. The total work force will bring together 170,000 employees. Agencies targeted for incorporation include the Immigration and Naturalization Service, the Secret Service, the Customs Service, the Federal Emergency Management Agency, the Transportation Security Administration, the Coast Guard, and the Border Patrol.

Originally President Bush had resisted the idea of creating a Department of Homeland Security. He preferred the establishment of an Office of Homeland Security within the White House. He established this office on October 8, 2001, by an executive order. Tom Ridge, whom Bush nominated to be the first secretary of the Department of Homeland Security, was selected to serve as the assistant to the president for Homeland Security. Bush's line of action produced a negative response from Congress on two counts. First, as an assistant to the president, Ridge's appointment was not subject to confirmation by the Senate, nor could he easily be compelled to testify. This angered congressional leaders who sought access to information from the Bush administration about intelligence leading up to the 9/11 attacks and about steps taken to prevent future terrorist attacks. Second, congressional dissatisfaction with the performance of the Central Intelligence Agency and the Federal Bureau of Investigation resulted in mounting pressure for organizational reform. Bush changed his position in June 2002, at which time he proposed creating the Department of Homeland Security.

The intent of both measures—the USA PATRIOT Act and the creation of the Department of Homeland Security—is to improve the ability of the U.S. intelligence community to respond to the terrorist challenge. In terms of the discussion of issues in this chapter, these measures raise two very different sets of concerns for the conduct of espionage and counterespionage. The USA

PATRIOT Act, along with laws and executive orders associated with it, is intended to make it easier to gather intelligence and conduct counterespionage operations. The principal concern expressed here centers on the potential excesses that may accompany this loosening of restraint. As has been seen, previous episodes in American history suggest that when espionage and counterespionage turn their attention away from foreign targets to domestic ones, the civil liberties of immigrants and members of radical political groups are frequently the first victims.

A related human rights concern that has been expressed deals with the conduct of interrogations by the CIA and foreign intelligence agencies of foreigners suspected of involvement in terrorist operations in or against the United States. It is not uncommon for those who do not cooperate with American interrogators to be turned over to foreign intelligence services for questioning. Among the practices reportedly employed by the CIA are sleep deprivation and requiring suspects to remain standing or kneeling for hours with black hoods over their heads. Some civil rights groups claim that these tactics are in violation of international human rights agreements and could be defined as torture. Other human rights experts disagree. Because Congress recognized the controversial nature of key provisions of the USA PATRIOT Act, it was to expire in 2005. In spring 2003 the Bush administration began preparing for a USA PATRIOT Act II that would make many of its provisions permanent. Attention has focused most closely on those expanding the authority of law enforcement officials to conduct telephone and Internet surveillance with minimal legal supervision and jail noncitizens for up to six months without any formal charges being presented. Early draft language would also allow the government to "infiltrate and monitor" worship services.

One of the most ambitious programs to come out of the increased concern with obtaining information on terrorists has been the FBI's attempt to enlist private citizens in espionage. A first attempt was the Operation TIPS program (Terrorism Information and Prevention System) in which truckers, bus drivers, and others would be asked to watch out for suspicious activity in the normal routine of their work and report it to authorities. The move was criticized by forces from both the political left and right, such as the American Civil Liberties Union and House Majority Leader Richard Armey (R-Texas). The bill creating the Department of Homeland Security outlawed the concept. In

December 2002 the FBI went forward on a different tack to accomplish the same end. It placed pictures of five individuals on its Web site who were believed to be in the United States illegally. The FBI asked the public to be on the lookout for them, although it acknowledged that it had no concrete information that they were connected to any potential terrorist activities.

The creation of the Department of Homeland Security raises a different sort of problem for espionage and counterespionage. Here, the question is one of effectiveness of effort. Commentators are concerned that it will take considerable time for the twenty-two agencies and 170,000 employees in the new department to meld into a coherent whole. At least three distinct tasks face those in charge of the new department. The first is building a sense of identity among those employed that will foster the achievement of common goals. Members of the new department are being drawn from organizations that currently differ in their internal bureaucratic cultures and value systems, standard operating procedures, and goals and priorities. A second task is to construct clear lines of accountability and control. Under the best of times a certain amount of trial and error can be expected that will lead to further reorganizations. But, in a turbulent operational environment such as the one the new department finds itself in, the pressure to demonstrate accomplishments competes with and may negate efforts at creating an administratively efficient body. Third, the Department of Homeland Security must establish working relationships with the other members of the intelligence community. One factor complicating this task is that it joins the intelligence community because of the perceived failings of other members, most notably the CIA and FBI. As was noted in the previous discussion of the intelligence community, it is a community in name only. In reality it is populated by competing organizations that jealously guard their turfs. Evidence of that is already emerging. The FBI, in particular, is concerned with proposals to create a new domestic spying agency and proclaims itself capable of carrying out this mission. As the year 2002 ended, the FBI and CIA had convinced the White House that the Department of Homeland Security should only receive summary intelligence reports and not raw intelligence.

Should those working to establish the Department of Homeland Security not be able to master these three tasks, twin dangers may be encountered. The first is that espionage and counterespionage efforts will not operate at their maximum potential. The second is that a new wave of recriminations and blame laying may be spawned that will prove damaging to the overall functioning of the intelligence system.

# Further Reading

The suggested further readings in this section are analytical in nature. They help place espionage and counterespionage in a conceptual context. Almost any comprehensive introductory college-level textbook on international relations will provide a solid analytic overview of world politics. Examples include Glenn Hastedt and Kay Knickrehm, *International Politics in a Changing World* (New York: Longman, 2003); John Rourke, *International Politics on the World Stage* (New York: McGraw-Hill/Dushkin, 2003); and Joshua Goldstein, *International Relations* (New York: Longman, 2001). Important accounts of the role of surprise in world politics include Roberta Wohlstetter, *Pearl Harbor: Warning and Decision* (Palo Alto, CA: Stanford University Press, 1962); and Epharim Kam, *Surprise Attack: The Victim's Perspectives* (Cambridge, MA: Harvard University Press, 1988).

Analytical treatments of the intelligence function and the operation of the intelligence community include Walter Laqueur, *A World of Secrets: The Uses and Limits of Intelligence* (New York: Basic, 1985); Scott Breckinridge, *The CIA and the U.S. Intelligence System* (Boulder, CO: Westview, 1986); Arthur Hulnik, *Fixing the Spy Machine: Preparing American Intelligence for the Twenty-First Century* (Westport, CT: Praeger, 1999); Harry Ransom, *The Intelligence Establishment* (Cambridge, MA: Harvard University Press, 1970); Alfred Maurer et al., eds., *Intelligence Policy and Process* (Boulder, CO: Westview, 1985); J. F. Holden-Rhodes, *Sharing the Secrets: Open Source Intelligence and the War on Drugs* (Westport, CT: Praeger, 1997); Glenn Hastedt, ed., *Controlling Intelligence* (London: Frank Cass, 1991); Mark Reibling, *Wedge: The Secret War between the FBI and CIA* (New York: Alfred Knopf, 1994 and 2002); Abraham Shulsky, *Silent Warfare* (Washington, DC: Pergamon-Brassey's, 1991); and Craig Eisendrath, ed., *National Insecurity: U.S. Intelligence after the Cold War* (Philadelphia: Temple University Press, 2000).

The field of economic intelligence is growing in importance, but much of the literature remains in the area of corporate spying, which is beyond the scope of this book. Also informative to read are hearings before congressional committees. For example, see *The Threat of Foreign Economic Espionage against U.S. Corporations*, Hearings before the Subcommittee on Economic and Commercial Law of the Committee of the Judiciary, House of Representatives, 102nd Congress, April 29, 1992; and *Economic Espionage, Technology Transfers, and National Security*, Hearings before the Joint Economic Committee, Congress of the United States, 105th Congress, June 17, 1997.

# References

Berkowitz, Bruce, and Allan Goodman. 1989. *Strategic Intelligence for American National Security*. Princeton, NJ: Princeton University Press.

Betts, Richard. 1982. *Surprise Attack: Lessons for Defense Planning*. Washington, DC: Brookings.

Central Intelligence Agency. 1975. *A Consumer's Guide to Intelligence*. Washington, DC: Central Intelligence Agency.

Chace, James, and Caleb Carr. 1988. *America Invulnerable: The Quest for Absolute Security from 1812 to Star Wars*. New York: Summit.

Demerest, Geoffrey. 1996. "Espionage in International Law." *Denver Journal of International Law and Policy* 24: 321–348.

Fialka, John. 1997. *War by Other Means: Economic Espionage in America*. New York: Norton.

Hitz, Frederick. 2002. "Unleashing the Rogue Elephant: September 11 and Letting the CIA Be the CIA." *Harvard Journal of Law and Public Policy* 25: 756–781.

Jervis, Robert. 1976. *Perception and Misperception in International Politics*. Princeton, NJ: Princeton University Press.

Johnson, Loch. 1988. *A Season of Inquiry: Congress and Intelligence*. Chicago: Dorsey.

———. 2000. "Spies." *Foreign Policy* 120: 18–28.

Martin, David. 1980. *Wilderness of Mirrors*. New York: Ballantine.

Richelson, Jeffrey. 1985. *The U.S. Intelligence Community*. Cambridge, MA: Ballinger.

Stein, Arthur. 1990. *Why States Cooperate: Circumstance and Choice in International Relations*. Ithaca, NY: Cornell University Press.

Wilensky, Harold. 1967. *Organizational Intelligence*. New York: Basic.

# 3

# Espionage around
# the World

It was noted in chapter 1 that espionage and the intelligence agencies that support it and seek to prevent it are not relics of the Cold War. The American experience with espionage dates back to the revolutionary period and continues into the present day. The reasons for the continued importance of espionage, along with the debate over its place in American foreign policy, were reviewed in chapter 2. This chapter will place espionage in a global context by presenting an overview that highlights its history and structure in other countries and then by reviewing significant cases of espionage involving these states.

Placing espionage in a global context is important for several reasons. First, most of the literature on American intelligence is written without any reference to espionage and intelligence organizations other than the United Kingdom and Soviet Union. It is not the case that only great powers engage in spying. The nature of world politics provides powerful incentives for countries of all sizes and political philosophies to engage in espionage. Second, context matters in studying espionage. For Americans the typical starting point for thinking about security concerns—and therefore the threat of espionage—is external. For other states, security threats are seen as coming both from external enemies and internal ones. This dual focus can be reflected in both the conduct of espionage and how it is bureaucratically organized. It explains why in some countries espionage is looked upon as a dirty activity that is permissible only in times of national emergency and why in others it is accepted as a political necessity. Third, the study of espionage and, more broadly, intelligence is not carried out in the same manner around the world. American studies of espionage are dominated by political science. British and Soviet studies of espionage are heavily historical in focus. Scholars examining intelligence practices and organizations in the developing world often use sociology and anthropology as the starting points for their studies (Godson, 1988).

Although the focus in this chapter is on espionage in post–World War II international politics, it is important to recognize the enduring role that espionage has played in political and military affairs throughout history. It is frequently noted that the Bible contains more than 100 references to spying and intelligence gathering. As early as 500 B.C. Sun Tzu, the Chinese strategist, argued that all war is based on deception and stressed the importance of intelligence in achieving victory. In the Middle Ages espionage was employed to protect the interests of the Crown from internal and external threats. Sir Francis Walsingham, who served Queen Elizabeth I, is credited with preventing her overthrow by Catholic forces aligned with Mary, Queen of Scots and by King Philip II of Spain through carefully constructed espionage operations. On the negative side it is also believed that he concocted many of the plots against Queen Elizabeth to enhance his own reputation for spy catching.

Two centuries later in France, Cardinal Richelieu set up an intelligence service, the Cabinet Noir, to keep track of the activities of French nobles who might threaten the reign of Louis XIII. Joseph Fouche is credited with establishing the first modern political espionage system, which was done in the service of Napoleon. It provided Napoleon with important information about Great Britain. Fouche, however, ultimately ran afoul of Napoleon, who came to suspect that he was a British spy and who sent him into exile. In Russia, the tsars set up an intelligence service that spied on revolutionary groups. This group, the Okhrana, established a system of spies and agents that successfully penetrated revolutionary groups in the period leading up to the Russian Revolution. Espionage could not, however, prevent the tsars' ultimate downfall. Once in power Vladimir Lenin would put together his own intelligence service, the CHEKA (All-Russian Extraordinary Commission for Combating Counterrevolution, Speculation, and Sabotage), under the leadership of Felix Dzershinsky to protect Bolshevik rule.

Frederick II of Prussia is considered by many to be the first architect of modern military intelligence organizations, and by World War I all major powers except the United States possessed such organizations. Russian intelligence was able to obtain Austria-Hungary's war plan by blackmailing a key Austrian army officer. The most famous spy in World War I was Margaretha Zelle. She was better known as Mata Hari. An exotic dancer, she became a German spy in 1914 and obtained information from her lovers. Not very skilled as a spy, Mata Hari soon came under suspicion and was later identified in a message that was intercepted and decoded by French authorities. She was shot in 1918.

During World War II all of the major combatants had intelligence organizations in place, although as noted in chapter 1, the United States again lagged behind the others with the creation of the Office of Strategic Services (OSS). In addition to their established intelligence organizations, the British set up a new unit in 1940, the Special Operations Executive (SOE). Like the Americans' OSS, the SOE combined multiple intelligence tasks including espionage, guerrilla warfare, and sabotage. A key task of theirs was to cooperate with resistance groups. The SOE's casualty rate was extraordinarily high. Of 393 agents sent to France between 1940 and 1944, 102 were killed.

Both of the United States's principal adversaries had multiple intelligence services. In Germany there was the Abwehr and the Sicherheitsdienst (SD). The Abwehr was the intelligence and covert operations unit of the armed forces. The SD was the intelligence arm of the Nazi Party. The two competed for political influence and primacy within the Third Reich throughout the war. Admiral Wilhelm Canaris, head of the Abwehr, was arrested in July 1944 and executed in April 1945 for his involvement in a failed plot to kill Adolph Hitler.

In Japan, the Tokko was responsible for domestic counterespionage. Formed in 1991, it was a branch of the Tokyo police that had prevented the spread of communism to Japan after World War I. Within the armed forces, the Kempei Tai was in charge of counterespionage. Within Japan it was responsible for keeping track of military personnel; abroad it was linked to atrocities in Singapore when it executed hundreds of Chinese people suspected of being security risks. Japanese naval intelligence successfully placed a spy in Hawaii prior to the attack on Pearl

Harbor. Arriving there in March 1941, he sent weekly reports to Japan through normal diplomatic channels about naval activity at Pearl Harbor (Melton 1996).

# Great Britain

The history of British espionage reaches back to the late sixteenth century and moves forward in century-long leaps of time. It begins when Francis Walsingham built up an intelligence network in France—to which he was the British ambassador—and throughout Europe, which alerted British authorities to Spanish naval plans for attacking Great Britain. The uniqueness of Walsingham was his employment of a network of agents to help him gather intelligence about people and events. Following his death in 1590, Great Britain returned to the more traditional practice of relying heavily on ambassadors for intelligence. It would be more than 100 years, in 1703, before the British would create a true intelligence agency. In that year the Decyphering Branch was established. It would be shut down in 1844 just as the electronic transmission of information (and its interception) became possible. One hundred years after the Decyphering Branch was created the first military intelligence unit was established, the Depot of Military Knowledge.

Excluding military intelligence organizations, four bodies have dominated the field of British intelligence in the twentieth century. The first is the Government Communications Headquarters (GCHQ). Its origins can be traced back to 1919 when Room 40 (the Naval intelligence communications intercept organization that deciphered the Zimmermann telegram) and MI-8 (the army's cryptographic unit) were combined into the Government Code and Cypher School. Among its notable espionage successes was breaking the American diplomatic code in use at the Washington Naval Conference. This organization was better known by its location, Bletchley Park, than by its formal name, the GCHQ.

Its mission is to monitor and decode electronic transmissions in and out of Great Britain including those by foreign embassies and companies. It also is responsible for developing codes for the British government and for safeguarding British communications. In order to accomplish its mission GCHQ directs the activities of all military electronic monitoring groups and maintains a number of overseas listening posts. Two major security breaches on record include the 1982 arrest of Geoffrey Prime, who provided the Soviet Union with GCHQ intelligence for fourteen years, and the 1981 loss of top secret material from a Hong Kong listening post that was targeted on Chinese space and missile launches.

The second major intelligence organization in Britain is the Secret Intelligence Service (SIS). The SIS was created in 1909 as a subcommittee of the Committee of Imperial Defence and was charged with establishing the nature and extent of foreign espionage in Great Britain. Based on the subcommittee's findings the British set up a Secret Service Bureau under the jurisdiction of the War Office. Very soon it settled into an organization that contained two branches, a Home Section and a Foreign Section. The Home Section evolved into MI-5 and then the civilian Security Service. The Foreign Section evolved into MI-6 and then the civilian Secret Intelligence Service.

The SIS is charged with the tasks of recruiting foreign spies within Great Britain and of engaging in covert operations and the clandestine collection of information abroad. Two notable SIS successes in the area of human espionage include East German agent Hans Joachim Koch, who provided important intelligence during the East Berlin uprising in 1953 and was arrested in 1955, and GRU Colonel Oleg Penkovsky, who provided information to British and American authorities from early 1961 until his arrest in October 1962. Technical espionage successes include placing microphones in the offices of the Polish Trade Mission in Brussels and the office of the Soviet commercial attaché in Copenhagen, and intercepting cables from the Imperial Hotel in Vienna, which served as the Soviet command center for occupied Austria during World War II.

The third organization, the Security Service, is internally focused. It conducts counterespionage operations against foreign targets, monitors domestic movements for possible acts of subversion, and conducts security investigations of individuals with access to secret information. Notable spies caught by this agency include John Vassall, who spied for the Soviet Union from 1954 to 1961. Reportedly he was being blackmailed by the Soviets for his homosexuality. Among the groups that the Security Service has conducted countersabotage operations against are the National Council for Civil Liberties and the Campaign for Nuclear Disarmament.

It is reported that the Irish embassy was once bugged by the Security Service. Ireland has been a special target of British intelligence since 1883 when the Irish Special Branch of the Metropolitan Police was set up to deal with Fenian bombings in London. The Fenians were a secret group that engaged in terrorism. They were organized in Ireland and the United States around 1858 for the purpose of winning Irish independence from Great Britain. All references to "Irish," as in the Irish Special Branch of the Metropolitan Police, were dropped in subsequent years, and the Special Branch now is charged with protecting key government personnel and buildings, investigating violations of the Official Secrets Act, and monitoring subversive organizations and aliens entering Great Britain. It also makes arrests for the Security Service (Richelson 1988). The fourth intelligence organization is the Special Branch that is a subdepartment of the Crime Department of the Metropolitan Police, which operates throughout Great Britain.

## Kim Philby

British intelligence was the victim of one of the most serious espionage penetrations in the Cold War. Harold Adrian Russell ("Kim") Philby was at the center of this storm. Kim Philby was a product of upper-class British society and enrolled in Cambridge in 1929. There he became radicalized by the Great Depression and by the failure of the Labour Party or the Tories (the conservative party) to respond effectively to it. Philby was recruited by the Soviets in 1933 with instructions that his long-term objective was to infiltrate the SIS. Before being able to do so he served as a journalist during the Spanish civil war. Philby achieved his assigned posting with the help of fellow spy Guy Burgess. Philby was initially assigned to the SIS section charged with carrying out acts of sabotage and stirring up resistance to Germany in Europe. World War I's end found Philby in charge of Section IX, the anti-Soviet section of the SIS. There he energetically advanced plans for a rapid expansion of the unit and for developing a network of agents in Eastern Europe. In this capacity he knew of postwar covert operations supporting East European resistance groups and British covert operations in Albania that were designed to bring an end to communist rule. Philby had also become the heir apparent to the position of director general of the SIS. In order to give him the needed field experience

Philby was sent to Turkey from 1947 to 1949. He was then posted to Washington where he served as the principal liaison between the SIS and the CIA and FBI.

One of the cases the Philby was privy to was the defection of Soviet spy William Weisband, who gave the Soviets a copy of some American codes. U.S. authorities decided not to prosecute Weisband, so as not to tip off the Soviets that they knew their codes had been compromised. Philby was also kept abreast of the accumulating evidence that fellow Cambridge alumni Donald Maclean, a member of the British diplomatic corps stationed in Washington, was a Soviet spy. Philby succeeded in warning Maclean of his impending arrest by passing a message through Burgess. By a stroke of fate Burgess had also been stationed in Washington but was being sent back to Great Britain because of alcoholism and associated behavior problems. Both Maclean and Burgess fled to Moscow in May 1951.

Less than one month later the FBI identified Philby as a spy, and the CIA informed the British that Philby was persona non grata in the United States and must leave. Philby resigned from the SIS shortly thereafter but was never prosecuted as a Soviet spy. He remained free for more than a decade before fleeing to the Soviet Union in 1963. In 1968 Philby wrote his memoirs, in which he admitted spying for the Soviet Union (Knightly 1988).

Evidence pointing to Philby as a spy had been building for some time. Among the earliest pieces of evidence was information provided by Soviet General Walter Krivitsky, who defected in 1938. Although unable to give names, Krivitsky indicated that the Soviets had succeeded in penetrating British intelligence. One, he said, was a young Scotsman who had entered the foreign service (Maclean) and the other a journalist who had reported on the Spanish civil war (Philby). Additional information was provided in 1945 by a defecting Soviet intelligence officer, Konstantin Volkov, who stated that he knew of two Soviet spies in the British foreign office and one in MI-6. Philby alerted the Soviets to Volkov's pending defection, and they arrested Volkov. That same year Igor Gouzenko defected to Canada. His information pointed to the existence of the atomic spies in the United States and to two penetrations of British intelligence. Ethel and Julius Rosenberg were the most notable atomic spies. They received this nickname because they stole secrets about the atomic bomb for the Soviet Union. Pursuit of these Soviet moles led them to British and American intelligence to incorrectly identify Maclean as one of these spies. After Philby's defection they recognized their mistake.

The true identity of one mole was Philby, but the identity of the second mole remained in doubt. The possibility that further penetrations beyond Philby, Burgess, and Maclean existed within British intelligence came from yet another Soviet defector. In 1961 Anatoliy Golitsyn defected; he had worked in the KGB's First Chief Directorate, which is responsible for foreign operations. He spoke of a "Ring of Five" Soviet agents within British intelligence. In 1964 Anthony Blount confessed to being a Soviet spy. This brought the known total to four spies. Speculation on the identity of the fifth spy came to center on Sir Roger Hollis, the director general of SIS from 1956 to 1965. Two separate investigations failed to establish that he was a Soviet spy.

# Israel

Israeli intelligence organizations trace their roots to the Zionist underground organizations that existed in Palestine after World War I when the League of Nations installed the British Mandate. The best known of these was the Sherut Yedioth, or International Service, which was popularly known as the SHAI. Operating between 1929 and 1948, the SHAI worked to create an independent Jewish state by infiltrating the British Mandate offices, penetrating Arab and anti-Zionist groups in the region. It obtained political intelligence that could further the Zionist cause and could provide security for Jewish settlers being smuggled into Palestine. Finally, it also spied on extremist Jewish groups on the political left and right. The SHAI was disbanded in 1948 when Israel became an independent state because the SHAI was a tool of a nonstate actor, the Zionist underground. In its place three organizations were created. The Israeli Defense Forces established a military intelligence service, the Political Department was established within the Foreign Ministry to collect intelligence abroad, and the General Security Service, the SHABAK or Shin Beth, was created to address internal security concerns.

Shin Beth is Israel's counterespionage and internal security service, with responsibility for gathering intelligence on and penetrating foreign intelligence organizations. Historically its two major targets have been Arab states and communist intelligence services. Domestically, Shin Beth is credited with having penetrated Israeli communist parties and running a well-developed network of Jewish and Arab informants who monitor the activity of foreigners and especially Arabs.

Shin Beth has uncovered several spies and spy rings operating in Israel. These include Israel Beer, a Soviet mole who assumed the identity of an individual who disappeared in 1938. Beer served in high-ranking intelligence positions early in Israel's history before his arrest in 1962. Shin Beth uncovered a Syrian spy ring operating in the Golan Heights in 1969. It was providing Syria with military intelligence on Israeli troop movements. In the early 1970s its investigations led to the arrest and conviction of a British electrical engineer on charges of spying for Jordan. Here again the material in question focused on military intelligence.

Shin Beth's aggressive pursuit of its mission on occasion has also placed it at the center of domestic controversy. In 1984 it responded to a Palestinian hijacking of an Israeli bus. The first story to emerge stated that all of the hijackers had been killed in the rescue raid. Subsequent photographs showed two of the hijackers in custody. They had been interrogated and beaten before their deaths, and Shin Beth was accused of altering evidence. Avraham Solon, head of Shin Beth, argued that he ordered the evidence changed with the approval of high-ranking political leaders. Israeli President Chaim Herzog issued a pardon to all involved, and one member of the government asserted: "Israel is in a state of war against terrorism . . . in a state of war the normal rules don't apply" (Richelson 1988, 288).

Perhaps the best-known Israeli intelligence organization is the Mossad, the Central Institute for Intelligence and Special Duties. It was created in 1951 and was originally charged with selecting targets and approving intelligence operations carried out by Israeli military intelligence. Today it is responsible for conducting covert action, counterterrorism, and intelligence collection operations. Two cases from the 1960s highlight Mossad's involvement in espionage. It recruited Eli Cohen to serve as a spy in Syria. Mossad gave him a false identity and sent him to Argentina to establish his business credentials. Cohen quickly established connections with the Syrian community there, and, upon returning to Syria, he was able to provide Israel with important information regarding Syrian military plans. Cohen was uncovered by Syrian intelligence in 1965 and publicly hanged. A second Mossad spy, Wolfgang Lutz, operated in Egypt, where he was able to obtain military secrets and even toured surface-to-air missile sites. He was arrested in 1965 and was subsequently exchanged for Egyptian POWs captured in the June 1967 Six Day War.

Another important force in Israeli intelligence is AMAN, the intelligence branch of the Israeli General Staff. It is tasked with collecting, producing, and disseminating economic, political, and military intelligence on states of concern to Israel. AMAN contains an Intelligence Corps that is charged with the covert and overt collection of intelligence. One means by which it does so is through signals intelligence. Another branch runs agents into neighboring countries. Israel's failure to be adequately prepared for the Egyptian and Syrian attacks in October 1973 is laid at the feet of AMAN. The failure here was not a collection failure but an interpretation one, as senior AMAN officials discounted warnings of an impending war.

The least-publicized Israeli intelligence unit engaged in espionage is LEKEM, the Bureau of Scientific Relations. It is responsible both for a major espionage success and for what is perhaps Israel's greatest espionage failure. The success involved acquiring the blueprints for key parts of the Mirage fighter-bomber. Israel's inventory of Mirages had been heavily depleted as a result of the June 1967 Six Day War. France, the manufacturer of the Mirage, had placed an embargo on weapons sales to Israel and was refusing to lift it. France, which had close relations with many of the Arab states in the region, imposed the arms embargo to protest Israel's actions and in an effort to gain political leverage over Israel's war decisions. Obtaining these blueprints allowed Israel to repair its own planes. Jonathan Jay Pollard's recruitment is considered a failure because the information he gave to Israel—valuable as it was—did not offset the political damage done to U.S.-Israeli security relations by the revelation that a trusted ally was spying on the United States or the split it produced within the Jewish community over whether or not the Israeli government should have moved quickly to protect Pollard.

## Jonathan Jay Pollard

Jonathan Jay Pollard joined U.S. Navy intelligence in 1979 after being rejected for a position by the CIA because of a history of occasional drug use while in college. He claims to have made the decision to spy for Israel in 1982 following his participation in a formal intelligence exchange between U.S. and Israeli intelligence organizations. Pollard was angry that the United States did not give Israel all of the intelligence it possessed. It was in 1984 that Pollard took his first steps toward becoming an Israeli spy. He told a friend about his interest in meeting Israeli Air Force Colonel Aviem Stella. The request was passed on to Stella, who sought instructions from the Israeli government on whether or not to meet Pollard. The Mossad, which as a general principle had no interest in running spy operations in or against the United States, conducted a background check on Pollard and concluded that the meeting should not take place. However, another Israeli intelligence organization, LEKEM, gave its approval.

The meeting between Stella and Pollard took place on May 29, 1984, at the Washington Hilton. Pollard wasted little time telling Stella he wished to spy for Israel. Stella had been authorized in advance to approve such a relationship, and it was agreed that a second meeting would be held. This occurred on July 7. To prove his worth, Pollard brought forty-eight documents with him. Per his instructions, Stella refused to accept them but did indicate to Pollard the type of intelligence Israel wished to obtain. Specifically excluded from this list was information on terrorism. Also following instructions, Stella raised the issue of financial compensation. Pollard resisted. He was volunteering his services as a spy out of a sense of commitment to Israel and not for monetary reasons. Israeli intelligence pressed the issue of financial compensation, as spies who provide their services on a volunteer basis are not considered trustworthy or good long-term agents.

The first exchange of intelligence came at a July 19, 1984, meeting. A second meeting occurred on July 28, at which time Pollard was paid $2,000. At a November meeting in Paris, Pollard received detailed instructions on the type of intelligence Israel was interested in. He also received $1,500 plus $10,000 for expenses. In the following months Pollard would steal secret information three times per week and make contact with his Israeli handlers every other week. The procedure was simple. Pollard brought the secret material to a safe house, where it was photocopied. Pollard would then return the originals to their places. In spring 1985 his monthly salary was raised from $1,500 to $2,500. While visiting Israel that summer at the request of his handlers, Pollard was offered $30,000 for each of the next ten years, to be placed in a Swiss bank account. The offer was accepted.

A sampling of the intelligence given to Israel by Pollard included all of the American information on Iraqi and Syrian chemical and biological warfare capabilities; exact details on Soviet arms shipments to Syria and other Arab states; and strategic information collected by the United States concerning Libya, Algeria, Iraq, and Pakistan. The most sensitive piece of information was the U.S. handbook on communications intelligence.

Things began to unravel for Pollard soon after returning to work in August 1985. He had made the decision to quit his job with naval intelligence by the end of the year. In his mind he would move on to some other espionage activity for Israel. Rather than curtailing his spying Pollard accelerated it, and in the process he drew attention to himself. In late October a coworker who disliked him reported seeing Pollard leave work with top secret intelligence. Armed with this information Jerry Agee, Pollard's boss, began to take an especially close look at Pollard's activity and concluded that Pollard was engaged in espionage.

Pollard was apprehended on November 18, 1985, sitting in his car as he was leaving work. During a break in the interrogations that followed he called his wife and by prearranged signal indicated that he was in trouble and she was to destroy all secret documents in their apartment. Pollard had been assured that an evacuation plan was in place for such a contingency, and he stalled and misled his interrogators in the expectation that it would be activated. In fact, no such plan existed, and when his Israeli contacts found out about his situation, they fled the United States. Initial searches of Pollard's apartment revealed seventy-five classified documents his wife had overlooked. After two days of questioning, realizing that no escape plan existed and that he would fail the polygraph test he was soon to be given, Pollard was able to make a bold dash to the grounds of the Israeli embassy because while undergoing questioning by U.S. intelligence officials, he and his wife were not put under arrest. This again reflects the differing perspectives of the traditional intelligence services, which are most interested in obtaining information about security breaches, and the FBI, which is most interested in arrests and convictions. Pollard was able to seek asylum by invoking the Law of Return. This principle asserts that all Jews have a right by law to citizenship in Israel and the right to reside there. To his amazement,

Pollard and his wife were forced to leave the embassy grounds, after which he was promptly arrested again. Anne Pollard was arrested the next day (Blitzer 1989).

On November 27, 1985, the same day that the Pollards were arraigned in court, a damage control committee in Israel completed its report. It stated that Pollard was part of a rogue intelligence operation that was taking place without the government's knowledge. This answer did not calm the Reagan administration's anger over being spied upon by a friendly power. Besides, sufficient evidence existed that pointed to the opposite conclusion. The Reagan administration sought the Israeli government's cooperation into investigating the matter and the return of the stolen documents. The Israeli government agreed but came under heavy domestic pressure for doing so. Pollard was deeply angered that the Israeli government would agree to participate in an investigation of his activities without first securing his release. Contributing to the U.S. government's anger was the suspicion that Pollard was not the only spy the Israelis were running. Fueling this suspicion were the detailed tasking requirements given to Pollard by his Israeli handlers. They referred to documents using terminology that could only have been provided by someone working in the U.S. intelligence community.

With the case against him bolstered through Israeli cooperation, Pollard had little choice but to enter into a plea bargain agreement in hopes of obtaining a light sentence for Anne. As part of the court hearings to establish what sentences should be imposed, Secretary of Defense Caspar Weinberger submitted a forty-six-page secret document. Parts of it have since been declassified; in these, Weinberger stated that Pollard's activities had caused significant harm to American national security. He also stated that "punishment, of course, must be appropriate to the crime, and in my opinion, no crime is more deserving of severe punishment than conducting espionage activities against one's own country."

On March 4, 1987, Jonathan Jay Pollard and his wife, Anne Henderson Pollard, appeared before Judge Aubrey Robinson for sentencing after having pleaded guilty to spying for Israel. Judge Robinson sentenced Jay Pollard to life imprisonment and Anne Pollard to five years imprisonment. Pollard's fate has remained a point of tension in U.S.-Israeli relations (Shaw 2001).

# China

The foundations for China's intelligence organizations were laid during the revolutionary period in which the Chinese Communist Party sought to establish its rule. In the early 1930s two intelligence organizations existed. One was centered in Shanghai in the Communist Party, the other in the Chinese communist government that existed in Kiangsi province where Mao Zedong ruled. This later intelligence unit proved to be the stronger of the two. By the late 1930s it was replaced by a newly created Social Affairs Department (SAD) within the Communist Party that was headed by a political ally of Mao. With the Communist Party's victory over Chiang Kai-shek's nationalist forces in 1949, a full array of government intelligence organizations were created to supplement party-based intelligence units such as SAD. The Ministry of Public Security was given jurisdiction over counter-subversion, counterintelligence, monitoring Chinese citizens who returned from abroad, running the labor reform camps, and conducting espionage in Macao, Hong Kong, and Taiwan. A reorganization in 1983 left the Ministry of Public Security with only traditional police functions. That year Chinese authorities announced that some 200 Chinese people had been accused of spying for the Soviet Union.

The Ministry of Public Security's counterespionage functions became the responsibility of the newly created Ministry of State Security (MSS). One reason for transferring counterespionage to the MSS was the apparent frustration with the high volume of secret information being leaked to the West. This was particularly true with regard to information about debates occurring within the Communist Party and reports of poor economic and social conditions within China. Students, both in China and abroad, have been a major concern of the MSS as Chinese leaders have struggled to deal with the fallout from the Tiananmen Square protests.

In addition to classical human espionage, China has also engaged in technological espionage activities. It has conducted photographic reconnaissance since 1970. By 1987 twenty-one such satellites had been launched. Ten of these are assumed to be military missions. China maintains a series of signals intelligence stations. Both photo reconnaissance and signals intelligence satellites are run by the Chinese military intelligence units (Richelson 1988).

# Larry Wu-tai Chin

In late 1982 a CIA informant inside the Chinese government noti-
fied the FBI that a Chinese-born American citizen held a sensitive
job inside the U.S. government and was spying for China. One
additional piece of information was soon provided. The Chinese
spy had flown aboard a Pan Am flight in the first week of
February in 1982. A check of individuals on those flights did not
produce any leads. The FBI was able to identify Chin as a possible spy by working backward: checking subsequent arrivals for
the returning spy.

Chin first made contact with American authorities in 1948
when he was hired as a translator and interpreter. Chin did not
take the job to spy on the United States, but to make money. Very
soon, however, he began to provide China with information. His
roommate, a fervent communist, recruited him. Chin left China in
1950 when the U.S. consulate moved to Hong Kong. He would
soon participate in the interrogation of Chinese prisoners captured during the Korean War. He passed the information thus
obtained back to China. According to some analysts, Chin's
actions prolonged the Korean War and were behind China's
demand that all prisoners from that particular war be repatriated.
Chin also identified many U.S. intelligence officers working out
of Hong Kong.

In 1965 Chin became a U.S. citizen and obtained a job with
the CIA. Chin, like other spies who are employed by U.S. intelligence agencies, must pass background checks on being hired.
These checks involve passing lie detector tests and having one's
life history examined for evidence of association with groups hostile to the United States or that one could be blackmailed into spying. No background check is foolproof. Lie detector tests can be
"beaten." Spies can have careers carefully constructed to pass
background checks as was the case with Kim Philby. And, as we
have seen with Hanssen, Pollard, Ames, and Walker, many who
turn to spying do so after they begin careers in intelligence. One
of the major critiques of counterespionage efforts in the United
States is the tendency to assume that those who have passed the
initial background security check and entered into the fraternity
of intelligence work are incapable of being spies. Time and time
again, evidence of spying or aberrant behavior was discounted or
not sought out. In the case of Chin we can surmise that having
gained employment first as a translator for the U.S. Army and

then in an American embassy, he faced little scrutiny in being hired as a translator by the CIA to monitor Chinese broadcasts in 1952. Any possible doubts about Chin's loyalty would have been further dampened when he became an American citizen in 1965.

In his capacity as a Chinese language intelligence officer, Chin had access to message traffic coming in and out of China. This included reports by American spies. He also had access to National Intelligence Estimates on China. In 1970 Chin became privy to information that President Richard Nixon was planning to open relations with China. He was able to provide Chinese leaders with advance warning of Nixon's plans and continued to provide them with information throughout the diplomatic negotiations leading up to the trip.

Chin retired from the CIA in 1981 with a medal for distinguished service. In 1982 he traveled to China, where he was feted with a farewell banquet and given $50,000. This sum was in addition to the estimated $200,000 that he had already been paid for engaging in espionage against the United States.

As a result of tips it had received, the FBI began monitoring Chin's movements in April 1983. It was not until November 22, 1985, however, that Chin was arrested. The key piece of evidence against him was his Chinese case file that detailed all of his actions. It had been secretly obtained by an American spy in the Chinese Ministry of State Security. Chin confessed at his trial in early February 1986. He claimed his intent was to help improve Sino-American relations. Later that month he committed suicide in his jail cell (Barron 1989).

# Soviet Union/Russia

As with China and Israel, Soviet and Russian intelligence organizations can trace their roots back beyond the founding of their respective political systems. A convenient point to mark the beginnings of intelligence organizations here is 1826, when Tsar Nicholas I established the Third Directorate to serve as a political force and protect the government from internal subversion. Its failing to do so led to its replacement by the Okhrana in 1880. It succeeded in penetrating revolutionary groups but also failed to protect the tsarist regime from domestic challengers.

The first communist intelligence organization to succeed the Third Directorate and Okhrana was the All-Russian Extraordinary

Commission for Combating Counterrevolution, Speculation, and Sabotage, the Vecheka. The Chekas (by its Russian language initials this organization was known as the CHEKA and those who worked in it were referred to as Chekas) pledged themselves to "annihilating enemy agents, counterrevolutionaries, and speculators." Along with its successor organization, the State Political Administration (GPU), these internal security organizations played major roles in solidifying Soviet rule and transforming Soviet society. In 1934 the GPU was absorbed into the just-established People's Commissariat for Internal Affairs (NKVD). It played a key role in carrying out Stalin's purges. Following Stalin's death in 1953 a power struggle broke out within the Soviet Union. Nikita Khrushchev emerged as the winner, and Lavrenty Beria, who once headed the NKVD, was one of the principal losers. He was removed from the Politburo, and in March 1954 a new political police force, the Committee of State Security (KGB), was established (Richelson 1988).

The KGB directed its energies at carrying out four tasks: frustrating and exposing the efforts of foreign spies, uncovering the political crimes of Soviet citizens, guarding Soviet borders, and protecting state secrets. Several of the KGB's internal units had jurisdiction over espionage-related matters. The First Chief Directorate was responsible for all foreign operations and intelligence gathering activities. The Second and Fifth Chief Directorates were responsible for internal political security matters. The Third Chief Directorate was responsible for military counterintelligence. The Seventh Chief Directorate was responsible for technical and human surveillance within the Soviet Union. The Eighth Chief Directorate was responsible for the security of Soviet communications, including its cipher systems. There is no Fourth Chief Directorate and the Sixth Chief Directorate deals with a range of issues that do not bear on intelligence work directly, such as finance, the physical security of the KGB, and operational analysis.

The end of the Soviet Union also spelled the end for the KGB. Just three months before its dissolution in December 1991, Mikhail Gorbachev abolished the KGB by decree. In its place he created three intelligence organizations: the Interrepublican Security Service, which was concerned with internal security; the Central Intelligence Service, which was put in charge of foreign intelligence; and the Committee for the Protection of the State Border.

The KGB did not completely disappear, however. In the chaotic period that characterized the last months of the Soviet

Union, a unified KGB remained alive and well at the republic level where Russian President Boris Yeltsin had insisted on its continued existence.

Yeltsin did move to disband the KGB once and for all when the Soviet Union collapsed. As head of the new Russian Federation, Yeltsin dispersed the KGB's functions among five different organizations. Foreign intelligence went to the Foreign Intelligence Service, and counterintelligence and surveillance went to the Ministry of State Security. Responsibility for communications was given to the Federal Agency for Government Communications and Information. Commentators note that this division of labor mirrors general Russian attitudes toward the KGB. Although its domestic surveillance powers were feared and resented, its foreign intelligence activities were never heavily criticized. There was general agreement that the West was hostile to the Soviet Union and that the KGB was needed.

Between 1975 and 1990 fifteen KGB agents were exposed as spies. Six were arrested in the Soviet Union, but the remainder defected. The rate of defection increased dramatically as the Soviet Union collapsed. Between March 1991 and September 1992 ten intelligence agents defected. In 1993 twenty more were arrested on espionage charges. Among the most notable defections was that of FIS Colonel Vladimir Konoplev, who was serving under the cover of first secretary of the Russian embassy in Brussels. His case led to several other Russian diplomats being identified as intelligence agents. Konoplev had, in fact, been spying for the United States for some time before his defection. Another case involved the defection of Viktor Oshchenko. Based on information he provided, several French citizens were charged with giving secret scientific information to Russia, and a British engineer whom Oshchenko had recruited to spy for Russia was exposed (Knight 1996).

The KGB did not have a monopoly over espionage-related intelligence activity in the Soviet Union. Military, scientific, and industrial espionage was conducted by the chief intelligence directorate (GRU) of the Soviet General Staff. Organizationally, its roots can be traced to 1920 when, acting on poor intelligence, the Red Army attacked Poland, expecting to set off an uprising. Instead, the army was badly beaten. In response to this failure an independent military intelligence unit was established that in time came to be the GRU. Politically, the GRU suffered two major setbacks. The first came in the 1930s when many of its most competent officials, including its founder and director, Yan Berzin, became victims of Stalin's purges. The second politically crippling setback came in the late 1950s and early 1960s when the GRU was rocked by two espionage cases. In 1958 it discovered that Lieutenant Colonel Pyotor Popov was an American spy; in 1962 Lieutenant Colonel Oleg Penkovsky was arrested for espionage. As a consequence of these penetrations the GRU appears to have lost political power within the Soviet system and fallen under the general direction of the KGB.

In between these two major setbacks the GRU did enjoy significant espionage successes. One such case involved Klaus Fuchs. Born in Germany and a communist supporter, he fled to England as Hitler rose to power. In late 1941 he volunteered to spy for the Soviet Union. Fuchs proved to be a valuable spy. He had obtained a Ph.D. in physics and was employed on a top secret British project to build an atomic bomb. In 1943 Fuchs moved to the United States and would soon join the project at Los Alamos labs in which the American atomic bomb was being put together. Fuchs's case demonstrates the dangers in relying heavily upon stolen material. He passed along to the Soviets work by Edward Teller, an American physicist born in Hungary who worked on the atomic bomb at Los Alamos and played a key role in its development, that contained flaws and that probably confused Soviet physicists in their efforts to build an atomic bomb. Fuchs was arrested in 1950 for spying and was sentenced to fourteen years in prison. Upon his release, he went to East Germany.

A second case involved Richard Sorge. Born to a German father and Russian mother, Sorge was educated in Germany and became a supporter of communism after the Russian Revolution. In the 1920s he was sent on several intelligence gathering missions by Russian intelligence and was then recruited by Berzin. Pretending to be a German journalist he was sent to run a spy ring out of Shanghai. After returning to Germany and establishing himself as a trustworthy member of the Nazi Party, Sorge was posted to Tokyo where he was to provide Soviet leaders with information pertaining to Japanese plans to attack the Soviet Union. Perhaps as much as 80 percent of the military information he obtained came from sources within the German embassy. Sorge was arrested by the Japanese for espionage in 1941 and executed in 1944. Although Sorge is praised in Soviet histories for his espionage exploits, controversy exists concerning the overall value of the intelligence sent by Sorge to his Soviet handlers. Some attribute greater importance to information provided by Soviet signals intercepts and treat Sorge's information as being used largely to confirm the validity of these intercepts.

During the Cold War the United States did not have a monopoly over satellite reconnaissance. The Soviet Union also had an active technically based spy program. The first two Soviet photo reconnaissance satellites, *Cosmos 10* and *11*, were launched in October 1962 and provided Soviet leaders with important information about U.S. military preparedness during the Cuban missile crisis. The Soviet effort at photo reconnaissance differed from its U.S. counterpart in a number of respects. First, Soviet reconnaissance satellite launches occurred much more frequently. Second, Soviet reconnaissance satellites were relatively simple. Unlike U.S. reconnaissance satellites that were specifically designed for espionage and contained highly sophisticated technology, Soviet spy satellites embodied relatively simple technologies and represented modifications of the *Soyux* space capsules. *Soyux* is a name given to the Russian space capsules like our *Gemini, Apollo,* and *Mercury* programs. Third, Soviet satellite reconnaissance was largely reactive in nature. Where U.S. satellite launches might require weeks of preparation, the Soviets were known to launch reconnaissance satellites within twenty-four hours of the onset of an international crisis. For example, during the 1973 Arab-Israeli War, the Soviet Union launched seven reconnaissance satellites in a three-week period, and instead of leaving them in orbit for the standard two-week period, they were brought down in less than six days in order to retrieve the film. Evidence suggests that the Soviet signals intelligence program mirrors that employed by the United States. Its first signals intelligence satellite was *Cosmos 148*. It was launched in March 1967, some five years after the U.S. program was initiated with the launching of *Ferret I* in May 1962.

## Oleg Penkovsky

Unlike the other spies whose stories are recounted in this chapter, Penkovsky spied for only a brief time before he was exposed. The information he provided on Soviet missile systems, however, is generally cited as having played an important role in U.S. decision making during the Cuban missile crisis. Penkovsky was a GRU colonel who had become angry with Soviet authorities for their discriminatory treatment of him. At issue was the fact that his father had been a tsarist judge and had fought with the white forces against the communists during the Russian civil war.

Penkovsky first tried to defect in August 1960 when he approached two American students after a performance of the Bolshoi Ballet. He told them that the U-2 spy plane piloted by Francis Gary Powers had not been shot down by surface-to-air missiles as the Soviets claimed and asked them to give an envelope to officials at the U.S. embassy that evening and relay his story to them. Inside the envelope was a letter in which he volunteered his services as a spy and gave instructions for a dead drop site. The CIA was interested in continuing contact with Penkovsky but did not succeed because it lacked personnel capable of eluding KGB surveillance. Penkovsky then switched his attention to the British. In December 1960 he approached a member of a British trade delegation offering him information and asking that it be delivered to the American embassy. The trade official rejected Penkovsky's approach but did report it to British authorities. British intelligence considered Penkovsky to be an agent provocateur, but U.S. intelligence officials sought to make still another contact with him. Working with British intelligence the CIA arranged for another British trade mission to go to the Soviet Union. Its leader, Greville Wynne, was instructed to try to make contact with the GRU. Wynne succeeded in making contact with Penkovsky. To the satisfaction of the CIA and British intelligence, Penkovsky was chosen to lead a Soviet trade delegation to Great Britain in 1961. In truth the mission was intended to obtain technological intelligence, but this did not matter to the CIA or MI-6.

No sooner had Penkovsky arrived in Great Britain in April than he gave Wynne a package of material containing secret information about Soviet rocket and missile systems. Penkovsky would also meet British and American intelligence officials in the evenings seventeen times during his stay and provide them with voluminous amounts of information about Soviet military capabilities, Soviet politics, and the identities of GRU agents operating in Western countries. Penkovsky requested that he be given some modest intelligence to bring back to the Soviet Union to prove that his mission was a success. He also demanded money and sexual favors for his services. He was offered $1,000 per month but found that sum unsatisfactory. Penkovsky requested, but was not granted, an audience with the queen. In a later meeting, Penkovsky was given British and American army uniforms to try on as part of a plan to stroke his ego. Ostensibly they were to be his uniforms and would be waiting for him when his espionage days were over.

Penkovsky went back to the Soviet Union with a tiny camera and a set of instructions about what types of information were desired. When Wynne returned to Moscow in late May to attend a French trade show, Penkovsky gave him three rolls of film and a briefcase full of papers. Wynne gave Penkovsky 3,000 rubles. In the coming months Penkovsky would pass additional information to his Western handlers, including a Soviet transcript of the Khrushchev-Kennedy summit conference in Vienna.

The KGB had begun to suspect Penkovsky of being a spy at least as early as January 1962. Following the discovery that Pyotor Popov was an American spy, the KGB began to undertake periodic and sustained surveillance of personnel stationed at the American and British embassies. This surveillance allowed the KGB to observe a meeting between someone in the British embassy and an unidentified Russian. Further surveillance of the British embassy showed that the Russian was Penkovsky.

As the case against Penkovsky built, the KGB moved to stop him from traveling abroad. They photographed him coming and going from meetings with his contact. They followed him in cars. A remote control camera directed at his apartment caught him listening to a radio and taking notes. The KGB rented the apartment above his and drilled a small hole into the ceiling, where they placed a camera. They would also secretly search his apartment. Penkovsky made his last drop in August and warned that the KGB was watching him.

Penkovsky was arrested on October 31, during the Cuban missile crisis. Wynne was arrested two days later. Wynne reportedly confessed in December, and Penkovsky was tried in May 1963. He was sentenced to death, and his execution was announced by *Pravda* (the Russian newspaper) on May 17. Within a year Wynne would be exchanged for a Soviet spy being held in Great Britain. The timing of Penkovsky's arrest has been remarked upon by many. Standard operating procedure would be to hold off on making an arrest for as long as possible in order to expose other members of the spy ring and to try to feed disinformation back to the United States. It has been suggested that the timing of Penkovsky's arrest during the Cuban missile crisis reflected a political decision made at the Politburo and one designed to move the crisis to a safer stage. It signaled to the United States that the information Penkovsky gave them was correct.

# Other States

Intelligence organizations and the practice of espionage are not the monopoly of the great world powers or of states whose history is characterized by frequent wars, such as Israel. Espionage is practiced by states of all sizes. In some cases the structure of a state's intelligence organizations can be traced to historically significant or relevant states. For example, Cuba's main foreign intelligence organization, the Directorate of General Intelligence (DGI), was founded in 1961 and modeled after the Soviet intelligence system. Not surprisingly, the United States is a principal intelligence target for Cuba. One estimate suggests that 40 percent of Cubans assigned to that country's United Nations mission in New York are DGI agents. Cuban intelligence also makes heavy use of the large émigré and refugee community in the United States in running agents. In addition to the standard politico-military targets, obtaining technology to help Cuba's ailing economy recover and grow.

Australia and India, both former British colonies, have intelligence activities that are patterned after British intelligence. The first intelligence service in India was established in 1892. A principal espionage target was Russia, which had imperial ambitions of its own in south Asia and which disguised intelligence officers as representatives of the British East India Company in order to collect information on British rule in India. In contrast, peacetime Australian intelligence is of much more recent origin. The Australian Security and Intelligence Organization, which is responsible for counterintelligence, was set up in 1949. The Australian Secret Intelligence Service was not set up until 1952. Senior British intelligence officers served as midwives in its creation. Among them was Roger Hollis, who would later serve as Director General of the British Security Service (MI-5) and come under suspicion for spying. A common heritage has not translated into similar espionage concerns for these two states, however. Australian intelligence became very much involved in the Cold War struggle. It sought to identify Soviet agents who arrived in Australia disguised as immigrants and bugged the

Soviet and Chinese embassies. In turn, the Australian government was the object of Soviet penetration efforts. For example, Soviet spies were placed within the Department of External Affairs. Of even greater concern to the West was the fact that two of the key British intelligence officers who helped set up the Australian intelligence system, Roger Hollis and C. H. "Dick" Ellis, later came under suspicion for being Soviet spies themselves. Neutral during the Cold War, India's intelligence service developed a more localized focus. Much of India's intelligence effort is directed at running intelligence agents in Pakistan and dealing with the Tamil separatist movement.

Postwar (West) German intelligence displays a rather different historical pedigree. The longtime head of West German intelligence was Richard Gehlen, who held the rank of major general during World War II and who headed Foreign Armies East, the Nazis' intelligence organization responsible for collecting information on Stalin's army. Anticipating an imminent surrender to American forces, Gehlen's organization microfilmed their information on the Soviet Union and buried it in the Austrian Alps. Gehlen surrendered to American military officials. Once in custody he used his position within German military intelligence to his advantage. He was flown to the United States where he met with American intelligence officials. There he entered into an agreement whereby he would use his network of agents to spy on the Russians and East Europeans in return for operational autonomy from American intelligence organizations and the eventual transfer of his intelligence organization to a new German government. After the war, Gehlen used the existence of this information as leverage to secure the release of many of his compatriots from internment camps and to set up an anticommunist intelligence organization that could run agents throughout Eastern Europe. Gehlen set up his postwar intelligence organization in 1946. In 1956 Gehlen's intelligence operation passed from loose American control to West German control and became the Federal Intelligence Service. Gehlen remained its director until his retirement in 1968.

Intelligence organizations and espionage are also vital to the security of states involved in regional struggles for power and dominance in the post–Cold War era. No longer can they count on the assistance of outside powers in pursuing their foreign policy objectives. Moreover, the pursuit of these objectives may place them in conflict with the United States. In such situations intelligence is invaluable because of its ability to act as a force multiplier. As in the distant past, intelligence organizations continue to serve as means for protecting the government from hostile domestic forces. The following section briefly surveys the intelligence and espionage operations of some of the most prominent states that fall into this category.

North Korea's umbrella intelligence organization is the National Intelligence Council (NIC) of the Central Committee of the Korean Workers Party. All North Korean intelligence units report to it. Among the most important of these for purposes of espionage is the Liaison Department, which runs operations in South Korea and Japan for purposes of gathering military information on U.S forces. The Reconnaissance Department infiltrates agents into the South Korean military. The State Security Department is responsible for counterintelligence.

Iraq possessed a well-developed intelligence system that was under the control of the National Security Council, which, in turn, was dominated by Saddam Hussein. Of particular interest was the Special Security Service, which operated a system of "dummy" companies used to obtain foreign equipment, technology, and supplies from the West. A second important intelligence organization was the Department of General Intelligence. It provided a springboard for Saddam Hussein to seize power and continued to be a critical foundation on which his rule was built. Within it was a special bureau that detectd and countered foreign intelligence operations.

Within Syria, air force intelligence has frequently been used to conduct operations against domestic Islamic opposition groups. A General Intelligence Directorate is responsible for surveillance over members of the ruling party, the government bureaucracy, and the public at large. In Libya intelligence organizations also play an important role in sustaining the government in power. Evidence suggests that Libyan and Syrian intelligence agencies have cooperated over the years to help "eliminate" opposition leaders in each other's countries. As in the case of Cuba, Libyan intelligence is patterned on the Soviet model. Libya also shares with Iraqi intelligence an interest in the clandestine acquisition of chemical and nuclear material. It is also important to note that intelligence officials may be engaged in more than the espionage or counterespionage activities. They may also take part in operational plans that one would associate with covert action. For example, two Libyan intelligence officers were implicated in the 1988 bombing of Pan Am flight 103 over Lockerbie, Scotland.

One common problem faced by works on espionage regardless of the country or time period under study is the paucity of data. Secrecy continues to surround espionage long after the act in question has occurred. This is why oral histories and memoirs play such a prominent role in the study of espionage. Secrecy also produces gaps in researchers' knowledge and leads to conflicting theories over how to fill in the missing information. This makes writing on espionage much more of an art than a science, with some scholars doubting that a single overarching theory of intelligence will ever emerge that can explain its conduct across countries and time. It also produces conflicting accounts of why an act of espionage occurred or how it was discovered, and what its ultimate importance is to national security concerns.

# Further Reading

Comparative studies of intelligence organizations remain a very underdeveloped field of inquiry. Typically accounts focus on the organizational structure of intelligence organizations, because little other information is available. See Richard Bennett, *Espionage: An Encyclopedia of Spies and Secrets* (London: Virgin, 2002). Also somewhat comparative in nature is Martin Alexander, *Knowing Your Friends: Intelligence inside Alliances and Coalitions from 1914 to the End of the Cold War* (London: Frank Cass, 1998). Valuable articles on foreign intelligence services can also be found in two journals, the *Journal of Conflict Studies* and the *International Journal of Intelligence and Counterintelligence*. More extensive are individual countries' treatments of intelligence and espionage.

On Great Britain see Nigel West and Oleg Tsarev, *The Crown Jewels* (London: HarperCollins, 1998); William Stevenson, *A Man Called Intrepid* (New York: Ballantine, 1976); Christopher Andrew, *Her Majesty's Secret Service: The Making of the British Intelligence Community* (New York: Penguin, 1986); Peter Wright, *Spy Catcher: The Candid Autobiography of a Senior Intelligence Official* (New York: Viking, 1987); Andrew Boyle, *The Fourth Man: The Definitive Account of Kim Philby, Guy Burgess, and Donald Maclean and Who Recruited Them to Spy for Russia* (New York: Dial, 1979); and Phillip Knightly, *The Master Spy: The Story of Kim Philby* (New York: Vintage, 1990).

On Russia/Soviet Union and other communist intelligence organizations see Oleg Kalugin, *The First Directorate: My 32 Years in Intelligence and Espionage against the West* (New York: St. Martin's, 1994); Markus Wolf, *Man without a Face: The Autobiography of Communism's Great*

*Spymaster* (New York: Random House, 1997); John Haynes and Harvey Klehr, *Venona: Decoding Soviet Espionage in America* (New Haven, CT: Yale University Press, 1999); Ronald Kessler, *Escape from the CIA* (New York: Pocket Books, 1991); David Murphy et al., *Battleground Berlin: CIA vs. KGB in the Cold War* (New Haven, CT: Yale University Press, 1997); Vladimir Sakharov, *High Treason* (New York: Ballantine, 1981); Jerold Schechter and Peter Duriabin, *The Spy Who Saved the World: How a Soviet Colonel Changed the Cold War* (New York: Charles Scribner's, 1992); Arkady Shevchencko, *Breaking with Moscow* (New York: Alfred A. Knopf, 1985); John Barron, *KGB: The Secret Work of Soviet Secret Agents* (New York: Bantam, 1974); V. E. Rarrant, *The Red Orchestra: The Soviet Spy Network inside Nazi Europe* (New York: John Wiley and Sons, 1995); and Oleg Gordievsky and Christopher Andrew, *KGB: The Inside Story of Its Foreign Operations from Lenin to Gorbachev* (New York: HarperCollins, 1990).

On Israel see Dan Raviv and Yossi Melman, *Every Prince a Spy: The Complete History of Israel's Intelligence Community* (New York: Houghton Mifflin, 1990) and Ian Black and Benny Morris, *Israel's Secret Wars: A History of Israel's Intelligence Services* (New York: Grove Weidenfeld, 1991).

# References

Barron, John. 1989. "Tracking China's Master Spy." *Reader's Digest* (December): 97–102.

Blitzer, Wolf. 1989. *Territory of Lies: The Exclusive Story of Johnathon Jay Pollard: The American Who Spied on His Country for Israel and How He Was Betrayed*. New York: Harper and Row.

Godson, Roy, ed. 1988. *Comparing Foreign Intelligence*. Washington, DC: Pergamon-Brassey's.

Knight, Amy. 1996. *Spies without Cloaks: The KGB's Successors*. Princeton, NJ: Princeton University Press.

Knightly, Phillip. 1988. *The Second Oldest Profession: Spies and Spying in the Twentieth Century*. New York: Penguin.

Melton, H. Keith. 1996. *The Ultimate Spy Book*. New York: DK Publishers.

Richelson, Jeffrey. 1988. *Foreign Intelligence Organizations*. Cambridge, MA: Ballinger.

Shaw, Mark. 2001. *Miscarriage of Justice: The Jonathan Pollard Story*. St. Paul, MN: Paragon.

# 4

# Biographical Sketches

This chapter provides brief biographical sketches of historical and contemporary figures that are important to the study of espionage in the United States and around the world. They can be grouped into three categories. The first group is made up of spies, individuals who participated in particularly damaging acts of espionage. The second group is made up of spy catchers, those who played important roles in catching spies. Often their significance lies not so much in whom they caught but in how they approached their job and the consequences that followed. The third and smallest group consists of those charged with overseeing the efforts of intelligence officials. Given the nature of the information available, these are Americans. They are neither spies nor spy catchers, so their role is often overlooked in the study of espionage. Their significance to the study of espionage is found in two areas. First, their actions set the broad legal parameters within which spies and spy catchers interact. Second, their actions also set the tone for thinking about the problem of intelligence reform. Both of these points are particularly important in the aftermath of the events of September 11, 2001, and the renewed interest in espionage and counterespionage within the United States.

## Rudolf Abel (1903–1971)

Rudolf Abel was a Soviet spy ring operator who ran agents in the United States from 1948 to 1957. Convicted of spying and two lesser charges in 1957, he was sentenced to thirty years in jail for espionage and an additional ten and five years on each of the other charges, respectively. In 1962 he was exchanged for Francis Gary Powers, who had been captured in May 1960 when his U-2 reconnaissance spy plane was shot down over Soviet airspace by a surface-to-air missile. Much is unknown both about Abel's early life and the extent of his espionage activities in the United States. He provided little information to American intelligence officials during his interrogation.

Though there is a Soviet biography of Abel, it is not considered to be authoritative. Histories tend to lack information on spies because the spies' very success depends on not leaving a trail of evidence. It is known, however, that Abel was born William Fisher in Great Britain, though he never went by his birth name in the United States. He was taken to the Soviet Union by his Russian-born father in 1921. In 1948 Abel came to Canada using the identity of Andrew Kayotis, an American citizen who had died in 1947 while visiting his Lithuanian homeland. It is believed that Abel arrived in New York City in 1950. He set up residence there as a photographer using the identity of Emil Goldfus, who had died forty-seven years earlier as an infant. In 1954 Abel was put into contact with Reino Hayhanen. He was a Soviet intelligence officer who would serve as a "cut-out" or courier for Abel. The relationship proved to be Abel's undoing. Hayhanen was an alcoholic who was not careful in practicing his trade, either in sending intelligence to the Soviet Union or in receiving intelligence information from members of Abel's spy ring. Concerned for the security of his operation, Abel had Hayhanen recalled to the Soviet Union. In 1957 on his way home during a stopover in Paris, Hayhanen made the decision to defect to the United States. The information he gave American intelligence officials allowed them to identify Abel as a Soviet spy. On October 14, 1957, Abel was charged with illegal entry into the United States, conspiring to obtain military secrets, and failing to register as a foreign agent. When a radio transmitter and microfilm were found in his apartment, Abel was convicted on all charges. The crime of conspiring to obtain military secrets carried the death penalty, but Abel's lawyer, James B. Donovan, successfully asked the court for clemency—in part on the grounds that Abel might be worth more alive than dead. Donovan suggested the possibility that Abel might be exchanged for a captured American spy at some future point in time. Exchanged for Powers in 1962, Abel died in the Soviet Union on November 16, 1971.

# Aldrich Ames (1941– )

Aldrich Ames began working in the CIA's Directorate of Operations in 1968. His first overseas posting came in 1969 with his assignment to Ankara, Turkey. His job was to recruit communist intelligence officials and diplomats as spies. Ames returned to Washington, D.C., in 1972 and in 1976 went to the CIA's Foreign Resources Division office in New York, which was in charge of operations against foreign targets. Ames's next posting took him to Mexico City, where he stayed from 1981 until 1983. As in Ankara he was supposed to recruit Soviet diplomats as spies; also as in Ankara, he received low performance evaluations. Ames's next assignment was as head of the Soviet branch of the counterintelligence group at CIA headquarters. Here he had access to highly secret information regarding CIA operations against Soviet intelligence agencies outside of the Soviet Union, and he supervised CIA assets inside the Soviet Union. He was also responsible for identifying possible Soviet spies within the CIA.

On April 16, 1985, Ames walked into the Soviet embassy and offered them his services as a spy. In return he sought $50,000. Ames claims that this was to have been a onetime act of espionage, but in mid-June of that same year Ames provided the Soviet Union with the identities of virtually all of the Soviet agents working for the CIA and other intelligence services. He did so without prompting and without demanding payment. From CIA headquarters Ames's next assignment took him to Rome in 1986 where he served as Soviet branch chief. Here Ames followed procedures he had initiated at CIA headquarters in spying for the Soviet Union. He simply walked out of the embassy with secret material and turned it over to the Soviets in return for cash payments. The CIA was slow to react to the consequences of Ames's betrayal. As a result of Ames's actions, some estimate that ten Soviet double agents were executed and another twenty or so most likely were turned into spies for the KGB and continued to work with the CIA or became "dangles," decoys for the CIA and therefore avenues of misinformation. It did not authorize an inquiry until October 1986. The FBI also began its own probe that month. The probe ended in 1987. In April 1991 a joint CIA-FBI investigation was launched in search of the Soviet mole. The joint investigative team issued its report in March 1993; it concluded that the CIA had been penetrated. The FBI formally opened another investigation that month. In May it opened a case file on

Ames, and he was placed under surveillance. He was arrested on February 21, 1994. Ames pled guilty to espionage. In return for cooperating with U.S. officials Ames received a life sentence with no possibility of parole.

## James Jesus Angleton (1917–1987)

James Angleton was born in Boise, Idaho, and grew up in Arizona and Italy. He did his undergraduate work at Yale and went on to Harvard Law School. Angleton joined the newly established Office of Strategic Services (OSS) in 1943 at the invitation of one of his professors from Yale. He was assigned to the Counterespionage (X-2) Branch and sent to Great Britain so that he could be trained by agents in the British Secret Intelligence Service. There he met Harold "Kim" Philby, a British intelligence agent who was also a Soviet spy. When World War II ended the OSS was disbanded and its functions split among other intelligence agencies. Angleton, who had risen to the position of head of OSS counterintelligence operations in Italy, stayed on with one of the OSS's successor organizations, the Strategic Services Unit. In its brief existence it would first become part of the Central Intelligence Group (CIG) in 1946 and then part of the Central Intelligence Agency, which replaced the CIG in 1947. Angleton would soon return to Washington to work at the CIA's headquarters, where he would become chief of its counterintelligence staff. The staff's functions included security operations and serving as the point of contact for friendly foreign intelligence organizations. Here again, Angleton came into contact with Philby. counterintelligence was by now Angleton's life work, and by all accounts he became increasingly suspicious of the motives of all those around him. Everything became part of a grand conspiracy to mislead the United States, including such major international developments as the Sino-Soviet split in the 1960s and Yugoslavia's earlier break with Stalin.

This same conspiratorial and paranoid outlook on events shaped his view of individuals. He believed that key American diplomats were Soviet agents. In what was perhaps the most damaging case to the ability of the CIA to conduct effective counterespionage operations against the Soviet Union, he became convinced that a Soviet spy, or mole, had penetrated the CIA. Key to Angleton's position was the word of Anatoliy Golitsyn, a KGB officer who defected in 1961. Golitsyn was turned over to Angleton, who wholeheartedly accepted his story of widespread

Soviet penetrations into Western intelligence organizations, even though Angleton was unsuccessful in searching for them within the CIA. He also accepted Golitsyn's assertion that others would defect and contradict his story in an effort to discredit him. Such a defector did appear in 1962 when Yuri Nosenko defected. He provided information that not only challenged Golitsyn but explained many troubling CIA cases such as the death of a long-time CIA spy within the Soviet military, Colonel Popov. For a fee of $100 per month, Popov had provided such intelligence as the names of Soviet agents who had been infiltrated into the West. Still, Angleton refused to budge from his support of Golitsyn.

So complete was Angleton's mistrust of others and the paralysis he inflicted on the CIA's intelligence and espionage units that some considered him to be a Soveit spy. His paranoia over the possibility of Soviet penetration into the CIA caused him to discount the information provided by other intelligence sources about Soviet espionage in the United States and information that challenged his beliefs. The result was a situation in which a reasonable evaluation of competing bodies of information was virtually impossible. Angleton's downfall began in 1973 when William Colby took over as director of the CIA. He began to cut back on Angleton's power. Angleton was stripped of his role as liaison between the CIA and the Federal Bureau of Investigation, and an illicit domestic mail-opening operation run by Angleton since 1955 was shut down. Angleton resigned shortly after evidence became public about the extent of illegal CIA domestic spying activities. They are chronicled in the Church Committee Report, excerpts of which are included in the document appendix. It was about this time that details of Angleton's Operation CHAOS were revealed. Set up with the approval of President Lyndon Johnson, it had secretly collected information on the anti–Vietnam War movement in hopes of ascertaining whether foreign governments or agents were manipulating the movement. After his retirement Angleton continued to work on behalf of a strong intelligence community, serving as chairman of a private organization that was active in intelligence-related issues, the Security and Intelligence Fund. Angleton was the last of the great American Cold War spy catchers. After him, a more bureaucratic culture came to dominate counterintelligence work. His downfall, along with the legacy left by J. Edgar Hoover, illustrates the danger inherent in counterintelligence when personal values are allowed to transcend societal ones.

# Benedict Arnold (1741–1801)

Benedict Arnold was a prominent military figure in the Continental army during the American Revolution who became a British spy. Arnold was born in Connecticut and became a successful merchant. When the American Revolution broke out with the battles of Lexington and Concord, Arnold organized an army and marched it to Boston. He thereupon began a military career that centered on the Lake Champlain region. Obtaining the rank of colonel and operating alongside Ethan Allen, Arnold captured the British outpost Fort Ticonderoga. After returning to Boston, Arnold then set out on a campaign against Quebec in the fall of 1775. Arnold had advocated an attack on Canada as a means of securing the St. Lawrence River Valley and preventing British attacks on the northern American frontier, but the operation failed. Arnold next helped put together and command a naval force to block a British southward advance. Although his forces were outnumbered and took heavy casualties, Arnold succeeded in blocking the British advance in a battle on October 11, 1776. Arnold would return to the region in 1777 and participate in the battles of Saratoga. Through all of this, Arnold quarreled with the Continental Congress over the lack of promotions and recognition for his military accomplishments and over the punishments handed out for his excessive and undisciplined behavior.

In 1778 after one of those disputes, Arnold was put in command of Philadelphia. There he married a reputed Tory sympathizer, Margaret Shippen, in April 1779 and became embroiled with civil authorities and Congress over charges of corruption and abuse of power. It was around this time that Arnold approached Sir Henry Clinton with an offer to sell military secrets. Arnold's delivery of secret information began in May 1779. He temporarily stopped sending information in December but resumed in May 1780 after he had been cleared of charges filed in a court martial suit.

Among the intelligence Arnold furnished to the British was information that a French expeditionary force was expected to arrive in Rhode Island. In late summer 1780 Arnold was given command of the American post at West Point, New York, overlooking the Hudson River. He worked out an arrangement with Clinton in which for 10,000 pounds he would defect and for another 20,000 pounds he would allow the British to seize West Point and its 3,000 troops. The plan collapsed when British Major

John Andre was captured in civilian clothes with incriminating documents. Andre was hanged, and Arnold fled to New York to join the British. He would lead British military campaigns in the Chesapeake region of Virginia and in Connecticut. After the British surrender, Arnold fled to Great Britain. In the latter part of his career he would engage in a failed commercial venture in Canada and one as a privateer in the West Indies, where he was arrested by French authorities as a British spy. He died in London on June 14, 1801.

## Lafayette Baker (1826–1868)

Lafayette Baker was a Union intelligence officer during the Civil War who founded an organization called the Secret Service after serving as a spy behind Confederate lines. Baker was born in New York and moved frequently throughout the United States before the Civil War. For a time he lived in San Francisco where he worked with vigilantes in trying to bring an end to the corruption and gambling there. In 1861 Baker volunteered to serve as a spy for Union General Winfield Scott. Posing as a photographer Baker crossed Union lines and entered into Virginia. His efforts met with frequent failure, although the information he provided Scott is considered to have been valuable. Several times he was arrested by both Union and Confederate forces as a spy, and he was imprisoned by Confederate forces in Fredericksburg.

On his return to the North, Baker was placed in charge of a counterespionage unit within the State Department. In February 1862 this organization was transferred to the War Department, where it became the National Detective Bureau. In this capacity Baker investigated charges of corruption in the Treasury Department and disloyalty within the military. He provided information about Confederate troop movements and a plot to capture Washington, D.C. Baker also captured Confederate spy Belle Boyd. Following Lincoln's assassination Baker took a leading a role in the search for and capture of John Wilkes Booth. Although his accomplishments were many, Baker operated with little regard for warrants or the constitutional rights of those he pursued. He is also reported to have employed brutal interrogation techniques in order to obtain information. Baker's fortunes declined dramatically after the end of the Civil War. He clashed with President Andrew Johnson, who dismissed Baker from the intelligence service on suspicion of spying on him. At issue was Baker's attempt to gain incriminating evidence against Lucy Cobb, a pardon broker, one who acts as an intermediary helping convicted people obtain a pardon by lobbying judicial officers, with whom Johnson was reputed to be having an affair. Baker had warned Johnson about Cobb's activities and had set a trap to catch her selling the documents needed to obtain a pardon. Baker testified at Johnson's impeachment hearings, falsely claiming that Johnson had been engaged in a correspondence with Jefferson Davis in which he expressed sympathies for the Confederate cause. Anxious to regain his former status within Washington, Baker lied about President Johnson as part of a conspiracy led by Republican Congressman James Ashley, who was a political opponent of Johnson. Baker was also indicted but he was acquitted on the extortion charge but convicted on the false imprisonment charge and fined a token $1.35. Baker died in Philadelphia shortly after Johnson's impeachment trial ended.

## Whittaker Chambers (1901–1961)

Whittaker Chambers was a communist spy who incriminated Alger Hiss, a former high-ranking State Department official, as being part of a 1930s spy ring in the United States. Whittaker's allegations set off one of the most complex and politically charged spy investigations in history. Conservatives of the time deeply distrusted the foreign policies of the Roosevelt and Truman administrations, believing they had sold out Eastern Europe to communism. In the months following the Hiss guilty verdict, Senator Joseph McCarthy would unleash his hunt for communists within the State Department.

Chambers was born in Philadelphia. He joined the Communist Party in 1924 and would become editor of its newspaper, the *Daily Worker*. He left the party briefly in 1929 after losing a power struggle for leadership within the Communist Party but returned in 1931. In 1932 he became an agent for the Soviet Union, working as a courier for a senior intelligence officer who had set up a network of communists (known as the Ware Group) within the Roosevelt administration. In 1937 Chambers had a change of heart and rejected communism, but he continued to work as a courier until the spring of 1938. In April of that year he defected and went into hiding. Chambers had been ordered back to the Soviet Union in 1937 but delayed going, fearing that he would become a victim of Stalin's purges. In 1939 Chambers came out of hiding, began working at *Time* magazine, and began ascending the corporate ladder there, moving from book reviewer to editor at large for special projects in 1945.

In 1939 he also went to Adolf Berle, an assistant secretary of state, and told him that several American senior government officials were members of the Communist Party. Chambers did not reveal his own former role as a communist agent in the Ware Group, but he did identify Hiss. Berle made a report, but no further action was forthcoming. Chambers also went to the Federal Bureau of Investigation with his charges but once again did not reveal that he too had spied. On August 3, 1948, Chambers testified before the House Un-American Activities Committee and accused Hiss of being a communist and a member of the Ware Group. Hiss denied knowing Chambers and rejected the charge that he was a communist. Hiss would soon identify Chambers as being George Crossley, a freelance journalist whom he did have dealings with in the 1930s. Hiss challenged Chambers to repeat his charges in the media so that he might sue Chambers for libel, which he did. Chambers then made the further accusation that Hiss was engaged in spying. By doing so, Chambers revealed his own involvement in espionage, but Hiss continued to deny the charges. Richard Nixon, then a junior member of the House Un-American Activities Committee, was assigned to investigate Chambers's allegation. Nixon became a staunch supporter and promoter of Chambers in the unfolding controversy. His career benefited greatly from Chambers's accusations against Hiss. It provided him with important media exposure and made him into a national political figure. To substantiate his position Chambers produced microfilm (previously hidden in pumpkins on his farm) containing information that he claimed Hiss had stolen from the State Department and given to him. Chambers had retained the evidence as a type of personal insurance policy when he had made the decision to leave the Communist Party. These documents sealed Hiss's fate. He was ultimately convicted by a grand jury of two counts of perjury and sentenced to five years in prison. The statute of limitations prevented any other conviction. Hiss continued to maintain his innocence.

Contradictions, incomplete revelations, and false statements made by Chambers about his involvement with Hiss made the verdict controversial. Evidence released by Russian authorities in the 1990s tends to confirm the truth of Chambers's allegations that Hiss was a communist spy. Chambers resigned from *Time* in

December 1948. In 1952 he wrote his autobiography, *Witness*, and went on to work for a short time for the conservative *National Review*. Chambers died on his Maryland farm on July 9, 1961. In 1984 he was awarded a posthumous Medal of Freedom by President Ronald Reagan.

## Frank Church (1924–1984)

Senator Frank Church (D-Idaho) gained notoriety in the 1970s when he chaired the Senate Select Committee to Study Government Operations with Respect to Intelligence Activities. His committee focused on the actions of the Central Intelligence Agency (CIA) with an emphasis on covert action. In the course of doing so it uncovered CIA misuse of intelligence agencies to spy on Americans.

Church was elected to the Senate in 1957 as an internationalist who pledged his support to President Dwight Eisenhower's Cold War foreign policies. The centerpiece was the concept of containment by which the United States sought to block any further Soviet expansion. Among the most prominent actions taken to carry out containment were the establishment of encircling military alliances such as the North Atlantic Treaty Organization (NATO) and covert action operations designed to bring down hostile governments such as those in Iran, Guatemala, and Indonesia. Once in office his foreign policy views had evolved such that by the mid-1960s he was opposing the Vietnam War. Because it was justified as necessary to stop the spread of communism, the Vietnam War was a logical outgrowth of the containment doctrine. Church rejected this rationale for the Vietnam War, arguing that the United States had become obsessed with communism and that America did not have legitimate national interests in Vietnam. Church was defeated in a 1980 reelection bid. He had become a primary target of conservatives who felt that he had crippled the United States's intelligence capabilities through his committee's hearings and his famous charge that the CIA was a "rogue elephant" in need of control. Church made an unsuccessful run for the Democratic presidential nomination in 1996.

## William Donovan (1883–1959)

William "Wild Bill" Donovan founded the Office of Strategic Services (OSS), the forerunner of the Central Intelligence Agency.

For this, he is often referred to as the "father of modern American intelligence." Donovan was born in Buffalo, New York. Prior to the American involvement in World War I, Donovan served in Europe as part of the Rockefeller Foundation's War Relief Commission. He left Europe when his National Guard unit was activated to serve along the Mexican border in 1916. After the United States entered World War I, Donovan saw combat in France as part of the 165th Regiment. He was wounded three times and received the Medal of Honor and other commendations. After the war he returned to Buffalo to practice law and delve into politics. He was the unsuccessful Republican candidate for lieutenant governor of New York in 1922 and for governor in 1932. In 1924 Donovan began work in the attorney general's office in the Criminal Division and then the Anti-Trust Division. He remained there until 1929 when he moved to New York City. Donovan had hoped to be named attorney general by President Hoover but did not obtain the position. As war grew nearer in the 1930s Donovan undertook several trips to Europe and Africa at his own expense to gather intelligence for the government. After war broke out, Donovan was sent on official intelligence missions to Europe under the sponsorship of Frank Knox, a friend and fellow Republican whom Franklin Roosevelt had appointed secretary of war. It was on these intelligence trips that Donovan was introduced to William Stephenson, chief of the Secret Intelligence Service (the British intelligence organization) in the United States.

It was conversations with Stephenson that convinced Donovan of the need to establish a central intelligence organization in the United States that combined intelligence analysis, espionage, and covert action. No such organization currently existed; intelligence responsibility at that time was divided among the military services, the State Department, and the Federal Bureau of Investigation. Donovan proposed such a system to Roosevelt, who agreed but stopped short of setting up as extensive and centralized a system as Donovan (and Stephenson) had proposed. Donovan was named coordinator of Central Intelligence on July 11, 1941. Within a year Roosevelt abolished the existing COI (Coordinator of Information) position and created the Office of Strategic Services (OSS) with Donovan as director. This moved intelligence a step closer to Donovan's proposal, but Roosevelt still stopped short of creating it as an independent agency. It was placed under the direction of the Joint Chiefs of Staff. Donovan proposed that the OSS be made a permanent institution after the war, but President Harry Truman rejected the plan and in October 1945 divided its intelligence duties among the existing intelligence organizations. Truman reversed course in 1947 when he created the CIA.

After leaving the OSS Donovan served for a short time as a prosecutor at the Nuremburg War Crimes trials and then as ambassador to Thailand during the Eisenhower administration. After retirement Donovan advocated a strong policy of anticommunism and covert action. He died in Walter Reed Army Hospital in Washington, D.C., on January 19, 1970.

## Allen Welch Dulles (1893–1969)

Allen Dulles was the third director of the Central Intelligence Agency (CIA). Along with his brother, John Foster Dulles, who was secretary of state, Allen Dulles played a key role in laying the foundations for American foreign policy in the second half of the twentieth century. He headed the CIA from 1953 to 1961. This was the height of the Cold War, and although Dulles's tenure in office is most associated with the high point of CIA covert action, it is also a time period in which some of its most notable espionage successes and failures took place. Although both covert action and espionage are clandestine activities occurring in secret, they differ in one important respect. The purpose of espionage is to collect information in another country. The spy does nothing else. The purpose of covert action is to influence or manipulate events in another country. This may be done by such means as leading a coup, supporting the career of a political official or military officer, or subsidizing a political party or magazine.

Dulles was born in Watertown, New York. He joined the Foreign Service in 1916 after completing law school and was assigned to Vienna. During World War I he was stationed in Berne, Switzerland. One of his assignments was to make contact with anticommunist Eastern European groups. His tour of duty in Switzerland produced one of the most famous stories in the lore of intelligence. Dulles claims that he received a phone call from Vladimir Lenin, who was living in exile in Switzerland. About to go off duty, Dulles put off Lenin's request for a meeting until the following day. That night Lenin left by train for Russia to help launch the communist revolution.

Dulles served on the staff of the American delegation to the Paris Peace Conference. After World War I ended he was posted in Washington, D.C., where he was head of the Near Eastern Division. In 1926 he left government service to enter into a New York–based law practice with his brother. Dulles continued to be involved in world politics, however, as he became affiliated with the Council on Foreign Relations. This was, and still remains, one of the most important and authoritative nongovernmental organizations involved in foreign policy. The Council on Foreign Relations sponsors meetings, workshops, and publications that examine foreign policy problems, and in the process influences the content of decisions. When World War II broke out Dulles joined the newly established Office of Strategic Services (OSS). He returned to Berne and from there operated a spy ring inside Germany. One agent of his provided more than 2,000 microfilmed copies of Nazi documents. Dulles also secured information about the Nazi V-2 rocket program and obtained proof that the Germans had broken the code used by the U.S. diplomatic mission in Berne. Reportedly it was during his service with the OSS that Dulles came into his strong anticommunist views.

After the war ended Dulles returned to private law practice, but his involvement in intelligence affairs continued. President Harry Truman asked him to help draft the 1947 National Security Act that created the CIA and then to serve on a committee to make recommendations on how it should operate. Dulles was called to Washington by the CIA's first director, Walter Bedell Smith, to help implement those recommendations. This led to Dulles's being appointed deputy director of the CIA in August 1951. In 1953 Dulles succeeded Smith as Director of Central Intelligence.

Among the notable espionage accomplishments during Dulles's stewardship of the CIA were digging a tunnel under the Berlin Wall for purposes of eavesdropping; the design, building, and flight of the U-2 spy plane; and obtaining a copy of Nikita Khrushchev's 1956 speech to the Soviet Communist Party elite in which he denounced Joseph Stalin for his excesses. Significant as these accomplishments were, they were also flawed efforts that have contributed to the mixed legacy Dulles is seen as having left the CIA. The Berlin tunnel is believed to have been compromised and used by the Soviet Union to send disinformation to the United States. A U-2 spy plane piloted by Francis Gary Powers was shot down during a critical period in U.S.-Soviet diplomacy. Khrushchev's speech was altered and released by CIA propagandists and thus lost some of its value.

President John F. Kennedy asked Dulles to resign in 1961 following the embarrassing failure of the Bay of Pigs invasion, which was intended to remove Fidel Castro from power. Conceived during the Eisenhower administration, it had evolved into a CIA-trained and -organized invasion by Cuban dissidents. Up until this failure, Dulles had overseen a series of successful, if now controversial, covert actions in Indonesia, Iran, and Guatemala. Dulles also left a mixed legacy in still another area: accountability. On the one hand, he protected CIA officials from the anti-communist investigations led by Senator Joseph McCarthy far better than his brother protected Foreign Service officers. On the other hand, Allen Dulles fiercely and successfully resisted meaningful congressional oversight of the CIA. Dulles remained in Washington, D.C., during his retirement and wrote one of the first textbook treatments of intelligence, *The Craft of Intelligence*. He also served on the Warren Commission that investigated the assassination of President Kennedy.

## Felix Dzershinsky (1877–1926)

Felix Dzershinsky was the founding force behind the Soviet secret police and the CHEKA intelligence body established by the Bolshevik government following their victory in the Russian civil war. Born into an aristocratic Polish family in 1877, Dzershinsky joined the Socialist Revolutionary Party as a youth. He followed Vladimir Lenin and joined the Bolshevik Party when the socialist revolutionary movement split into the Bolshevik and more moderate Menshevik factions. Prior to the Russian revolution Dzershinsky served as a courier between revolutionaries in Russia and Russian exiles abroad. It took him only six months after the revolution to transform his antiespionage commission, the All-Russian Extraordinary Commission for Combating Counterrevolution, Speculation, and Sabotage (CHEKA), into a powerful bureaucratic force. He divided his organization into two units. One dealt with counterespionage; the other dealt with secret, or covert, operations. Those in his employ were personally loyal but also brutal in their approach to intelligence. Such was the government's dislike of CHEKA that in December 1921 a government reorganization replaced it with a new organization, the State Political Administration (GPU). Less than two years later it was replaced by the United States Political Administration (OGPU). Dzershinsky remained in charge of Soviet intelligence throughout these changes. He also constructed an anticommunist front organization, the Trust, that he used to attract and identify opponents to communist rule. operating as the Moscow Municipal Credit Association, it was able to trap British agent Sidney Reilly. Reportedly Reilly revealed all of his contacts before being executed.

Disagreement surrounds Dzershinsky's death. Some claim he died of natural causes on July 20, 1926. Others have him being assassinated by his successor, Vyachesiav Menzhinsky.

## Klaus Fuchs (1911–1985)

Considered by many to be the most important of the Soviet "atomic spies," Fuchs was born in Germany and fled to Great Britain in 1933. A staunch anti-Nazi, Fuchs was also and openly pro-communist. Fuchs was a physicist and became involved in the British effort to build an atomic bomb. Participation in this project required that Fuchs pass a security clearance and become a British citizen, which he did in 1942.

In 1943 Fuchs went to Columbia University to work on the atomic bomb and in 1946 would become head of the theoretical physics center of atomic research at Harwell, a research lab roughly equivalent to Los Alamos in the United States, where work on the atomic bomb was conducted. Fuchs is described as becoming head of the Theoretical Physics Division of the Atomic Research Center there. In 1949 the Federal Bureau of Investigation uncovered a spy ring in the United States that was passing secrets to the Soviet Union. One of the members of the spy ring was identified as a British physicist. Fuchs quickly became a suspect. He was confronted after inquiring as to whether his father's appointment to a position at the University of Leipzig in East Germany would cause problems for his security clearance. Fuchs confessed and was arrested in Great Britain. He was sentenced to the maximum term of fourteen years in prison. Upon his release Fuchs returned to East Germany where he became head of the Nuclear Research Institute at Dresden.

## Rose O'Neal Greenhow (1815?–1864)

Rose O'Neal Greenhow was born in Maryland; during her early teens she lived with her aunt, who owned the Old Capitol Boardinghouse. Located near Capitol Hill, it served as home for many prominent political figures including Senator John C.

Calhoun. She married Robert Greenhow, a linguist in the State Department, in 1835. Rose Greenhow soon became immersed in a series of diplomatic intrigues that often placed her in the role of spy or provocateur. She became a confident of then-Secretary of State and later President James Buchanan. During Buchanan's administration Greenhow would become an outspoken advocate of succession by the South. Earlier she had been suspected of spying for Great Britain during negotiations over the Oregon Territory, and in 1849 Greenhow was associated with a plan to annex Cuba and bring it into the United States as a slave state.

Widowed in 1854, Greenhow was recruited as a Confederate spy by Colonel Thomas Jordan who was then an officer in the U.S. Army but would soon resign and join the Confederate army. There Jordan served as an adjunct general to General P. G. T. Beauregard who commanded Confederate troops at the Battle of Bull Run. Her place in Washington society provided her with a vast network of social and political contacts to obtain intelligence from. The established mythology of the Civil War has Greenhow's greatest intelligence coup as being that of providing information to General P. G. T. Beauregard prior to the First Battle of Bull Run. Other research suggests, however, that this account is unlikely to be true or that the role it played in the Confederate victory has been greatly exaggerated. Greenhow was unschooled in the techniques of espionage tradecraft and made little secret of her Southern sympathies. It came as no surprise, then, that she was arrested by Thomas Pinkerton—who served as director of intelligence for the Union and was the founder of the Pinkerton detective agency—for spying, along with many of the other members of the espionage ring she belonged to. First placed under house arrest before being imprisoned in the Old Capitol Boardinghouse that her aunt had owned, Greenhow was permitted to go to Richmond in June 1862. The following year Greenhow went to Europe and published her memoirs. In August 1864 she sailed back to the Confederacy carrying messages from Confederate agents. She drowned off the coast of North Carolina when the ship she was on sank while she was trying to run a Union blockade.

## Nathan Hale (1755–1776)

Nathan Hale was one of the first heroes of the American Revolution and perhaps the first American spy to die in the service of his country. A statue honoring him stands at the headquarters of the Central Intelligence Agency, and his last words, "I only regret that I have but one life to lose for my country," are engraved in its main entranceway.

Hale was born in Connecticut and entered Yale at age fourteen. Upon graduation he became a schoolteacher. When the American Revolution began in April 1775 with the battles of Lexington and Concord, Hale left to join the Continental army at Boston. He quickly proved himself in combat and was promoted to the rank of captain on January 1, 1776. Soon he was chosen to lead a company of Knowlton's Rangers, the first intelligence reconnaissance unit of the American army. Established by George Washington and led by Lieutenant Colonel Thomas Knowlton, its purpose was to provide forward intelligence on British forces and engage in sabotage. In August of that year General George Washington's troops retreated to Manhattan; eager for intelligence about the disposition of the British forces opposing him, Washington asked Knowlton's Rangers to provide a spy. No one volunteered until Hale stepped forward. Disguised as a schoolteacher, Hale began his mission on September 12 knowing little if anything about the practice of espionage. After collecting information and making drawings of British fortifications, Hale sought to return to Washington's army. He was captured by the British on the night of September 21 attempting to cross their lines. British General William Howe ordered him hanged. He was executed the following day, September 22, 1776.

## Lee H. Hamilton (1931– )

Lee Hamilton (D-Indiana) was first elected to Congress in 1964 and served seventeen terms before retiring at the end of the 105th Congress. Hamilton was the Democrats' pick to replace retired Senator George Mitchell as its ranking member on the bipartisan committee to investigate the performance of the intelligence community leading up to the events of September 11, 2001. Henry Kissinger had been the Republicans' choice to chair the committee, but he resigned and was replaced by former New Jersey Governor Thomas Keane. A domestic conservative who opposed big government and spending on social welfare programs, he was nevertheless an internationalist in foreign policy and opposed isolationist conservative foreign policy initiatives such as cutting foreign aid. Hamilton rose to prominence in the House for his involvement in foreign policy matters. During the Reagan era he chaired the House Intelligence Committee and chaired the special House committee that investigated the Iran-Contra scandal. Hamilton's belief that foreign policy was the prerogative of the president led him to take a restrained and generally sympathetic view to the Reagan administration's handing of the matter.

During Clinton's presidency Hamilton emerged as a vocal supporter of that administration's foreign policy toward events in the former Yugoslavia. From his position as senior ranking Democrat on the House International Relations Committee, Hamilton worked to prevent a lifting of the Bosnian arms embargo. He also authored an amendment to a House resolution that was critical of Clinton's handling of the peacekeeping operation in Bosnia. Hamilton's amendment permitted the administration to keep U.S. forces in Somalia according to the administration's timetable rather than insisting on their prompt withdrawal.

## Philip (Robert) Hanssen (1945– )

Philip Hanssen (also known as Robert Hanssen) was arrested for spying in February 2001. He was a twenty-seven-year FBI veteran who specialized in counterintelligence. Hanssen was excellently placed to spy on the U.S. intelligence system. From 1987 to 1990 he was deputy chief of the FBI's Soviet Analytical Unit. In the mid-1980s he was active in the FBI's domestic spying program, which monitored the activities of Americans thought to be Soviet spies. From 1995 until January 2001 Hanssen was on assignment from the FBI to the State Department's Office of Foreign Missions, which is responsible for monitoring foreign diplomats believed to be working with international terrorists.

The U.S. government asserts that Hanssen received some $600,000 in cash and diamonds, along with $800,000 escrowed in Russian bank accounts, for his efforts. Included among the charges leveled at Hanssen were fourteen charges that were punishable by death. In all, he turned over twenty-six computer disks and more than 6,000 pages of U.S. documents to Soviet officials. Hanssen pled guilty to spying as part of a deal to avoid the death penalty.

## Alger Hiss (1904–1996)

Alger Hiss was a prominent member of the American foreign policy establishment who was accused by Whittaker Chambers of being a communist spy. Hiss steadfastly claimed his innocence

during a complex series of congressional hearings and court proceedings in the 1950s. After one hung jury, Hiss was retried and
found guilty, but because the statute of limitations had expired
Hiss could not be charged with espionage. He was convicted of
two counts of perjury in 1950 and was sentenced to a five-year
prison sentence, which was commuted to four years for good
behavior in 1954. After his release he wrote a book defending
himself, *In the Court of Public Opinion*. Documents released by
Russia after the fall of communism in the Soviet Union point to
his guilt.

Hiss was born in Baltimore and attended Harvard Law
School. In 1929 he obtained a clerkship with Supreme Court
Justice Oliver Wendell Holmes. After briefly serving in Franklin
Roosevelt's administration in the Agricultural Adjustment
Administration and then on the Nye Committee (which investi-
gated charges that the arms industry was responsible for involv-
ing the United States in World War I), Hiss followed one of his
Harvard professors into the State Department in 1936. Before he
resigned in 1947 to become president of the Carnegie Endowment
for International Peace, Hiss rose to the upper levels of the State
Department. He served as advisor to Secretary of State Edward
Stettinus at the Yalta Conference in 1945 and played a key role in
establishing the United Nations.

Things began to unravel for Hiss in 1948 when Whittaker
Chambers, a onetime communist spy but now fervently anticommunist, accused him of having belonged to a communist cell in
the 1930s. Hiss denied the allegations, and the House Un-
American Activities Committee, before which Whittaker had
made the charges, established a subcommittee to investigate the
matter. Richard Nixon, then a first-term congressman from California, was placed in charge of the investigation.

Hiss would identify Chambers as George Crossley, a freelance journalist he had once known, but he continued to deny
Chambers's allegations of belonging to a communist cell. Hiss
then sued Chambers for libel, and a federal grand jury began
investigating the charge that Hiss was a communist. Before that
trial could begin, Chambers expanded on his charges against Hiss.
He now accused Hiss of not only being a communist but of engaging in espionage. As proof he produced microfilm copies of some
of the material that Hiss had allegedly given him; Chambers had
kept this microfilm stored in hollowed-out pumpkins on his farm.
Soon Chambers would be testifying against Hiss in multiple

venues and was giving contradictory testimony. Still, the weight
of evidence began to point to Hiss's guilt, and he was indicted by
a grand jury on two counts of perjury in December 1948. One
count was for lying that he had turned over State Department
documents to Chambers and the other for lying that he had not
seen Chambers after 1937. His first trial began on May 31, 1949,
and ended in a hung jury. His retrial began on November 17,
1949, and he was convicted on both counts of perjury on January
21, 1950. After several appeals were denied Hiss began serving
his sentence on March 22, 1951.

## John Edgar Hoover (1895–1972)

J. Edgar Hoover was director of the Federal Bureau of Investigation (FBI) for forty-eight years. In that capacity he became the
self-proclaimed expert on domestic communist subversion in the
United States. A classic example of a bureaucratic entrepreneur,
Hoover rose steadily through the ranks of the Justice Department,
escaping blame for policy excesses and adroitly working with the
media to establish his image as an indispensable defender of freedom. As the height of the Cold War competition gave way to
détente, and Hoover's obsession with subversion extended
beyond communists to include black civil rights activists, anti-
Vietnam war protestors, and others on the political left.

Hoover was born in Washington, D.C., and after completing
law school there he joined the Alien Enemy Bureau of the Justice
Department in 1917. Two years later he became a special assistant
to Attorney General Mitchell Palmer and was placed in charge of
a newly established General Intelligence Division. Its charge was
to collect intelligence on radical individuals and groups. There he
planned and directed the "Palmer Raids" that paid little respect
to civil liberties and that led to the arrest of thousands of political
radicals and the deportation of such notable figures as anarchist
Emma Goldman. Most of those arrested were released, however,
and not deported.

Hoover survived the political backlash against the Palmer
Raids and the allegations of widespread corruption that plagued
the FBI in the early 1920s. The next decade of his career was spent
improving the FBI's efficiency as a crime-fighting organization
from his position as director of the Federal Bureau of Investigation.
In the early 1930s he became involved in highly publicized battles

with celebrity criminals such as John Dillinger. By the late 1930s Hoover was again involved in collecting information on potential subversives. President Franklin Roosevelt had secretly ordered him to spy on the leadership of the American Nazi movement.

During World War II Hoover clashed with British intelligence officials in their efforts to coordinate counterespionage and intelligence activities. Such was his intransigence that the British, through William Stephenson, helped Bill Donovan create the Office of Strategic Services (OSS). Hoover was reluctant to cooperate with anyone, inside or outside the U.S. government. The British needed to act, and when Hoover displayed little interest, they had to look elsewhere. The British then turned to Donovan because of his ties to Roosevelt and perceived willingness to embrace the idea of a central intelligence organization. Hoover's major success in this bureaucratic war was to keep the OSS out of Latin America, where the FBI was active in anti-Nazi surveillance efforts.

With the onset of the Cold War, Hoover turned his attention to communist subversion within the United States. Dissatisfied with the Truman administration's pursuit of communists within the government, Hoover struck out on his own and in cooperation with Republicans on the House Un-American Activities Committee to expose this threat. These efforts led to the arrest of Klaus Fuchs in 1950 and the 1951 convictions of Ethel and Julius Rosenberg.

A key tool in Hoover's pursuit of domestic communist spies was the Smith Act. Passed in 1940, the Smith Act made it illegal to advocate overthrowing the government of the United States or belonging to an organization that did. Members of the Communist and Socialist Parties were especially vulnerable to arrest. In 1956, however, a Supreme Court ruling severely limited its utility to Hoover. He then adopted a different strategy, one that would later place him at the center of controversy. Hoover established a Counterintelligence Program (COINTELPRO) that employed "dirty tricks" to disrupt the activities of the American Communist Party. He then expanded the program to include attacks on the Ku Klux Klan, the Black Panthers, and student groups. One of Hoover's main targets became Dr. Martin Luther King, who had spoken out criticizing the FBI's handling of civil rights cases. As part of his campaign against King, Hoover secretly collected information on King's personal life that could be used for blackmail. It was a practice that Hoover also employed against many government officials, including presidents.

The national traumas of Vietnam and Watergate produced a series of investigations and exposés of the intelligence community. One of the most thorough was that conducted by Senator Frank Church's Committee to Study Government Operations with Respect to Intelligence Activities. Its report concluded that Hoover had engaged in a "sophisticated vigilante operation" against domestic political dissenters. Hoover remained director of the FBI until his death on May 2, 1972. Controversy continues to surround his tenure in office and is fueled by the fact that his personal files were destroyed after his death by his secretary and his lifelong assistant.

## Joseph McCarthy (1908–1957)

In 1952 Senator Joseph McCarthy became chairman of the Senate Committee on Government Operations and headed its Subcommittee on Investigations. He used those positions to launch what is commonly described as a witch-hunt for communist sympathizers within the government. He was known for his bullying tactics, deceit, and loose use of facts. McCarthy eventually left the Senate in disgrace.

McCarthy was born in Wisconsin. His first foray into politics was an unsuccessful bid for district attorney as a Democrat. In his next attempt he was elected as a circuit judge. McCarthy won this position handily in a nonpartisan election in which he misrepresented facts about the incumbent. McCarthy joined the military in 1942 in hopes of laying a foundation that would advance his postwar political career. For most of the war he served as an intelligence officer and saw minimum combat duty. In his political campaigns he would embellish this record to make it appear that he was a war hero. In 1946 McCarthy pulled off a stunning upset of Republican Senator Robert La Follette Jr. in the primary and went on to win election to the Senate. Both campaigns were marked by innuendo and falsehoods on McCarthy's part.

McCarthy accomplished little during his first term. With his reelection campaign in the offing, McCarthy made his most famous speech on February 7, 1950, in Wheeling, West Virginia. He boldly announced that he had in his possession the names of 205 known communists in the State Department. The allegations were not new; they had first been raised in 1946 and were investigated at that time, with some seventy-nine people being fired.

Spies were known to exist in and outside of the State Department. Alger Hiss had recently been convicted for perjury, and Klaus Fuchs confessed to sending atomic secrets to the Soviet Union. Moreover, McCarthy did not have such a list, nor was he an expert on espionage. His allegations created a sensation due to their timing. China had "fallen" to the communists, Russia had exploded an atomic bomb, and the Korean War was on the horizon. The country was looking for answers as to why the United States's security was threatened, and the specter of spies from within provided a plausible answer.

Emboldened by the positive public response to his charges, McCarthy went on the offensive. He referred to Secretary of State Dean Acheson as the "Red Dean of Fashion" and called Secretary of Defense George Marshall a traitor. Republican senators who had once shunned him now urged him on, hoping to weaken the Truman administration. McCarthy's first series of public hearings into communist influence within the government were held in 1953 and produced little that was newsworthy. Hearings held in the fall of that year, though, accomplished all that McCarthy hoped. He now targeted the army for harboring a spy ring at Fort Monmouth, New Jersey, and for coddling communists. Army officials were constantly on the defensive, and McCarthy pressed his case.

By spring 1954, however, the political tide had turned against McCarthy. Republican leaders expressed concern about the impact of "McCarthyism" on what was now a Republican foreign policy bureaucracy, and President Dwight Eisenhower, who had resisted engaging in "politics" with McCarthy, was now angry with McCarthy and wished to see him stopped. In April 1954 the Senate held thirty-six days of televised hearings into McCarthy's conflict with the army. They proved to be McCarthy's undoing, as he came across to the American public not as a defender of freedom but as a bully. In December 1954 the Senate censured McCarthy for bringing "dishonor and disrepute" to that body by a vote of 67–22. Just as rising Cold War tensions had earlier helped McCarthy, they now conspired against him. The Korean War had ended, Joseph Stalin had died, and European postwar economic recovery was under way. The world no longer appeared to be quite as threatening. McCarthy was now politically isolated within the Senate. He died on May 2, 1957, in a Bethesda, Maryland, military hospital of hepatitis, reportedly brought on by alcoholism.

# Robert S. Mueller III (1944– )

Robert Mueller was serving as director of the Federal Bureau of Investigation (FBI) at the time of the September 11, 2001, terrorist attacks. He had been nominated for the position by President George W. Bush and sworn in on September 4, 2001. In private legal practice before entering government service in 1976, Mueller's practice had consisted largely of white-collar crime, internal corporate investigations, establishing compliance programs, and complex civil litigation matters. Prior to becoming FBI director, Mueller held a series of positions within the Justice Department. From 1976 to 1988 he served in California and Massachusetts in the U.S. attorney general's office.

In 1989 Mueller came to Washington, D.C., as an assistant to Attorney General Richard Thornburgh. He soon moved on to become assistant attorney general in charge of the Criminal Division. In that capacity he investigated the Libyan terrorist attack on Pan Am flight 103 that crashed over Lockerbie, Scotland. From 1995 to 2001 Mueller again worked in the U.S. attorney general's office, first in the District of Columbia and then in California.

Mueller has put forward a spirited defense of the FBI in the face of charges that it failed to anticipate the September 11, 2001, terrorist attacks or to work closely with other intelligence agencies in preventing it from happening. He has argued against creating a new domestic spy agency and asserts that the FBI can adapt and transform itself into such an agency. Because he assumed the post of FBI director only days before the attack, his stewardship of the bureau has not been called into question. Rather, his challenge now is to deal with allegations of poor past performance and weak leadership in the FBI.

# Richard Milhous Nixon (1913–1994)

Richard Nixon served as the thirty-seventh president of the United States. He held office from 1969 until 1974 when he resigned as a consequence of the Watergate scandal, which led to impeachment proceedings being brought against him by the Senate. Nixon is best known for his foreign policy initiatives during his presidency. Along with his national security advisor and later Secretary of State Henry Kissinger, Nixon redirected American foreign policy away from an attitude of Cold War confrontation with the Soviet Union to one of détente. As part of this strategy the United States and Soviet Union entered into a series of arms control talks. The United States also began the process of normalizing relations with China during this period. Détente was the centerpiece of Nixon's post-Vietnam strategy for the United States. For Nixon, the domestic politics of extracting the United States from the Vietnam War proved every bit as challenging as the foreign policy of doing so and placed him in constant conflict with an antiwar movement.

Nixon entered national politics in 1946 when he defeated incumbent Democrat Jerry Voorhis for the U.S. Senate seat from California. During the campaign Nixon implied that Voorhis was a communist sympathizer. (He used a similar tactic in his successful 1950 senatorial campaign.) In 1948 Nixon cosponsored a bill with Senator Karl Mundt that would have required communists and communist organizations to register with the government. That same year he joined the House Un-American Activities Committee and gained national attention for his work on the Whittaker Chambers case. It was largely because of this exposure that Nixon was selected by the Republicans to run as Dwight Eisenhower's vice presidential candidate in 1952. Nixon served two terms as vice president and stepped in for the president during his 1955 heart attack and 1957 stroke. Nixon was the Republican Party's nominee for president in 1960 but lost to John Kennedy. Nixon then left public life briefly, angry at the press for its treatment of him during the campaign, but he made a stunning political comeback to win the presidency in 1968.

## A. Mitchell Palmer (1872–1936)

A. Mitchell Palmer had a tumultuous political career that reached its most controversial point during his service as President Woodrow Wilson's attorney general from 1919 to 1921. Palmer worked his way quickly up the ranks of the Democratic Party in Pennsylvania. Loyal to the party, elected to Congress, and a gifted speaker, he served as Woodrow Wilson's floor manager—a highly important position since this person was in charge of managing the candidate's day-to-day campaign at the party's presidential nominating convention—in the 1912 Democratic presidential convention. Following Wilson's election as president, he offered Palmer the position of secretary of war, but Palmer declined, citing his Quaker background and beliefs. Remaining in Congress,

Palmer established himself as a champion of workers' rights. In 1914 he failed to obtain a seat in the Senate, because his candidacy was opposed by organized labor. In 1919 Wilson appointed Palmer to be attorney general. With Wilson largely incapacitated by a stroke and World War I not yet officially over, Palmer moved vigorously to end strikes by miners and railroad workers by invoking wartime powers.

Allied with J. Edgar Hoover, who would later be director of the Federal Bureau of Investigation, Palmer unleashed a campaign against political radicals, claiming to have uncovered a worldwide communist conspiracy. Palmer's legal justification for acting in this matter was the Immigration Act of 1917, which as amended allowed for the deportation of alien anarchists and those who supported organizations that advocated violence. More than 3,000 suspected anarchists and members of the Communist Party were arrested, often without warrants. These "Palmer Raids" are widely considered to be among the most notorious in American history because of the widespread violations of civil liberties they produced. Few of his arrests were later upheld.

Politics figured prominently in Palmer's thinking. Having helped create the "Red Scare," he had no choice but to take forceful action. This was especially the case because he was an active candidate for the 1920 Democratic presidential nomination. He failed to get the nomination, in part because party leaders feared that labor would not support his ticket in the general election. Palmer continued to be active in Democratic Party politics in his later life. At Franklin Roosevelt's invitation he played a central role in writing the party's 1932 platform, and he died while working on the 1936 platform.

# Oleg Vladimirovich Penkovsky (1919–1963)

Oleg Penkovsky is arguably the most important (known) spy the United States had in the Soviet Union during the Cold War. Information he provided on Soviet missiles in Cuba during the Cuban missile crisis is often cited as having been crucial to the formation of American strategy and the outcome of the conflict.

Born in 1919, Penkovsky never knew his father, a civil servant in the tsarist government who had died fighting Bolshevik forces in the Russian civil war. Penkovsky's father's tsarist past, though, played a significant role in Penkovsky's career and apparently contributed to his decision to spy for the United States.

As a youth Penkovsky joined the Komsomol, or communist youth league, and in 1937 he enlisted in the army. Connections made during World War II helped secure him a postwar berth in the Frunze Military Academy. In 1949 he accepted a post with the GRU, the soviet military intelligence organization. While serving there Penkovsky attended the Military Diplomatic Academy, where he studied intelligence.

His career then took a number of abrupt turns. In 1955 he was sent to Turkey as an assistant military attaché but was disciplined and sent back to Moscow after a dispute with his superior. After a two-year sojourn studying missile technology at the Dzershinksy Military Artillery Engineering Academy, Penkovsky was sent back to intelligence work with an assignment to India as a military attaché. However, before he could take the position his father's political background was discovered, and Penkovsky's assignment was changed to a desk job in Moscow. Shortly thereafter, however, Penkovsky was able to secure a more prestigious position as a senior officer in the GRU's Third Division, which was responsible for collecting scientific and technical intelligence from the West. It was now that Penkovsky approached Great Britain and the United States about spying.

After several failed attempts, he made contact with these intelligence agencies and established his credibility. It was arranged that he would work through Greville Wynne, a British citizen with business interests in the fields of science and technology. Penkovsky accompanied a Soviet trade mission to London in April 1961 and began providing key information to the West. He continued to do so either in Moscow or on trips to the West for the next eighteen months. One estimate suggests that he passed along more than 5,000 photographs during this period. Penkovsky was arrested on October 22, 1962, while the Cuban missile crisis was under way. Wynne was arrested shortly thereafter in Hungary. Both were tried by the Soviets on charges of espionage and were convicted. Wynne was later exchanged for a captured Soviet spy, Gordon Lonsdale, who operated in Great Britain. Penkovsky's death was announced by the Soviet press on May 16, 1963. He was shot.

Controversy surrounds Penkovsky's espionage career on two counts. The first concerns whether or not the Soviets knew he was spying but allowed him to continue to feed information and/or disinformation to the West. Some accounts suggest that Soviet intelligence knew of his espionage for several months. The possibility has been raised that Penkovsky was a triple agent. A triple agent is one who is employed as a spy for one country, agrees to become a double agent by secretly spying on his country for the country he was supposed to spy on, while in fact continuing to spy on that country for the first country, which knows that he has been employed as a double agent by them. The second controversy about Penkovsky concerns why he was arrested during the Cuban missile crisis and executed so quickly. Some suggest that it was an effort by Soviet authorities at crisis management, signaling to the United States that the information he had given them was accurate.

## Harold "Kim" Philby (1912–1988)

Harold Adrian Russell "Kim" Philby was among the most significant of the Soviet Union's Cold War espionage placements in Great Britain. Prior to his exposure as a possible Soviet spy, Philby had been considered a leading candidate to one day head British counterintelligence. In addition to passing vital intelligence information to Soviet authorities, Philby compromised a series of covert action operations in Eastern Europe. His success is attributed at least in part to the refusal of British intelligence officials to believe that anyone with the proper social background and education was not trustworthy.

Philby was born in British-ruled India in 1912. In 1929 he entered Trinity College at Cambridge University, where he became a socialist and then a communist. It was at Cambridge that Philby met Donald Maclean and Anthony Blount, who would also become Soviet spies. After graduation Philby went to Vienna, Austria, where he helped smuggle leftists out of the country while right-wing oppression was becoming commonplace. While there he met and married Alice Litzi, an ardent communist, in 1934. (He would divorce her in 1946 and would eventually marry three more times.) Philby and his wife then returned to London, where Philby was approached by Soviet intelligence about becoming a spy. He agreed and, along with fellow Cambridge graduate Guy Burgess, began to build a cover for himself by becoming active in right-wing causes. In the 1930s Philby covered the Spanish civil war for a London newspaper. It is suggested that in reality he was spying on General Franco for the Soviet Union. When World War II began Philby joined British forces in France as a war correspondent. There he put British intelligence in contact with a Soviet espionage network that was spying on Nazi Germany. This was done with the approval of Philby's Soviet handler; it was in Russia's interest that Great Britain be as effective as possible in fighting the Germans.

In 1940 with the help of Burgess, Philby joined MI-6, Britain's Secret Intelligence Service, which was responsible for counterintelligence operations. In that position he came into contact with William Donovan, Allen Dulles, and James Angleton, all of whom were founding figures in the American espionage and counterespionage effort. Such was his position that he produced a report for British intelligence on Boris Krotov, the Russian spy master who had run Philby and other Cambridge spies in the 1930s.

Philby was nearly exposed as a Soviet spy in the late 1940s when a would-be Russian defector, Konstantin Volkov, the Soviet counsel-general in Turkey, had offered to identify high-ranking soviet agents working in Turkey, where Philby was now posted. But Philby was able to take charge of the case and alert Soviet officials, who captured Volkov before he could provide this information to the British. With his true identity secure, Philby went on to Washington, D.C., in 1949 where he served as British liaison with the Central Intelligence Agency and Federal Bureau of Investigation. It was here that he betrayed Western covert operations designed to unseat communist governments in Albania, Poland, Latvia, and the Ukraine. As fate would have it, Philby was soon joined in Washington by Guy Burgess.

In May 1951 Philby was alerted by Blount (who worked in MI-5) that Maclean was under suspicion of being a spy. With some simplification, two major British intelligence services can be identified. The Secret Intelligence Service (MI-6) is a civilian intelligence service charged with gathering information. The Security Service (MI-5) is charged with protecting British secrets from spies and preventing sabotage. Maclean at that time worked in the American department of the British Foreign Office in London. Philby in turn alerted Maclean, who fled to Russia. Unfortunately, Burgess fled as well, and this raised suspicions about Philby, given their close association in the past. Although J. Edgar Hoover was convinced that Philby was the "third man" involved in the now-uncovered spy ring, there was not enough evidence to convict him. Philby resigned "in disgust" from MI-6 only to be rehired and sent to Lebanon in 1956. His career began to unravel there. He became depressed and an alcoholic. New information provided by a Soviet defector, Anatoliy Golitsyn, surfaced and again pointed to Philby as a spy. He was confronted with this evidence in January 1963 and quietly escaped to the Soviet Union, where he received the rank of major general in the KGB and where he spent the remainder of his life. In 1968 he wrote an autobiography, *My Silent War.*

## Allan Pinkerton (1819–1884)

Allan Pinkerton founded one of the United States's most famous detective agencies and served as director of intelligence for the Union during the Civil War. His success in that role was limited, however; the intelligence he provided was often inaccurate, and his key agent was captured and executed by Confederate forces.

Pinkerton was born in Glasgow, Scotland. Due to police persecution for his involvement in a workers' protest movement, he fled Scotland in 1842, going first to Canada and then to the United States. Ultimately settling in Chicago in 1850, he became that city's first detective, setting up the North West Police Agency, which later became Pinkerton's National Detective Agency. Pinkerton had entered the detective business accidentally when in 1847 Pinkerton had helped break up a rural counterfeiting ring and in the process earned a reputation as a detective.

Railroads provided the main source of employment for Pinkerton's firm. Railroad companies had dramatically increased the miles of track laid in the 1850s to the point that they could no longer police or secure the property themselves. Pinkerton focused his efforts on dishonest employees and set up an espionage system to uncover corrupt behavior. Not only was he successful; his successes were also highly publicized and contributed to rising labor tensions within the railroad industry. In early 1861 while he was investigating the possibility of Confederate sabotage against the Philadelphia, Wilmington, and Baltimore Railroad, Pinkerton claimed to have uncovered a plot to assassinate president-elect Abraham Lincoln. He met with Lincoln's advisors and organized a plan to get Lincoln safely to Washington for his inauguration.

Pinkerton met with newly elected President Lincoln about the establishment of a federal secret service, but nothing came of the discussions. In May 1861 Pinkerton was asked by General George McClellan to set up a spy ring that could be used to gain information from the Confederacy. Pinkerton's successes were well publicized but not extensive. In the area of counterespionage he did succeed in capturing Confederate spy Rose O'Neal

Greenhow, but his own espionage efforts provided little intelligence of value and were restricted in scope. When McClellan was relieved of command in 1862, Pinkerton returned to his detective business. Railroad companies continued to provide an important segment of his business. He now expanded the scope of his efforts from policing employee honesty to pursuing railroad robbers and bank robbers such as the Dalton gang and the James brothers.

## Jonathan Jay Pollard (1943– )

Jonathan Jay Pollard joined U.S. Navy intelligence in 1979. He claims to have made the decision to spy for Israel in 1982 because he was angry that the United States did not give Israel all of the intelligence it possessed. In 1984 Pollard met with Israeli intelligence officials and expressed his interest in becoming a spy. To prove his worth as a spy Pollard brought forty-eight documents with him to the meeting, but they were not accepted by the Israelis. The first exchange of intelligence came at a July 19, 1984, meeting. In the following months Pollard would remove secret information three times per week. Each time Pollard brought the secret material to a safe house, where it was photocopied. Pollard would then return the originals.

Pollard's career as a spy ran into difficulty in August 1985. He had made the decision to quit his job with naval intelligence by the end of the year, and he hoped to move on to other espionage activities for Israel. He became careless in his tradecraft and drew attention to himself. Pollard was apprehended on November 18, 1985, sitting in his car as he was leaving work. He had been led to believe (incorrectly) that an evacuation plan existed for him and his wife and was in place for such a contingency, so after two days of questioning, the Pollards drove onto the grounds of the Israeli embassy and sought asylum. They were turned down and forced to leave. Pollard was sentenced to life imprisonment, and his wife, Anne, received a five-year prison sentence. His arrest and the handling of the matter by Israel elevated the case into a recurring source of tension in U.S.-Israeli relations.

## Francis Gary Powers (1929–1977)

Francis Gary Powers was a U-2 reconnaissance aircraft pilot whose spy plane was shot down over Russia in 1960. The United States first denied that it was involved in spying, but when Russian authorities produced Powers, they were forced to recant their story. Powers's failed mission led to the discontinuation of a Paris summit conference between President Dwight Eisenhower and Soviet leader Nikita Khrushchev that was under way at the time.

Powers was born in Kentucky and enlisted in the air force upon graduation from Milligan College. Commissioned in 1952, he was assigned to the Strategic Air Command. In January 1956 Powers and other pilots were recruited by the Central Intelligence Agency (CIA) to fly the new U-2 high-altitude reconnaissance aircraft on spy missions over the Soviet Union and other key sites. For example, in 1956 Powers flew missions over the Mediterranean Sea to provide information on the Suez crisis. Powers's unit was based at Incerlik Air Force Base at Adana, Turkey, and operated under the cover of the Weather Observational Squadron of the National Advisory Committee for Aeronautics. This was the predecessor body to the National Aeronautics and Space Administration (NASA).

Powers flew his first mission over the Soviet Union in November 1956. He would fly his last on May 1, 1960. On that date he was flying a mission that was to take him from Peshawar, Pakistan, to Bodo, Norway. As his plane approached Sverdlovsk, Soviet Union, it was hit by a surface-to-air missile. The Soviets had known about the U-2 overflights from the beginning and had protested about them to the United States. Initially they lacked the capacity to shoot down these planes due to the high altitude at which they flew, some 80,000 feet, but that capacity improved. The CIA had provided Powers with suicide poison, but he chose to eject from the aircraft. On the ground he was captured with documents identifying him as a CIA agent. Under interrogation he admitted to being a spy. Khrushchev made his confession public along with some of the aerial photographs he had been taking, thereby nullifying the American cover story that a weather plane was missing along the Soviet border.

Powers was put on trial by Soviet authorities in August 1960. He pled guilty to spying and was sentenced to ten years in prison. Two years into his sentence he was exchanged for Soviet spy Rudolf Abel on February 10, 1962, at one of the checkpoints along the Berlin Wall. Powers died on August 1, 1977, when the helicopter he was piloting as part of his job as a traffic reporter for a radio station in Los Angeles crashed. With the permission of President Jimmy Carter, Powers was buried in Arlington National Cemetery.

## Thomas Joseph Ridge (1945– )

Nine days after the September 11, 2001, terrorist attacks on the World Trade Center and Pentagon, Tom Ridge was selected by President George W. Bush to be director of the cabinet-level Office of Homeland Security. At the time, Ridge was serving his second term as governor of Pennsylvania. Having won a hotly contested election in 1994, Ridge had established himself as a popular governor and had easily won reelection. He is characterized by many as moderate and pragmatic and as having bridged the gap between social and economic conservatives. Ridge had served six terms in Congress before winning the governorship. Ridge was mentioned as a possible vice presidential running mate for both Robert Dole in 1996 and George W. Bush in 2000. In each case his pro-choice abortion views reportedly kept him off the ticket.

As president-elect, Bush considered Ridge for the position of secretary of defense. Colin Powell reportedly supported his nomination, but it was rejected by conservative Republicans who objected to his Reagan-era record of opposition to the Strategic Defense Initiative, the MX missile, and U.S. policy in Nicaragua. Nevertheless, he remained on good terms with Bush, who, in his announcement appointing Ridge to the head of the Office of Homeland Security, referred to him as a "trusted friend." In November 2002 Bush nominated Ridge for the position of secretary of the Department of Homeland Security. In some ways Ridge was seen as an unconventional choice due to the low profile he kept in the White House and his lack of experience and success in bureaucratic infighting, a skill seen as vital for trying to establish the new department's place in the national security bureaucracy.

## Julius Rosenberg (1918–1953) and Ethel Rosenberg (1915–1953)

Julius and Ethel Rosenberg, a husband and wife, were convicted of spying for the Soviet Union in 1951 and were executed in 1953. Both steadfastly proclaimed their innocence. Their case sparked domestic and international protests that they had been falsely convicted as part of an upswing in anti-Semitic and anticommunist hysteria that gripped the United States in the early 1950s. The case remains controversial, although evidence released from the National Security Agency's VENONA project in 1995 strongly points to their guilt.

Ethel and Julius Rosenberg were born and grew up in New York City in orthodox Jewish families in a Jewish neighborhood. In their youth both were politically active, Julius in left-wing student groups and Ethel in the labor movement. They were married in 1939, and in 1940 Julius began working as a junior engineer for the Army Signals Corps. He lost that job in 1945 due to allegations (which he denied) that he was a communist. Julius would eventually enter into a struggling machine shop business with his brother-in-law, David Greenglass. Ethel stayed at home with their two sons. During World War II Greenglass had served in the army and had worked as a machinist in the Los Alamos, New Mexico, laboratories that produced the atomic bomb. In June 1950 Greenglass was arrested for spying for the Soviet Union. He was accused of having given the Soviet Union vital information about the triggering mechanism for detonating the bomb.

Julius Rosenberg was arrested on July 17, 1950, and charged with being the central figure in a World War II atomic spy ring. Ethel was similarly charged with espionage on August 11 following her testimony to a federal grand jury. The case against Ethel was far weaker than that against Julius, and speculation exists that she was indicted in hopes of pressuring Julius to confess in order to obtain a lenient sentence for her. In fact, Julius and Ethel were identified as spies by Greenglass in an effort on his part to obtain a more lenient sentence for himself. The Rosenbergs' trial began on March 6, 1951, with the principal evidence against the Rosenbergs being presented by Greenglass, who detailed his own espionage activities in the process. He also indicated that he had been recruited into spying by the Rosenbergs. One of the lawyers assisting in the prosecution was Roy Cohen, who would go on to assist Senator Joseph McCarthy in his search for communist infiltrators of the U.S. government. The Rosenbergs' attorney was Emanuel Bloch, who put forward a weak and ineffective defense. He failed to cross-examine either Greenglass or Harry Gold, another witness who admitted being a courier for the spy ring.

The Rosenbergs were convicted of espionage on April 5, 1951, and sentenced to death by Judge Julius Kaufman. The Rosenbergs appealed their conviction and were supported by thousands in the United States and abroad. However, neither the Truman nor Eisenhower administrations granted them a stay of execution, although the Eisenhower administration did offer to commute the sentence if they confessed. They were executed in Sing Sing prison on June 19, 1953. They were the first American civilians executed for espionage. Their arrest, trial, and execution occurred against a backdrop of rising Cold War anxieties. The Rosenbergs were arrested less than one year after the Soviet Union exploded their first nuclear weapon, and their indictment came shortly after the Korean War began. The Rosenbergs' two sons, Robert and Michael Meeropol, worked to establish their parents' innocence after their parents' execution, and a National Committee to Re-Open the Rosenberg Case now exists. Their case remains one that scholars and commentators revisit and continue to disagree about.

## Sir William Samuel Stephenson (1896–1989)

A Canadian, Sir William Stephenson was instrumental in establishing the Office of Strategic Services (OSS), the forerunner of the Central Intelligence Agency. He did so while covertly working for British intelligence under the guise of the British Security Coordination Office in New York City. This office, which he headed, was charged with conducting a propaganda campaign and secret diplomacy in the United States to bring it into the war as well as engaging in a full range of intelligence operations against Nazi targets in the Western Hemisphere.

Stephenson had served with honor in World War I as a fighter pilot. In one encounter Stephenson's plane was shot down, and he was imprisoned in a prisoner-of-war camp, from which he escaped. After the war Stephenson became a millionaire from his patenting of a machine that made possible the radio transmission of photographs. From there he expanded into a number of other business ventures including steel mills. When World War II broke out, he used his knowledge of a range of targets for the British to pursue to help British intelligence and took part in a failed sabotage mission. British intelligence next asked him to serve as a liaison with American officials in order to ferret out German espionage and sabotage programs in the United States. When his efforts to work with Federal Bureau of Investigation director J. Edgar Hoover produced few positive results, Stephenson turned his attention to one of President Franklin Roosevelt's many confidants, William "Wild Bill" Donovan. He accompanied Donovan on a trip to London in 1940 during which Donovan was evaluating the strategic situation in Europe and the Mediterranean for Roosevelt. Bad weather delayed their flight for eight days, and Stephenson used the time to press his case for a centralized American civilian intelligence agency that would engage in covert action, espionage, and analysis. Donovan proved to be far more receptive to Stephenson's message than had Hoover, and he produced a report for Roosevelt urging the creation of such an organization. Donovan's proposal led to the creation first of the Office of the Coordinator of Information and then the OSS.

Stephenson worked closely with these bodies in order to provide them with the necessary skills to carry out their missions and to ensure that their activities were consistent with British objectives. At war's end Stephenson went back into private business. He was knighted in 1945 and also received the U.S. Medal of Merit.

## George J. Tenet (1953– )

George Tenet was director of the Central Intelligence Agency (CIA) at the time of the September 11, 2001, terrorist attacks. In this post he was both head of the Central Intelligence Agency and of the broader intelligence community. Tenet was appointed to the CIA position by President Bill Clinton and sworn in on July 11, 1997. He had previously served as deputy director of central intelligence and later as acting director of central intelligence. Prior to coming to the CIA Tenet had served as special assistant to the president and senior director for intelligence programs at the National Security Council under Clinton. Among the projects he supervised were ones on U.S. counterterrorism effectiveness and U.S. remote-sensing space capabilities. Tenet assumed the head CIA post after having served on Clinton's presidential transition committee and before that as staff director on the Senate Select Committee on Intelligence.

Tenet's background is typical of more recent appointments to the position of director of the CIA in that he is an intelligence outsider, unlike Allen Dulles, Richard Helms, or William Colby, who all had extensive careers in the CIA. Outsiders such as Tenet have come to be favored by presidents because they are uncertain of the political loyalty and foreign policy perspectives of those who have had extensive experience in the intelligence community. Presidents and foreign policy bureaucrats routinely approach foreign policy issues with differing perspectives. A president's time frame, or period of interest on a problem, is limited by electoral politics, as are his evaluation of policy options. Career foreign policy bureaucrats (for example, intelligence officials, diplomats, soldiers) tend to have a longer perspective and view issues not in terms of what is best for the president but what is best for their organization. In an effort to minimize the potential conflict here and stop "political end runs" by the foreign policy bureaucracies to friendly congresspeople and senators, presidents have opted to avoid placing careerists with strong ties to an organization in charge of them. In that regard, Tenet is seen as a team player, and it is noteworthy that the Bush administration assigned him an unprecedented task in sending him to the Middle East to mediate the Palestinian-Israeli dispute. It falls upon Tenet to improve the CIA and the intelligence community's performance and standing with the public and elected officials following the September 11 terrorist attacks.

## Ralph H. Van Deman (1865–1952)

Ralph Van Deman is considered by many to be the father of American military intelligence because it was under his direction that the War Department's Military Intelligence Branch became a viable organization and developed a counterespionage capability. Van Deman was born in Ohio and joined the U.S. Army as a surgeon in 1893. He soon undertook a career change within the army and in 1897 he was assigned to the Military Information Division (MID) of the Adjunct General's Office. At the time this unit was responsible for army intelligence. During the Spanish-American War he saw duty in both Cuba and the Philippines, and after the war ended he stayed on in the Philippines as part of the occupying army, working with the Bureau of Insurgent Records in the army's Philippines Department. From there he went to the Army War College in Washington, D.C., as a student, and then in 1906 he was sent on a secret intelligence mission to China to collect basic intelligence regarding China's transportation system and topography.

Van Deman made his biggest impact on military intelligence when, in the years prior to the United States's entry into World War I, he lobbied for the creation of a separate division of the General Staff that would be devoted to intelligence. Not only did Van Deman succeed in having such an office created, he was placed in charge of it. He held that position from May 1917 until June 1918 when he was transferred to France to serve in General John Pershing's intelligence unit. Van Deman attended the Paris

Peace Conference and was responsible for security and counterespionage at the conference. He retired in 1929 and went on to establish a private counterespionage and countersubversion operation that compiled information on suspected subversives and foreign agents. Van Deman made this information available to the Federal Bureau of Investigation and military intelligence units. During World War II he served as an advisor on intelligence matters to the War Department.

## Elizabeth Van Lew (1818–1900)

Elizabeth Van Lew was a Union spy in Richmond, Virginia, during the Civil War. She ran a highly successful spy ring, the Richmond Underground, which engaged in espionage and sabotage. She financed her spy ring out of her own funds, which she had because her father had moved to Richmond in his youth and over time established himself as a prosperous merchant.

Van Lew's parents were born in the North, but she as a native of Richmond. She was a fervent abolitionist who freed all of her father's slaves upon his death. Little is known about her activities as a spy; after the Civil War ended Van Lew obtained all of the War Department documents detailing her activities and destroyed them. It is believed that Van Lew began spying for the Union in 1863 or 1864. Reportedly among her agents was Mary Elizabeth Bowser, one of her own former slaves, who was now a servant in the home of Jefferson Davis, president of the Confederacy. Van Lew also obtained access to Confederate prisons, where she worked with Union soldiers and helped some escape. She was credited by General U. S. Grant's intelligence officer with providing key intelligence in support of his advance on Richmond in 1864. When Congress refused to reimburse Van Lew for the cost of running the Richmond Underground after the war ended, President Grant appointed her postmaster of Richmond, a post she held until Rutherford Hayes became president and removed her. After having held a civil service position in Washington, Van Lew lived the last years of her life in Richmond and died there.

## John Walker (1938– )

John Walker was the head of a spy ring that he created. He began spying for the Soviet Union in 1968, using his position with the

U.S. Navy to gather information. He was the classic "walk-in," appearing at the Soviet embassy in January of that year to volunteer. To prove his credentials, he brought with him the key lists for the past thirty days to the KL-47 cipher machine (a spy code). Walker wanted to be paid $1,000 per week to spy for the Soviets. In February Walker met with a KGB officer who paid him $5,000 without even looking at the material Walker was delivering. For the next two years, Walker provided the Soviet Union with information that for all practical purposes allowed them to read all messages to and from American submarines and supporting ships. In 1970 Walker was transferred to San Diego and from there to the USS *Niagara Falls*, a supply ship where he was placed in charge of guarding all cryptographic material.

In the late 1970s Walker began his own spy ring. He recruited fellow navy officer Jerry Whitworth, who by a quirk of fate would come to hold Walker's old job on the USS *Niagara Falls.* In September 1978 Whitworth delivered to the Soviets the complete diagrams for several cipher machines, along with keys for ships deployed in the Pacific. Walker next recruited his son, Michael, into his spy ring. Walker was arrested on May 20, 1985. The next day, Whitworth and Michael Walker were also arrested.

## Herbert Yardley (1889–1958)

Herbert Yardley is generally regarded as the father of American cryptology. Born in Indiana, Yardley moved to Washington, D.C., in 1912 where he obtained work as a telegrapher and code clerk in the State Department. Working on his own and with no formal training Yardley was able to break the codes used by the State Department. When the United States entered World War I, Yardley convinced Major Ralph Van Deman, head of military intelligence, to have him assigned to the War Department, where he was put in charge of MI-8, a newly created cryptological section of military intelligence. Under his supervision MI-8 succeeded in breaking most of the codes used in German diplomatic and army communications and established new codes for use by the American army. Yardley accompanied the American mission to the Paris Peace Conference in 1919 as chief cryptologist. With the war over, the initial response of the American government was to disband MI-8, which was retained and was simply renamed as the Cipher Bureau, and since Yardley successfully resisted the move, he was placed in charge of the renamed Cipher Bureau. It was jointly funded by the War Department and the State Department. As by law the State Department could not spend funds within the boundaries of Washington, D.C., the Cipher Bureau set up operations in New York City under cover as the Code Compilation Company, which produced commercial codes. Its New York location gave it easy access to Western Union and Postal Telegraph messages.

Once again Yardley's operation enjoyed great success. In December 1919 it broke the Japanese diplomatic code, which allowed the United States to have access to the negotiating instructions given to the Japanese delegation at the Washington Conference on the Limitations of Arms. This was one of the first modern disarmament conferences and was called to avoid a naval arms race in the Pacific Ocean. Yardley's bureau was closed in 1929 when Secretary of State Henry Stimson concluded it was not essential to American security. It was Stimson's position that "gentlemen do not read each other's mail." By that time the Cipher Bureau had read more than 45,000 secret telegrams from more than twenty countries. Yardley had referred to his operation as the American Black Chamber. He named it after the French Black Chamber, which he had visited in Europe in 1918.

Now unemployed, Yardley wrote his memoirs, *The American Black Chamber*. It was first serialized in the *Saturday Evening Post* and then published as a book. His story caused a sensation. Yet, even though confronted with stories of code breaking, the U.S. government denied the existence of the Cipher Bureau. Later in his life Yardley would go on to write several novels that involved cryptology. He was also hired in 1938 by Chiang Kai-shek's government in China and then by the Canadian government to make and break codes.

# 5

# Documents

Given the clandestine nature of espionage it is not surprising to find that many key documents are secret. For example, secrecy continues to engulf the annual budget of the intelligence community. Many of the organizations involved in espionage were not established through laws passed by Congress or through published executive orders. The National Reconnaissance Office, the Defense Intelligence Agency, and the National Security Agency, for example, were created by secret intelligence directives. Likewise, lines of action have been authorized by references to vague phrases or secret directives.

The general authority for covert action lies in the 1947 National Security Act, which authorizes the Central Intelligence Agency (CIA) to undertake "other duties as directed." Today specific covert action operations are authorized through presidential findings that are shared with congressional intelligence committees. Here again the authorization may be quite specific, or it may be stated in broad generalities. It is not unusual to have key information emerge as part of a congressional or presidential investigation into acts of alleged wrongdoing by the intelligence community or as deliberate leaks by people within the government who oppose a course of action.

The documents presented here were chosen because they provide an overview of the legal and institutional environment in which the spies and spy catchers have operated in the United States. The documents in this section are organized under three sections: Organizational Procedures and Authorities, Laws, and Evidence of Domestic Spying.

# Organizational Procedures and Authorities

This section presents the founding documents of five intelligence organizations.

## Presidential Order, July 11, 1941

*This document is the presidential order establishing the office of the Coordinator of Information (COI). One of the major weak points in the pre–World War II American intelligence system was the absence of any centralized unit within the U.S. government with responsibility for analyzing intelligence. The idea for such a position was advanced by William "Wild Bill" Donovan, who served as President Franklin Roosevelt's personal envoy to Europe. In his dealings with Great Britain, Donovan worked closely with Sir William Stephenson, an intelligence agent of the British government, who helped steer Donovan's thinking in this direction. The COI was to collect and analyze information for senior government officials and was intended to report directly to President Roosevelt. The COI was replaced by the Office of Strategic Services (OSS) once the United States became involved in World War II.*

Coordinator of Information
    By virtue of the authority vested in me as President of the United States and as Commander in Chief of the Army and Navy of the United States, it is ordered as follows:

1. There is hereby established the position of Coordinator of Information, with authority to collect and analyze all information and data, which may bear upon national security; to correlate such information and data available to the President and to such departments and officials of the Government as the President may determine; and to carry out, when requested by the President, such supplementary activities as may facilitate the securing of information important for national security not now available to the Government.

2. The several departments and agencies of the Government shall make available to the Coordinator of Information all and any such information and data relating to national security as the Coordinator, with the approval of the President, may from time to time request.

3.  The Coordinator of Information may appoint such committees, consisting of appropriate representatives of the various departments and agencies of the Government, as he may deem necessary to assist him in the performance of his functions.

4.  Nothing in the duties and responsibilities of the Coordinator of Information shall in any way interfere with or impair the duties and responsibilities of the regular military and naval advisers of the President as Commander in Chief of the Army and Navy.

5.  Within the limits of such funds as may be allocated to the Coordinator of Information by the President, the Coordinator may employ necessary personnel and make provision for the necessary supplies, facilities, and services.

6.  William J. Donovan is hereby designated as Coordinator of Information.

Franklin D. Roosevelt
The White House
July 11, 1941

# Military Order, June 13, 1942

*This Military Order established the Office of Strategic Services (OSS). The OSS replaced the Coordinator of Information that was established on July 11, 1941. The OSS is the forerunner of the Central Intelligence Agency (CIA). Unlike the COI, which reported to the president, the OSS reported to the Joint Chiefs of Staff. The OSS was the United States's first true independent intelligence agency. It had responsibility in a broad array of intelligence areas. Its Research and Analysis branch was charged with conducting economic, social, and political analysis of events abroad. Open sources such as foreign newspapers and periodicals provided much of the information it relied upon. A Secret Intelligence branch secretly collected information in enemy and neutral states. A Special Operations branch engaged in covert action abroad and worked with resistance groups in German-occupied territories. A Counterespionage branch was charged with protecting American secrets and institutions from foreign penetrations. The Morale Operations branch engaged in propaganda targeted on the populations of enemy states. Operational Groups conducted guerrilla warfare. Finally, a Maritime Unit carried out maritime sabotage operations.*

*William Donovan became the head of the OSS. President Harry Truman disbanded the OSS by executive order on October 1, 1945, and distributed its duties among other existing departments. For example, the Research and Analysis branch went to the State Department, and the Secret Intelligence and Special Operations branches went to the War Department.*

Office of Strategic Services

By virtue of the authority vested in me as President of the United States and as Commander in Chief of the Army and Navy of the United States, it is ordered as follows:

1. The office of Coordinator of Information established by Order of July 11, 1941, exclusive of the foreign information activities transferred to the Office of War Information by Executive Order of June 13, 1942, shall hereafter be known as the Office of Strategic Services, and is hereby transferred to the jurisdiction of the United States Joint Chiefs of Staff.
2. The Office of Strategic Services shall perform the following duties:
   (a) Collect and analyze such strategic information as may be required by the United States Joint Chiefs of Staff.
   (b) Plan and operate such special services as may be directed by the United States Joint Chiefs of Staff.
3. At the head of the Office of Strategic Services shall be a Director of Strategic Services who shall be appointed by the President and who shall perform his duties under the direction and supervision of the United States Joint Chiefs of Staff.
4. William J. Donovan is hereby appointed as Director of Strategic Services.
5. The Order of July 11, 1941, is hereby revoked.

Franklin D. Roosevelt
Commander in Chief

# The Central Intelligence Agency (National Security Act of 1947, July 26, 1947, Excerpts)

*The National Security Act of 1947 is widely regarded as the foundation document for establishing the contemporary national security bureaucracy. It combined the War and Navy Departments along with the air force into a single bureaucratic unit, the Department of Defense, and provided for the position of a civilian secretary of defense. Furthermore, it provided for unified military commands but prohibited the merger of the military services into a single force. The need for this reorganization had been recognized during World War II.*

*The National Security Act of 1947 also created the Central Intelligence Agency (CIA). During World War II the United States had established the Office of Strategic Services (OSS) as its first central intelligence unit. President Truman disbanded the OSS after the war and scattered its responsibilities and units among the State Department and War Department. Several studies were conducted after the war as to how to organize defense and intelligence functions. One of the most influential was the Eberstadt Report, which recommended the creation of a central intelligence unit that would synthesize departmental intelligence.*

*Truman acted on this advice and issued an executive order on January 22, 1946, creating the Central Intelligence Group (CIG). Along with analytic responsibilities the CIG was also permitted to engage in clandestine operations by this executive order. The new CIG was headed by a Director of Central Intelligence. The CIG was the immediate predecessor of the CIA. Interestingly, the creation of the CIA was not controversial. Virtually everyone recognized the need for a more centralized intelligence agency in the rapidly shifting geopolitical landscape of the immediate post–World War II international system. Most of the debate on the National Security Act of 1947 focused on the merits of defense reorganization and the degree to which the services should be brought under a single authority.*

National Security Act of 1947, July 26, 1947

An act to promote the national security by providing for a Secretary of Defense; for a National Military Establishment; for a Department of the Army, a Department of the Navy, and a Department of the Air Force; and for the coordination of the activities of the National Military Establishment with other departments and agencies of the Government concerned with the national security.

*Be it enacted by the Senate and House of Representatives of the United States of America in Congress assembled,*

SHORT TITLE

That [50 U.S.C. 401 note] this Act may be cited as the "National Security Act of 1947."

DECLARATION OF POLICY

Section 2. [50 U.S.C. 401] In enacting this legislation, it is the intent of Congress to provide a comprehensive program for the future security of the United States; to provide for the establishment of integrated policies and procedures for the departments, agencies, and functions of the Government relating to the national security; to provide a Department of Defense, including the three military

Departments of the Army, the Navy (including naval aviation and the United States Marine Corps), and the Air Force under the direction, authority, and control of the Secretary of Defense; to provide that each military department shall be separately organized under its own Secretary and shall function under the direction, authority, and control of the Secretary of Defense; to provide for their unified direction under civilian control of the Secretary of Defense but not to merge these departments or services; to provide for the establishment of unified or specified combatant commands, and a clear and direct line of command to such commands; to eliminate unnecessary duplication in the Department of Defense, and particularly in the field of research and engineering by vesting its overall direction and control in the Secretary of Defense; to provide more effective, efficient, and economical administration in the Department of Defense; to provide for the unified strategic direction of the combatant forces, for their operation under unified command, and for their integration into an efficient team of land, naval, and air forces but not to establish a single Chief of Staff over the armed forces nor an overall armed forces general staff.

CENTRAL INTELLIGENCE AGENCY
Section 102. [50 U.S.C. 403]

   (a)   There is hereby established under the National Security
         Council a Central Intelligence Agency with a Director of
         Central Intelligence who shall be the head thereof, and with a
         Deputy Director of Central Intelligence who shall act for, and
         exercise the powers of, the Director during his absence or
         disability. The Director and the Deputy Director shall be
         appointed by the President, by and with the advice and
         consent of the Senate, from among the commissioned officers
         of the armed services, whether in an active or retired status,
         or from among individuals in civilian life: *Provided, however,*
         That at no time shall the two positions of the Director and
         Deputy Director be occupied simultaneously by
         commissioned officers of the armed forces, whether in an
         active or retired status. . . .

   (d)   For the purpose of coordinating the intelligence activities of
         the several government departments and agencies in the
         interest of national security, it shall be the duty of the Agency,
         under the direction of the National Security Council—

         (1)   to advise the National Security Council in matters
               concerning such intelligence activities of the Government
               departments and agencies as relate to the national
               security;

         (2)   to make recommendations to the National Security
               Council for the coordination of such intelligence
               activities of the departments and agencies of the
               Government as relate to the national security;

(3)   to correlate and evaluate intelligence relating to the
national security, and provide for the appropriate
dissemination of such intelligence within the
Government using where appropriate existing agencies
and facilities: *Provided,* That the agency shall have no
police, subpoena, law-enforcement powers, or internal
security functions: *Provided further,* That the departments
and other agencies of the Government shall continue to
collect, evaluate, correlate and disseminate departmental
intelligence: *And provided further,* That the Director of
Central Intelligence shall be responsible for protecting
intelligence sources and methods from unauthorized
disclosure;

(4)   to perform, for the benefit of existing intelligence
agencies, such additional services of common concern as
the National Security Council determines can be more
efficiently accomplished centrally;

(5)   to perform such other functions and duties related to
intelligence affecting the national security as the National
Security Council may from time to time direct.

# Executive Order 13228 Establishing the Office of Homeland Security and the Homeland Security Council

*This executive order established the Office of Homeland Security as a
unit within the Office of the President in the White House. It followed
in the wake of the September 11, 2001, terrorist attacks on the World
Trade Center and the Pentagon. The move was welcomed by most as a
necessary response to the threat of terrorism in the United States. Still,
points of controversy arose. By placing the Office of Homeland Security
in the White House, President George W. Bush was not required to have
its head, the assistant to the president for Homeland Security, confirmed
by the Senate, nor was the Senate empowered to force this person to ever
testify about the Office of Homeland Security's actions. Republican
Pennsylvania Governor Thomas Ridge was selected by President Bush
to be the head of this new office.*

*The second controversy, which was linked to the first, involved the
role that the Office of Homeland Security would play in detecting and
coordinating efforts to obtain information about terrorist threats.
Concerns were raised about the potential for violating civil rights and
liberties when the efforts of the Office of Homeland Security were combined with other initiatives put into place by President Bush and*

*Attorney General John Ashcroft that made it easier to obtain informa-*
*tion on individuals and to detain them without being charged or having*
*access to counsel.*

By the authority vested in me as President by the Constitution and the
laws of the United States of America, it is hereby ordered as follows:

Sec. 1. Establishment. I hereby establish within the Executive
Office of the President an Office of Homeland Security (the "Office") to
be headed by the Assistant to the President for Homeland Security.

Sec. 2. Mission. The mission of the Office shall be to develop and
coordinate the implementation of a comprehensive national strategy to
secure the United States from terrorist threats or attacks. The Office
shall perform the functions necessary to carry out this mission,
including the functions specified in section 3 of this order.

Sec. 3. Functions. The functions of the Office shall be to coordinate
the executive branch's efforts to detect, prepare for, prevent, protect
against, respond to, and recover from terrorist attacks within the
United States.

(a) **National Strategy.** The Office shall work with executive
departments and agencies, State and local governments, and
private entities to ensure the adequacy of the national
strategy for detecting, preparing for, preventing, protecting
against, responding to, and recovering from terrorist threats
or attacks within the United States and shall periodically
review and coordinate revisions to that strategy as necessary.

(b) **Detection.** The Office shall identify priorities and coordinate
efforts for collection and analysis of information within the
United States regarding threats of terrorism against the
United States and activities of terrorists or terrorist groups
within the United States. The Office also shall identify, in
coordination with the Assistant to the President for National
Security Affairs, priorities for collection of intelligence
outside the United States regarding threats of terrorism
within the United States.

(i) In performing these functions, the Office shall work with
Federal, State, and local agencies, as appropriate, to:

(A) facilitate collection from State and local governments
and private entities of information pertaining to
terrorist threats or activities within the United States;

(B) coordinate and prioritize the requirements for
foreign intelligence relating to terrorism within the
United States of executive departments and

agencies responsible for homeland security and provide these requirements and priorities to the Director of Central Intelligence and other agencies responsible for collection of foreign intelligence;

(C) coordinate efforts to ensure that all executive departments and agencies that have intelligence collection responsibilities have sufficient technological capabilities and resources to collect intelligence and data relating to terrorist activities or possible terrorist acts within the United States, working with the Assistant to the President for National Security Affairs, as appropriate;

(D) coordinate development of monitoring protocols and equipment for use in detecting the release of biological, chemical, and radiological hazards; and

(E) ensure that, to the extent permitted by law, all appropriate and necessary intelligence and law enforcement information relating to homeland security is disseminated to and exchanged among appropriate executive departments and agencies responsible for homeland security and, where appropriate for reasons of homeland security, promote exchange of such information with and among State and local governments and private entities. . . .

(d) **Prevention.** The Office shall coordinate efforts to prevent terrorist attacks within the United States. In performing this function, the Office shall work with Federal, State, and local agencies, and private entities, as appropriate, to:

(i) facilitate the exchange of information among such agencies relating to immigration and visa matters and shipments of cargo; and, working with the Assistant to the President for National Security Affairs, ensure coordination among such agencies to prevent the entry of terrorists and terrorist materials and supplies into the United States and facilitate removal of such terrorists from the United States, when appropriate;

(ii) coordinate efforts to investigate terrorist threats and attacks within the United States; and

(iii) coordinate efforts to improve the security of United States borders, territorial waters, and airspace in order to prevent acts of terrorism within the United States, working with the Assistant to the President for National Security Affairs, when appropriate.

## The Department of Homeland Security: Homeland Security Act of 2002, November 25, 2002 (Excerpts)

*The Homeland Security Act replaced the Office of Homeland Security, a unit in the Office of the President, with a new cabinet-level department, the Department of Homeland Security. The primary mission of the department is defined in terms of preventing terrorist attacks within the United States, reducing the vulnerability of the United States to terrorism, and minimizing the damage from terrorist attacks that do occur and speeding the recovery from those attacks. The Department of Homeland Security is also charged with the responsibility for investigating and prosecuting terrorism. It is here that the primary linkage to espionage exists.*

*As was repeatedly noted in this book's overview of American espionage, the outward-looking orientation of espionage and spy catching has turned inward and focused on Americans who held unpopular views or were recent immigrants. Support for the establishment of a Department of Homeland Security was widespread and reflected a sense that the established intelligence agencies charged with espionage, counterespionage, and analysis (the Central Intelligence Agency and the Federal Bureau of Investigation) had failed to meet the terrorist challenge. Still, the Homeland Security Act met with considerable opposition within the Senate, principally from Democrats. Their opposition was based less on the issue of counterespionage excesses than on concerns for the rights of federal employees who were being brought into the new department. The George W. Bush administration sought maximum flexibility in the hiring, firing, and management of personnel.*

*A second concern was related to the size of the Department of Homeland Security. Among the intelligence-related agencies brought under its umbrella were the Immigration and Naturalization Service, the U.S. Coast Guard, and the Federal Emergency Management Agency. In all, 170,000 employees from twenty-two agencies were united into the Department of Homeland Security. The Department is divided into four units: a Border and Transportation Security unit; an Emergency Preparedness and Response unit; a Chemical, Biological, Radiological, and Nuclear Countermeasures unit; and an Information Analysis and Infrastructure Protection unit. The Homeland Security Act passed with relative ease after the November 2002 election, in which the Republican Party won control of both houses in the upcoming Congress. Thomas Ridge, who headed the Office of Homeland Security, became the first secretary of the Department of Homeland Security.*

PUBLIC LAW 107-296 [H.R. 5005]
NOV. 25, 2002 HOMELAND SECURITY ACT OF 2002
107 P.L. 296; 116 Stat. 2135; 2002 Enacted H.R. 5005; 107 Enacted
H.R. 5005
An Act
To establish the Department of Homeland Security, and for other
purposes.
TITLE I—DEPARTMENT OF HOMELAND SECURITY
[*101] Sec. 101. EXECUTIVE DEPARTMENT; MISSION.
(a) Establishment.—There is established a Department of
Homeland Security, as an executive department of the United
States within the meaning of title 5, United States Code.
(b) Mission.—
(1) In general.—The primary mission of the Department is
to—
(A) prevent terrorist attacks within the United States;
(B) reduce the vulnerability of the United States to
terrorism;
(C) minimize the damage, and assist in the recovery,
from terrorist attacks that do occur within the
United States;
(D) carry out all functions of entities transferred to the
Department, including by acting as a focal point
regarding natural and manmade crises and
emergency planning;
(E) ensure that the functions of the agencies and
subdivisions within the Department that are not
related directly to securing the homeland are not
diminished or neglected except by a specific explicit
Act of Congress;
(F) ensure that the overall economic security of the
United States is not diminished by efforts, activities,
and programs aimed at securing the homeland; and
(G) monitor connections between illegal drug
trafficking and terrorism, coordinate efforts to sever
such connections, and otherwise contribute to
efforts to interdict illegal drug trafficking.
(2) Responsibility for investigating and prosecuting
terrorism.—Except as specifically provided by law with
respect to entities transferred to the Department under
this Act, primary responsibility for investigating and
prosecuting acts of terrorism shall be vested not in the
Department, but rather in Federal, State, and local law
enforcement agencies with jurisdiction over the acts in
question.

## Coordination of Counterintelligence Activities (Title 50, Section 402 of the U.S. Code, Excerpts)

*One of the most enduring criticisms of the operation of the U.S. intelligence community in the areas of espionage and counterespionage is the lack of coordination and cooperation among units. This has especially been the case with regard to the behavior of the Central Intelligence Agency (CIA) and the Federal Bureau of Investigation (FBI). Often this is presented as a matter of personality; the counterespionage efforts of both of these bureaucracies have been led by strong-willed individuals, most notably J. Edgar Hoover in the FBI and James Angleton in the CIA. Several other factors contribute to this problem as well. One is the natural tendency to trust one's own people. As can be seen in the case studies of espionage in this book, the tendency is to blame improper tradecraft and communication intercepts first before blaming one's own people for security breaches. A second impediment to cooperation is how these two agencies define their missions. The CIA sees counterespionage as a threat that is to be countered, neutralized, and—if possible— exploited. The FBI sees counterespionage as leading to prosecutions that may demand evidence the CIA is unwilling to make available. It should also be noted that the charge of noncooperation has been made in the areas of intelligence analysis and covert action, and that it is not simply a problem of counterespionage. This document lays out a bureaucratic attempt to legislate cooperation among members of the intelligence community. The document is important not so much for what it has accomplished but because it recognizes the problem and provides a basis for joint action. Because coordinating intelligence is a key issue in counterespionage efforts, presented here is a core document that details how this coordination is to occur.*

    (a)   Establishment of Counterintelligence Policy Board
        There is established within the executive branch of Government a National Counterintelligence Policy Board (in this section referred to as the "Board"). The Board shall report to the President through the National Security Council.
    (b)   Function of Board
        The Board shall serve as the principal mechanism for—
        (1)  developing policies and procedures for the approval of the President to govern the conduct of counterintelligence activities; and

(2)   resolving conflicts, as directed by the President, which may arise between elements of the Government which carry out such activities.

(c)   Coordination of counterintelligence matters with [the] Federal Bureau of Investigation

(1)   Except as provided in paragraph (5), the head of each department or agency within the executive branch shall ensure that—

(A)   the Federal Bureau of Investigation is advised immediately of any information, regardless of its origin, which indicates that classified information is being, or may have been, disclosed in an unauthorized manner to a foreign power or an agent of a foreign power;

(B)   following a report made pursuant to subparagraph (A), the Federal Bureau of Investigation is consulted with respect to all subsequent actions which may be undertaken by the department or agency concerned to determine the source of such loss or compromise; and

(C)   where, after appropriate consultation with the department or agency concerned, the Federal Bureau of Investigation undertakes investigative activities to determine the source of the loss or compromise, the Federal Bureau of Investigation is given complete and timely access to the employees and records of the department or agency concerned for purposes of such investigative activities.

(2)   Except as provided in paragraph (5), the Director of the Federal Bureau of Investigation shall ensure that espionage information obtained by the Federal Bureau of Investigation pertaining to the personnel, operations, or information of departments or agencies of the executive branch, is provided through appropriate channels in a timely manner to the department or agency concerned, and that such departments or agencies are consulted in a timely manner with respect to espionage investigations undertaken by the Federal Bureau of Investigation which involve the personnel, operations, or information of such department or agency.

(3)   (A) The Director of the Federal Bureau of Investigation shall submit to the head of the department or agency concerned a written assessment of the potential impact of the actions of the department or agency on a counterintelligence investigation.

(B) The head of the department or agency concerned shall—

    (i) use an assessment under subparagraph (A) as an aid in determining whether, and under what circumstances, the subject of an investigation under paragraph (1) should be left in place for investigative purposes; and

    (ii) notify in writing the Director of the Federal Bureau of Investigation of such determination.

(C) The Director of the Federal Bureau of Investigation and the head of the department or agency concerned shall continue to consult, as appropriate, to review the status of an investigation covered by this paragraph, and to reassess, as appropriate, a determination of the head of the department or agency concerned to leave a subject in place for investigative purposes.

(4) (A) The Federal Bureau of Investigation shall notify appropriate officials within the executive branch, including the head of the department or agency concerned, of the commencement of a full field espionage investigation with respect to an employee within the executive branch.

(B) A department or agency may not conduct a polygraph examination, interrogate, or otherwise take any action that is likely to alert an employee covered by a notice under subparagraph (A) of an investigation described in that subparagraph without prior coordination and consultation with the Federal Bureau of Investigation.

(5) Where essential to meet extraordinary circumstances affecting vital national security interests of the United States, the President may on a case-by-case basis waive the requirements of paragraph (1), (2), or (3), as they apply to the head of a particular department or agency, or the Director of the Federal Bureau of Investigation. Such waiver shall be in writing and shall fully state the justification for such waiver. Within thirty days, the President shall notify the Select Committee on Intelligence of the Senate and the Permanent Select Committee on Intelligence of the House of Representatives that such waiver has been issued, and at

that time or as soon as national security considerations permit, provide these committees with a complete explanation of the circumstances which necessitated such waiver.

# Laws

This section presents key documents that relate to espionage and counterespionage. The first is an executive order that established procedures for a loyalty program within the government. The second originally comes from the 1917 Espionage Act, which was the first law governing espionage in the United States. The third is a recent law governing economic espionage.

## Loyalty Programs: Executive Order 9835, 1947 (Excerpts)

*Spying against one's own country is an act of treason that has been punished by the ultimate penalty in both the United States and abroad. Julius and Ethel Rosenberg were convicted of stealing atomic secrets and passing them to the Soviet Union in the 1950s and were executed. So too was Oleg Penkovsky. He was captured by Soviet authorities for spying on behalf of the United States. Such is the nature of espionage, however, that spies are not always damned and viewed with dishonor. During the War for Independence, Nathan Hale was executed for spying on Great Britain in an effort to aid the cause of the American revolutionaries. His statue now adorns the entranceway to the headquarters of the Central Intelligence Agency and serves as a symbol of sacrifice and patriotism. Given the seriousness of espionage it is not surprising that establishing the loyalty of those who work in sensitive government positions is a constant concern. Lie detector tests and background checks are performed as a matter of routine for new employees. The often haphazard nature of security checks for those employed in the intelligence community has emerged as a key contributing factor to the success of individuals spying on the United States. At the same time, concerns exist that the search for spies can lead to uncontrolled witch-hunts in which the rights of individuals are trampled if those inquiries are not conducted according to clearly prescribed rules. The early 1950s McCarthyite investigations into the loyalty of members of the national security bureaucracies and the blackballing of entertainers for their political beliefs stand as vivid examples of this excess. This document from 1947 is an example of an effort to set standards and procedures for investigating loyalty among employees of the executive branch.*

Prescribing Procedures for the Administration of an Employees Loyalty Program in the Executive Branch of the Government

WHEREAS each employee of the Government of the United States is endowed with a measure of trusteeship over the democratic processes which are the heart and sinew of the United States; and

WHEREAS it is of vital importance that persons employed in the Federal service be of complete and unswerving loyalty to the United States; and

WHEREAS, although the loyalty of by far the overwhelming majority of all Government employees is beyond question, the presence within the Government service of any disloyal or subversive person constitutes a threat to our democratic processes; and

WHEREAS maximum protection must be afforded the United States against infiltration of disloyal persons into the ranks of its employees, and equal protection from unfounded accusations of disloyalty must be afforded the loyal employees of the Government:

NOW, THEREFORE, by virtue of the authority vested in me by the Constitution and statutes of the United States, including the Civil Service Act of 1883 (22 Stat. 403), as amended, and section 9A of the act approved August 2, 1939 (18 U.S.C. 61i), and as President and Chief Executive of the United States, it is hereby, in the interest of the internal management of the Government, ordered as follows:

PART I—INVESTIGATION OF APPLICANTS
1. There shall be a loyalty investigation of every person entering the civilian employment of any department or agency of the executive branch of the Federal Government.
   a. Investigations of persons entering the competitive service shall be conducted by the Civil Service Commission, except in such cases as are covered by a special agreement between the Commission and any given department or agency.

PART V—STANDARDS
1. The standard for the refusal of employment or the removal from employment in an executive department or agency on

grounds relating to loyalty shall be that, on all the evidence, reasonable grounds exist for belief that the person involved is disloyal to the Government of the United States.

2. Activities and associations of an applicant or employee which may be considered in connection with the determination of disloyalty may include one or more of the following:

   a. Sabotage, espionage, or attempts or preparations therefor[e], or knowingly associating with spies or saboteurs;

   b. Treason or sedition or advocacy thereof;

   c. Advocacy of revolution or force or violence to alter the constitutional form of government of the United States;

   d. Intentional, unauthorized disclosure to any person, under circumstances which may indicate disloyalty to the United States, of documents or information of a confidential or non-public character obtained by the person making the disclosure as a result of his employment by the Government of the United States;

   e. Performing or attempting to perform his duties, or otherwise acting, so as to serve the interests of another government in preference to the interests of the United States[;]

   f. Membership in, affiliation with or sympathetic association with any foreign or domestic organization, association, movement, group or combination of persons, designated by the Attorney General as totalitarian, fascist, communist, or subversive, or as having adopted a policy of advocating or approving the commission of acts of force or violence to deny other persons their rights under the Constitution of the United States, or as seeking to alter the form of government of the United States by unconstitutional means.

6. Executive Order No. 9300 of February 5, 1943, is hereby revoked.


Harry S. Truman
The White House,
March 21, 1947

## Laws Governing Espionage:
## Title 18 of the U.S. Code Sections 793, 794, 798, 783b (Excerpts)

*Espionage is a crime. This document is a compilation of key sections of the U.S. Code that define espionage and specify permissible punishments. The laws center on the gathering, transmitting, or losing of defense information; the gathering or delivering of defense information to aid foreign governments; the disclosure of classified information; and the communication of classified information. The first espionage law was written in 1917, and provisions have been added in subsequent years. For those not familiar with the legal writings, this document is important because it sheds light on the degree to which espionage laws seek to cover all potentialities both as to the material being stolen or the nature of activities involved. Note that in some cases the punishment is defined as being fined "not more than $10,000 or imprisoned not more than ten years or both" (18 U.S.C. 793 f) and in other cases "death or imprisonment for any term of years or life" (18 U.S.C. 794 a).*

18 U.S.C. Sec. 793
Gathering, transmitting or losing defense information

(a)  Whoever, for the purpose of obtaining information respecting the national defense with intent or reason to believe that the information is to be used to the injury of the United States, or to the advantage of any foreign nation, goes upon, enters, flies over, or otherwise obtains information concerning any vessel, aircraft, work of defense, navy yard, naval station, submarine base, fueling station, fort, battery, torpedo station, dockyard, canal, railroad, arsenal, camp, factory, mine, telegraph, telephone, wireless, or signal station, building, office, research laboratory or station or other place connected with the national defense owned or constructed, or in progress of construction by the United States or under the control of the United States, or of any of its officers, departments, or agencies, or within the exclusive jurisdiction of the United States, or any place in which any vessel, aircraft, arms, munitions, or other materials or instruments for use in time of war are being made, prepared, repaired, stored, or are the subject of research or development, under any contract or agreement with the United States, or any department or agency thereof, or with any person on behalf of the United States, or otherwise on behalf of the United States, or any prohibited place so designated by the President by proclamation in time of war or in case of national emergency in which anything for the use of the Army, Navy, or Air Force is being prepared or constructed or stored, information as to which prohibited place the President has determined would be prejudicial to the national defense; or

(b)    Whoever, for the purpose aforesaid, and with like intent or reason to believe, copies, takes, makes, or obtains, or attempts to copy, take, make, or obtain, any sketch, photograph, photographic negative, blueprint, plan, map, model, instrument, appliance, document, writing, or note of anything connected with the national defense; or

(c)    Whoever, for the purpose aforesaid, receives or obtains or agrees or attempts to receive or obtain from any person, or from any source whatever, any document, writing, code book, signal book, sketch, photograph, photographic negative, blueprint, plan, map, model, instrument, appliance, or note, of anything connected with the national defense, knowing or having reason to believe, at the time he receives or obtains, or agrees or attempts to receive or obtain it, that it has been or will be obtained, taken, made, or disposed of by any person contrary to the provisions of this chapter; or

(d)    Whoever, lawfully having possession of, access to, control over, or being entrusted with any document, writing, code book, signal book, sketch, photograph, photographic negative, blueprint, plan, map, model, instrument, appliance, or note relating to the national defense, or information relating to the national defense which information the possessor has reason to believe could be used to the injury of the United States or to the advantage of any foreign nation, willfully communicates, delivers, transmits or causes to be communicated, delivered, or transmitted or attempts to communicate, deliver, transmit or cause to be communicated, delivered or transmitted the same to any person not entitled to receive it, or willfully retains the same and fails to deliver it on demand to the officer or employee of the United States entitled to receive it; or

(e)    Whoever having unauthorized possession of, access to, or control over any document, writing, code book, signal book, sketch, photograph, photographic negative, blueprint, plan, map, model, instrument, appliance, or note relating to the national defense, or information relating to the national defense which information the possessor has reason to believe could be used to the injury of the United States or to the advantage of any foreign nation, willfully communicates, delivers, transmits or causes to be communicated, delivered, or transmitted, or attempts to communicate, deliver, transmit or cause to be communicated, delivered, or transmitted the same to any person not entitled to receive it, or willfully retains the same and fails to deliver it to the officer or employee of the United States entitled to receive it; or

(f) Whoever, being entrusted with or having lawful possession or control of any document, writing, code book, signal book, sketch, photograph, photographic negative, blueprint, plan, map, model, instrument, appliance, note, or information, relating to the national defense, (1) through gross negligence permits the same to be removed from its proper place of custody or delivered to anyone in violation of his trust, or to be lost, stolen, abstracted, or destroyed, or (2) having knowledge that the same has been illegally removed from its proper place of custody or delivered to anyone in violation of his trust, or lost, or stolen, abstracted, or destroyed, and fails to make prompt report of such loss, theft, abstraction, or destruction to his superior officer—Shall be fined not more than $10,000 or imprisoned not more than ten years, or both.

(g) If two or more persons conspire to violate any of the foregoing provisions of this section, and one or more of such persons do any act to effect the object of the conspiracy, each of the parties to such conspiracy shall be subject to the punishment provided for the offense which is the object of such conspiracy.

June 25, 1948, c. 645, 62 Stat. 736; Sept. 23, 1950, c. 1024, Title I, § 18, 64 Stat. 1003.
18 U.S.C. Sec. 794
Gathering or delivering defense information to aid foreign government

(a) Whoever, with intent or reason to believe that it is to be used to the injury of the United States, or to the advantage of a foreign nation, communicates, delivers, or transmits, or attempts to communicate, deliver, or transmit, to any foreign government, or to any faction or party or military or naval force within a foreign country, whether recognized or unrecognized by the United States, or to any representative, officer, agent, employee, subject, or citizen thereof, either directly or indirectly, any document, writing, code book, signal book, sketch, photograph, photographic negative, blueprint, plan, map, model, note, instrument, appliance, or information relating to the national defense, shall be punished by death or by imprisonment for any term of years or for life.

(b) Whoever, in time of war, with intent that the same shall be communicated to the enemy, collects, records, publishes, or communicates, or attempts to elicit any information with respect to the movement, numbers, description, condition, or disposition of any of the Armed Forces, ships, aircraft, or war materials of the United States, or with respect to the plans or conduct, or supposed plans or conduct of any naval or military operations, or with respect to any works or measures undertaken for or connected with, or intended for the fortification or defense of any place, or any other information relating to the public defense, which might be useful to the enemy, shall be punished by death or by imprisonment for any term of years or for life.

(c) If two or more persons conspire to violate this section, and one or more of such persons do any act to effect the object of the conspiracy, each of the parties to such conspiracy shall be subject to the punishment provided for the offense which is the object of such conspiracy.

June 25, 1948, c. 645, 62 Stat. 737; Sept. 3, 1954, c. 1261, Title II, § 201, 68 Stat. 1219.
18 U.S.C. 798
Disclosure of Classified information

(a) Whoever knowingly and willfully communicates, furnishes, transmits, or otherwise makes available to an unauthorized person, or publishes, or uses in any manner prejudicial to the safety or interest of the United States or for the benefit of any foreign government to the detriment of the United States any classified information—

   (1) concerning the nature, preparation, or use of any code, cipher, or cryptographic system of the United States or any foreign government; or

   (2) concerning the design, construction, use, maintenance, or repair of any device, apparatus, or appliance used or prepared or planned for use by the United States or any foreign government for cryptographic or communication intelligence purposes; or

   (3) concerning the communication intelligence activities of the United States or any foreign government; or

(4) obtained by the processes of communication intelligence from the communications of any foreign government, knowing the same to have been obtained by such processes—

Shall be fined not more than $10,000 or imprisoned not more than ten years, or both.

(b) As used in subsection (a) of this section—

The term "classified information" means information which, at the time of a violation of this section, is, for reasons of national security specifically designated by a United States Government Agency for limited or restricted dissemination or distribution;

The terms "code," "cipher," and "cryptographic system" include in their meanings, in addition to their usual meanings, any method of secret writing and any mechanical or electrical device or method used for the purpose of disguising or concealing the contents, significance, or meanings of communications;

The term "foreign government" includes in its meaning any person or persons acting or purporting to act for or on behalf of any faction, party, department, agency, bureau, or military force of or within a foreign country, or for or on behalf of any government or any person or persons purporting to act as a government within a foreign country, whether or not such government is recognized by the United States;

The term "communication intelligence" means all procedures and methods used in the interception of communications and the obtaining of information from such communications by other than the intended recipients;

The term "unauthorized person" means any person who, or agency which, is not authorized to receive information of the categories set forth in subsection (a) of this section, by the President, or by the head of a department or agency of the United States Government which is expressly designated by the President to engage in communication intelligence activities for the United States.

(c) Nothing in this section shall prohibit the furnishing, upon lawful demand, of information to any regularly constituted committee of the Senate or House of Representatives of the United States of America, or joint committee thereof.

Added Oct. 31, 1951, c. 655, § 24(a), 65 Stat. 719.
50 U.S.C 783(b)

Communication of classified Information by Government officer or employee

(b)   It shall be unlawful for any officer or employee of the United States or of any department or agency thereof, or of any corporation the stock of which is owned in whole or in major part by the United States or any department or agency thereof, to communicate in any manner or by any means, to any other person whom such officer or employee knows or has reason to believe to be an agent or representative of any foreign government or an officer or member of any Communist organization as defined in paragraph (5) of section 782 of this title, any information of a kind which shall have been classified by the President (or by the head of any such department, agency, or corporation with the approval of the President) as affecting the security of the United States, knowing or having reason to know that such information has been so classified, unless such officer or employee shall have been specifically authorized by the President, or by the head of the department, agency, or corporation by which this officer or employee is employed, to make such disclosure of such information.

## Laws Governing Economic Espionage: Economic Espionage Act of 1996 (Excerpts)

*Economic espionage is not necessarily a problem that governments need to concern themselves with. Firms have long been engaged in spying on one another in order to obtain an advantage or to negate an existing one. Yet there are cases in which economic espionage is a national security concern. The conceptual starting point for this view is the idea of a strategic trade policy. According to such a policy, "potato chips are not computer chips." That is, what matters is not just how much you produce and trade but what you produce and trade. Competitiveness in a globalized economy depends upon obtaining and holding a technological edge. Moreover, many of the key technologies that produce an economic advantage in the private sector are dual use technologies; they also hold significant military applications. Under these circumstances governments as well as firms have an incentive to engage in economic espionage. This document presents a definition of economic espionage as it relates to trade secrets and sets forward punishments for engaging in economic espionage.*

PUBLIC LAW 104-294 [H.R. 3723]
OCTOBER 11, 1996
ECONOMIC ESPIONAGE ACT OF 1996
1831 Sec. 1831. Economic espionage

(a) In General.—Whoever, intending or knowing that the offense will benefit any foreign government, foreign instrumentality, or foreign agent, knowingly—

   (1) steals, or without authorization appropriates, takes, carries away, or conceals, or by fraud, artifice, or deception obtains a trade secret;

   (2) without authorization copies, duplicates, sketches, draws, photographs, downloads, uploads, alters, destroys, photocopies, replicates, transmits, delivers, sends, mails, communicates, or conveys a trade secret;

   (3) receives, buys, or possesses a trade secret, knowing the same to have been stolen or appropriated, obtained, or converted without authorization;

   (4) attempts to commit any offense described in any of paragraphs (1) through (3); or

   (5) conspires with one or more other persons to commit any offense described in any of paragraphs (1) through (3), and one or more of such persons do any act to effect the object of the conspiracy, shall, except as provided in subsection (b), be fined not more than $500,000 or imprisoned not more than 15 years, or both.

(b) Organizations.—Any organization that commits any offense described in subsection (a) shall be fined not more than $10,000,000.

1832 Sec. 1832. Theft of trade secrets

(a) Whoever, with intent to convert a trade secret, that is related to or included in a product that is produced for or placed in interstate or foreign commerce, to the economic benefit of anyone other than the owner thereof, and intending or knowing that the offense will, injure any owner of that trade secret, knowingly—

   (1) steals, or without authorization appropriates, takes, carries away, or conceals, or by fraud, artifice, or deception obtains such information;

   (2) without authorization copies, duplicates, sketches, draws, photographs, downloads, uploads, alters, destroys, photocopies, replicates, transmits, delivers, sends, mails, communicates, or conveys such information;

(3)   receives, buys, or possesses such information, knowing the same to have been stolen or appropriated, obtained, or converted without authorization;

(4)   attempts to commit any offense described in paragraphs (1) through (3); or

(5)   conspires with one or more other persons to commit any offense described in paragraphs (1) through (3), and one or more of such persons do any act to effect the object of the conspiracy, shall, except as provided in subsection (b), be fined under this title or imprisoned not more than 10 years, or both.

(b)   Any organization that commits any offense described in subsection (a) shall be fined not more than $5,000,000.

# Evidence of Domestic Spying

As has been noted throughout this book, the effort to catch spies in the United States has often resulted in excesses and illegalities. The two sets of documents in this section are found in the Church Committee Hearings [Select Committee to Study Governmental Operations with Respect to Intelligence Activities, October and November, 1975].

## Statement by Senator Frank Church, October 21, 1975

*The Church Committee, more formally known as the Senate Select Committee to Study Governmental Operations with Respect to Intelligence Activities, was established by a vote of 82–4 on January 27, 1975. It followed the publication of a story by Seymour Hirsh in the New York Times barely a month earlier, on December 22, 1974, revealing that the Nixon administration had engaged in a "massive, illegal domestic intelligence operation" against the anti–Vietnam War movement and other political dissident groups. Talk had already been under way in Congress over the need for an investigation into the operations of the intelligence community, but Hirsh's story dramatically escalated the pressure for action. Much of the material in his story had originally come from an in-house Central Intelligence Agency (CIA) inquiry directed by John McCone that came to be known as the "family jewels." One of the first casualties of the revelations was the resignation of long-time CIA counterintelligence chief James Angleton, who had led an illegal mail-opening operation.*

In early January 1975 President Gerald Ford sought to avert congressional investigations by establishing a special commission chaired
by Vice President Nelson Rockefeller, but the move failed because it did
not avert these investigations. The Church Committee, a congressional
investigation that Ford did not want, consisted of six Democrats and
five Republicans. Frank Church (D-Idaho) chaired the committee, and
John Tower (R-Texas) was its cochair. It operated largely by consensus,
but its deliberations were often complicated by Church's presidential
ambitions in the upcoming 1976 election. At the height of its operation
the committee had 150 staffers. It conducted more than 800 interviews.
Its work was broken into three broad stages. The first stage consisted of
a closed-door examination of CIA involvement in assassination plots.
The second stage consisted of twenty-one days of public hearings into
illegal activities of the intelligence community. The final stage involved
the writing and release of its report. In the course of its investigations
the Church Committee had very different relations with the CIA and
the FBI.

On two occasions the White House refused to allow members of the
executive branch to testify. One occasion involved the illegal activities of
the National Security Agency, and the other involved covert operations
in Chile that led to the downfall of the Allende government. The CIA,
through McCone, who now headed the agency, was largely cooperative,
although this stance was not popular in the White House. The FBI was
largely uncooperative. The committee held 126 full committee meetings,
40 subcommittee meetings, and 250 executive committee hearings. Its
full report runs 110,000 pages and consists of 14 public volumes of hearings and reports. Three chapters of the final report, dealing with
"Cover," "Espionage," and "Budgetary Oversight," were not released.
Its final report presented 183 recommendations concerning the future of
the intelligence community.

The two documents that follow are from the second stage of the
Church Committee's operation. In this second stage the committee heard
testimony regarding the unauthorized storage of toxic agents; the
Huston Plan, a plan proposed by Nixon's White House advisor Tom
Charles Huston that called for using the capabilities of the intelligence
community to spy on American citizens through such measures as electronic surveillance, mail openings, and infiltrating campus radical
groups; the Internal Revenue Service; mail openings; the National
Security Agency; the FBI; and covert action.

Beginning in 1953 and ending finally in 1973, the figures show that there was a total volume of letters coming through the *New York Post* Office that was subject to culling and opening and photographing by the CIA, in this particular program, a total of 28,322,796. Of that number, based as we have heard now on certain watch lists that were established, but in the main, on random selection accounting for two-thirds of the inspections, there was a total of 2,705,726 envelopes that were photographed plus 389,324 envelopes that were copied.

And the number of those letters that were illegally opened and whose contents were photographed came to 215,820, of which the photographed contents were distributed as follows: 57,846 were sent to the FBI; 31,436 were sent to the Soviet division of the CIA; and 57,894 were sent to other departments, largely counterintelligence departments of the CIA.

## Project MINARET: Domestic Spying on Antiwar Protestors

*Among the most controversial aspects of the Church Committee's investigation was its examination of the actions of the National Security Agency (NSA) and Fourth Amendment rights. It held two days of public hearings on this subject. The NSA was established by a secret administrative order in 1952; this was the first time its director had testified in public before members of the Senate. One topic examined was Project MINARET. It ran from 1967 to 1973. Under Project MINARET the NSA monitored the cables and telephone calls of more than 1,600 Americans. Its initial focus was the anti–Vietnam War movement and allied domestic protesters. Soon, however, the "watch list" expanded as the CIA, FBI, Defense Intelligence Agency, and Bureau of Narcotics and Dangerous Drugs provided additional names.*

*A second topic examined was Operation SHAMROCK. It ran from 1947 to 1975. Under Operation SHAMROCK the NSA secretly obtained copies of cables sent by Americans through RCA, Western Union, and ITT. In neither undertaking did the CIA obtain a judicial warrant. The public disclosure of these two programs sharply divided the committee. One faction, led by Senator John Tower, argued that public disclosure was unacceptable because it provided information to the enemy on the espionage capabilities and operation of the intelligence community. The other faction, led by Church, argued that the public release of this information was necessary in order to pass legislation to prevent its recurrence. The following document is part of the record of the Church Committee hearings on Project MINARET. Exhibits 1 and 2 are planning documents.*

The National Security Agency and Fourth Amendment Rights
Exhibit 1
[October 20, 1967]
FM Yarborough ACSI DA Washington
TO Carter Dir of NSA

1.  As you know, the Department of the Army is, and expects to
    be for sometime to come, involved in the civil disturbances
    taking place within the CONUS. With respect to this
    involvement, my counterintelligence staff is tasked with
    keeping the DA staff apprised of the counterintelligence
    matters pertaining to such disturbances, including
    involvement of individuals and organizations. Concerning
    the anti-Vietnam demonstration of 21–22 October 1967, the
    Department of the Army has been designated as the
    executive agency to support civilian authorities with regard
    to this activity.
2.  I am particularly interested in determining whether or not
    there is evidence of any foreign action to develop or control
    these anit-Vietnam [sic] and other domestic demonstrations.
    Realizing, of course, that this is the "big" question, I
    nevertheless feel that we should make every effort to obtain
    the answer. Since your agency is a major US intelligence
    collector, I would appreciate any information on a continuing
    basis covering the following:
    A.  Indications that foreign governments or individuals and
        organizations acting as agents of foreign governments
        are controlling or attempting to control or influence the
        activities of US "peace" groups and "black power"
        organizations.
    B.  Identities of foreign agencies eerting [sic] control or
        influence on US organizations.
    C.  Identities of individuals and orgainzations [sic] in US in
        contact with agents of foreign governments.
    D.  Instructions or advice being given to US groups by
        agents of foreign governments.

Exhibit 2
Date: 01 Jul 69
Charter for Sensitive SIGINT Operation MINARET (C)
1.  MINARET (C) is established for the purpose of providing more
    restrictive control and security of sensitive information
    derived from communications as processed which contain (a)
    information on foreign governments, organizations or

individuals who are attempting to influence, coordinate or control U.S. organizations or individuals who may foment civil disturbances or otherwise undermine the national security of the U.S. (b) information on U.S. organizations or individuals who are engaged in activities which may result in civil disturbances or otherwise subvert the national security of the U.S. An equally important aspect of MINARET will be to restrict the knowledge that such information is being collected and processed by the National Security Agency.

2.  MINARET specifically includes communications concerning individuals or organizations involved in civil disturbances, anti-war movements/demonstrations and military deserters involved in anti-war movements.

3.  MINARET information will not be serialized, but will be identified for reference purposes by an assigned date/time. Information will be classified TOP SECRET, stamped "Background Use Only" and addressed to named recipients. Further, although MINARET will be handled as SIGINT and distributed to SIGINT recipients, it will not be identified with the National Security Agency.

## Project SGPOINTER/HGLINGUAL: Mail Openings

*The CIA's mail-opening program ran from 1953 until 1973. During that time it handled 28,322,796 letters in the New York Post Office. The CIA is prohibited from operating in the United States. James Angleton was able to establish the mail-opening program by arguing that mail openings were necessary to support its foreign operations. The Federal Bureau of Investigation did not find out about the operation until 1958 when it sought to begin a similar operation and was told by the Post Office that the CIA was already conducting such an operation. Church condemned the operation as a clear example of how the CIA saw itself as living outside the law and beyond the law. Former Director of Central Intelligence Richard Helms testified that the operation had provided valuable intelligence on Mexican terrorists being trained in North Korea and Americans being trained as guerrillas in Algeria. Two former postmasters defended the programs and an official in the CIA's inspector general's office asserted that since the Russians intercepted and opened mail coming in and out of the Soviet Union, the CIA was justified in doing so. This document provides an overview of the mail-opening program.*

Mail Opening
EXHIBIT 1
Inspector General's Survey of the Office of Security
Annex II
Project SGPOINTER/HGLINGUAL

1.   This project is a sensitive mail intercept program started by
     the Office of Security in 1952 in response to a request from
     the SR Division. Under the original project, named SGPOINTER,
     representatives of the Office of Security obtained access to
     mail to and from the USSR and copied the names of the
     addressees and addressors. In 1955 the DD/P transferred the
     responsibilities in his area for this program from SR Division
     to the CI Staff, the program was gradually expanded, and its
     name was changed to HGLINGUAL. Since then the program has
     included not only copying information from the exteriors of
     envelopes, but also opening and copying selected items.
2.   The activity cannot be called a "project" in the usual sense,
     because it was never processed through the approval system
     and has no separate funds. The various components involved
     have been carrying out their responsibilities as a part of their
     normal staff functions. Specific DD/P approval was obtained
     for certain budgetary practices in 1956 and for the
     establishment of a TSD lab in 1960, but the normal
     programming procedures have not been followed for the
     project as a whole. However, the DCI, the DD/P, and the
     DD/S have been aware of the project since its inception and
     their approvals may thus be inferred.
3.   The mechanics of the project can be summarized as follows.
     Mail to and from the USSR and other countries is processed
     through the branch post office at LaGuardia Airport in New
     York City. The postal authorities agreed to a screening of mail
     by Agency representatives at this central point, and office
     space has been established there for three Agency officers and
     one representative of the postal service. As mail is received it
     is screened by the Agency team and the exteriors of the
     envelopes are photographed on the site. The volume being
     photographed at the time for the inspection was
     approximately 1,800 items per day. From this total the
     Agency team selects approximately 60 items a day which are
     set aside and covertly removed from the post office at the end
     of the day. These are carried to the Manhattan Field Office
     (MFO) and during the evening they are steamed open,
     reproduced and then resealed. The letters are replaced in the

mails the following morning. The films are forwarded to the Office of Security at headquarters and thence to the CI Staff, where dissemination is controlled.

6.  The principal guidance furnished to the interception team is the "watch list" of names compiled by the CI Staff. Names may be submitted by the SR Division, the FBI, the CI Staff, or the Office of Security. The list is revised quarterly to remove names no longer of interest, and it ranges between 300 or 400 names. The list itself is not taken to the LaGuardia Airport post office, and the three team members have to memorize it. Headquarters has compared the actual watch list intercepts with the photographs of all exteriors, and there has not yet been a case of a watch list item having been missed by interceptors. Of the total items opened, about one-third are on the watch list and the others are selected at random. Over the years, however, the interceptors have developed a sixth sense or intuition, and many of the names on the watch list were placed there as a result of interest created by the random openings. A limited amount of guidance is given in specific area or topical requirements, but this is not very satisfactory. The interception team has to rely largely on its own judgment in the selection of two-thirds of the openings, and it should have more first-hand knowledge of the objectives and plans of operational components which levy the requirements. Information is now filtered through several echelons and is more or less sterile (that is, it cannot be traced to any one individual making the request for an intercept and as such, no paper trail of responsibility for ordering a mail opening exists) by the time it is received in New York.

14. There is no coordinated procedure for processing information received through the program; each component has its own system. The Office of Security indexes selected portions of the information in its Security Records Division. The CI Staff indexes the opened mail as well as a large percentage of the photographed exteriors. The SR Division maintains its own file system, and the information sent to [the] SR Division by the CI Staff is frequently indexed by the Records Integration Division while it is in transit. The FBI is one of the largest customers and it is assumed that it also indexes the material it receives. The same material could thus be recorded in several indices, but there is no assurance that specific items would be caught in ordinary name traces.

The CI Staff uses its IBM index cards to make fan-folds which are distributed monthly, quarterly, and semi-annually on a need-to-know basis.

15. The general security of the project has always been maintained at a very high level. When intelligence information is disseminated the source is concealed and no action can be taken until a collateral source is found.

# 6

# Chronology

**1765**  Sons of Liberty formed, a.k.a Liberty Boys. Widely considered to be the ancestor of all American intelligence services. It was created as a reaction to the Stamp Act, which was a revenue bill passed by the British Parliament in 1765. It was the first direct tax imposed on the American colonies and was to raise funds for the defense of the colonies. It produced outcries of opposition from colonial authorities because of the lack of colonial representation in Parliament.

**1775**  Continental Congress created the Committee of Secret Correspondence. It was the first American government organization formally charged with collecting foreign intelligence.

**1790**  American secret foreign intelligence activities received official endorsement when Congress appropriated funds to pay people for advancing American interests abroad. This set up the President's Contingent Fund for Foreign Intercourse, known informally as the Secret Service Fund. The executive branch could send agents overseas for various tasks, including intelligence gathering and covert operations.

**1861**  Allen Pinkerton offered his services as a spy for General George McClellan.

| | |
|---|---|
| **1882** | U.S. Navy established the Office of Intelligence within its Bureau of Navigation. Later it became the Office of Naval Intelligence (ONI). It had two functions. One was to gather information about foreign navies; the other was to acquire new technology from abroad to build the new America navy. |
| **1885** | War Department created the Military Information Division as part of the army's Adjunct General's Office. |
| **1908** | Bureau of Investigation established by Attorney General Charles J. Bonaparte on orders from President Theodore Roosevelt. Its purpose was to combat German espionage and sabotage within the United States. It later became the Federal Bureau of Investigation. |
| **1909** | Secret Intelligence Service is established in Great Britain. |
| **1924** | J. Edgar Hoover named to head the Federal Bureau of Investigation. Hoover had gained prominence working with Attorney General A. Mitchell Palmer investigating anarchists and communists. |
| **1941** | Office of the Coordinator of Information (COI) established by presidential order. It was headed by William J. Donovan. |
| | Richard Sorge, a Russian spy in Tokyo who posed as a German, was captured by the Japanese. He was executed in 1944. |
| **1942** | Organization of Strategic Services (OSS) established, replacing the COI. Its White Propaganda unit was split off and established as a separate, independent agency, the Office of War Information. By a presidential order the remainder of the COI was placed under the command of the Joint Chiefs of Staff and renamed the OSS. |

Thirty-three members of a Nazi spy ring headed by Frederick Duquesne are sentenced to a total of more than 300 years in jail. The key witness against them was William Sebold, who was recruited by the spy ring and who worked as a double agent.

1943    Project VENONA began. It allowed the United States to intercept and decipher diplomatic exchanges between Moscow and various Soviet embassies. It was compromised by William Weisband, an army cipher clerk. VENONA ended in 1980.

1945    President Truman dissolved the OSS by presidential order.

1946    President Truman issued a presidential directive creating the Central Intelligence Group (CIG). The CIG had no personnel or budget of its own but drew on the resources of the Departments of State, Navy, and War. The CIG was placed under the overall guidance of a Director of Central Intelligence (DCI).

1947    Central Intelligence Agency (CIA) created by 1947 National Security Act.

1950    Klaus Fuchs was convicted of spying for the Soviet Union and providing them with information about the atomic bomb. He was sentenced to fourteen years' imprisonment.

1951    Russian spies Guy Burgess and Donald Maclean, who penetrated British intelligence, fled to the Soviet Union.

The Mossad was established in Israel.

1952    A presidential directive created the National Security Agency.

1953    Julius and Ethel Rosenberg, Soviet spies, were executed for stealing nuclear weapons information.

1954    KGB was established in the Soviet Union.

**1955**     Operation GOLD was begun. It was a Berlin tunnel used to tap phone lines used by Soviet intelligence. It was compromised by a British intelligence officer.

**1957**     Colonel Rudolf Abel was convicted of spying for the Soviet Union against the United States. The key witness against him was KGB Lieutenant Colonel Reino Hayhanen, who defected to the United States in 1957. In 1962 Abel was exchanged for U-2 pilot Francis Gary Powers.

**1960**     U-2 spy plane piloted by Francis Gary Powers was shot down over the Soviet Union. United States denied spying, then was forced to admit the truth when Powers was brought forward by Soviet authorities.

**1961**     Anatoliy Golitsyn, a KGB officer, defected to the United States. He would later provide information about a CIA penetration. He served as a confidant for James Angleton, who headed the CIA's counterintelligence operation and was obsessed with finding the Soviet mole.

**1963**     Oleg Penkovsky was executed for spying for the United States. He had begun passing documents to the United States in 1961. Over a sixteen-month period he provided more than 5,000 documents dealing with Soviet missiles. He was arrested in 1962.

Kim Philby fled to the Soviet Union. Along with Guy Burgess and Donald Maclean he formed part of a Soviet spy ring that infiltrated British intelligence. He began spying in 1933 and was uncovered in 1951. Philby was allowed to resign from SIS (the Secret Intelligence Service) in 1951 when Burgess and Maclean fled to the Soviet Union.

**1964**     American officials discover forty eavesdropping devices in the U.S. embassy in Moscow.

**1970s**    Operation IVY BELLS took place. It was a joint navy-NSA project that tapped undersea Soviet communication cables in the Sea of Okhotsk. It was compromised in 1980 by Ronald Pelton.

1978   A secret tunnel under the U.S. embassy in Moscow is discovered containing eavesdropping technology.

1979   Operation TAW, a CIA project that tapped a top secret communications center outside Moscow, was compromised by Edward Lee Howard.

1980s   Operation ABSORB was conducted, in which the CIA placed nuclear warhead detection equipment on a cargo container in a train crossing the Soviet Union. Aldrich Ames compromised this operation.

1980   CIA agent David Barnett pleaded guilty to spying for the Soviet Union while based in Indonesia between 1976 and 1979. He was the first CIA agent convicted of espionage. Barnett exposed thirty U.S. agents during his spy career.

Soviet Union finds eavesdropping equipment in a Washington apartment complex used by their officials.

1984   Navy intelligence analyst Samuel Loring Morison arrested and charged with passing classified reconnaissance satellite photographs of a Soviet naval shipyard to *Janes' Defence Weekly*. He was sentenced to two years in prison.

American officials find listening devices in typewriters used since 1962 in the U.S. embassy in Moscow.

1985   Retired navy chief John Walker, his brother, navy retiree Arthur Walker, and his son, navy seaman Michael, along with Jerry Whitworth, were arrested for spying for the Soviet Union. John Walker had been passing cryptographic information to the Soviet Union for more than seventeen years. He was given two concurrent life sentences. Arthur was given one life sentence. Michael was sentenced to twenty-five years in prison. Jerry Whitworth was sentenced to 365 years.

**1985**      Former CIA clerk Sharon Scrange, yet still employed
*(cont.)*     by the CIA, who was stationed in Ghana, gave infor-
              mation about CIA methods and the names of CIA
              agents to her Ghanaian lover. Some informants were
              killed. Scrange received a five-year prison sentence;
              her lover received twenty years. Both were immedi-
              ately exchanged for some Ghanaians who allegedly
              worked for the United States.

              Suspected spy and former CIA employee Edward Lee
              Howard eluded FBI surveillance in New Mexico and
              fled to Moscow. The CIA had suspected Howard of
              engaging in espionage and had allowed him to retire,
              but did not tell the FBI. Howard was charged with
              passing information to the Soviets that allowed them
              to arrest U.S. sources and to expel U.S. intelligence
              personnel from the embassy in Moscow.

              Jonathan Jay Pollard, a civilian navy intelligence ana-
              lyst, and his wife, Anne, were arrested for spying for
              Israel. Pollard received a life sentence; Anne received
              five years. Four Israeli coconspirators were not
              indicted.

              Former CIA employee Larry Wu-tai Chin was con-
              victed of having passed documents to China for thirty
              years.

              Former NSA employee Ronald Pelton was arrested for
              passing exceptionally sensitive information to the
              Soviet Union dealing with American communications
              intercepts. He received a life sentence in prison.

              Vitaly Yurchenko, security officer for all Soviet oper-
              ations in North America, defected to the United
              States. Yurchenko defected in August and provided
              the CIA with a wealth of information about Soviet
              penetrations. The case took a bizarre twist when in
              November Yurchenko defected back to the Soviet
              Union, claiming he had been drugged and kidnapped
              by the CIA.

Listening devices are discovered in the pillars, beams, and floors of the new U.S. embassy in Moscow.

1986    Marine Sergeant Clayton Lonetree surrenders to the CIA station chief in Vienna because of lost information. He was convicted of thirteen counts of espionage, committed while he had been stationed in Moscow. He received a twenty-five-year prison sentence.

1988    Douglas Tsou, an American, was arrested for spying for Taiwan.

1989    Foreign Service Officer Felix Bloch was suspended by the State Department after being captured on a video monitor passing information to a Soviet agent in Paris.

1991    The KGB presented the United States with blueprints showing where listening devices were placed in the U.S. embassy. The KGB gave the United States this information because the Cold War was over and this was part of an attempt at moving U.S.-Soviet relations into a new era that would be characterized by less conflict.

1994    CIA counterintelligence officer Aldrich Ames and his wife, Rosario, pleaded guilty to charges of spying for the Soviet Union. His was considered the most damaging spy case in U.S. history. Ames spied between 1985 and 1994. His information was linked to the deaths of at least nine agents.

1996    CIA official Harold Nicholson was arrested by the FBI and charged with spying for the Soviet Union. At the time of his arrest he was carrying rolls of exposed film containing secret and top secret information. In 1997 he pleaded guilty and was sentenced to twenty-three years in prison.

1997    FBI agent Earl Pitts was charged with espionage for the Soviet Union. The FBI was tipped off to Pitts by a double agent. Pitts pleaded guilty and was sentenced to twenty-seven years.

1998        David Boone, an army signals analyst for the National Security Agency, was arrested for spying for the Soviet Union between 1988 and 1991. He was sentenced to twenty-four years and four months in prison.

1999        Wen Ho Lee was accused of spying for China while working as a physicist at Los Alamos. The government's case was compromised by revelations that FBI agents had lied and accusations that Lee was targeted because he was Chinese. Lee pleaded guilty to one count of mishandling information, and the other fifty-eight counts were dropped.

2000        Retired Army Reserve Colonel George Trofimoff was accused of spying for the Soviet Union and Russia for more than twenty-five years. In 2001 he was sentenced to life in prison without parole.

            Mariano Faget, a senior immigration official based in Miami, was charged with spying for Cuba. In 2001 he received a five-year sentence.

2001        Philip (Robert) Hanssen was arrested for spying for the Soviet Union after he was videotaped leaving a package of classified documents to be picked up by his Russian handlers. He began spying in 1979 and turned over 6,000 pages of documents to the Soviets. In 2002 he was sentenced to life imprisonment.

            A navy surveillance plane collided with a Chinese military jet over international airspace. The plane and crew land in China. The Chinese pilot died and the American crew was returned to the United States.

            The USA PATRIOT Act is passed following the September 11, 2001, terrorist attacks on the World Trade Center and the Pentagon.

2002        Ana Belan Montes, a senior Cuban analyst for the Defense Intelligence Agency, pleaded guilty to spying for Cuba for more than sixteen years.

Brian Regan, a retied air force master sergeant, was charged with trying to spy for Iraq, Libya, and China. In 2003 he received a life sentence.

The United States expelled a United Nations–based Iraqi diplomat on charges that he was spying on the United States.

In response to the September 11, 2001, terrorist attacks on the World Trade Center and the Pentagon, a Department of Homeland Security was established.

2003        Katrina Leung is arrested as a Chinese spy. A longtime fund-raiser for the Republican Party in California, she acted as a double agent. The FBI paid her to provide false information to China when she was actually a Chinese agent. The FBI stated that every Chinese counterintelligence case since 1991 may have been compromised.

# 7

# Print and Nonprint Resources

## Books

Adams, James. *The New Spies: Exploring the Frontiers of Espionage.* London: Hutchinson, 1994. 380p.

Adams presents an overview of the challenges facing intelligence agencies in the post–Cold War era. It is not intended to serve as a text or a comprehensive handbook on espionage. Rather, Adams seeks to highlight key issues that he feels are central to the broader question of the future of intelligence agencies and espionage. Adams writes as a sympathetic observer and supporter of the intelligence community but is fearful that intelligence organizations will remain wedded to the status quo and fail to adapt to the changing global environment. Country-focused discussions cover the United States, Great Britain, and Russia. Thematic chapters examine economic espionage, terrorism, weapons of mass destruction, and drugs. Readers will find interesting the extended discussion of the espionage problem as it relates to the Irish Republican Army. Adams concludes with chapters on intelligence reforms.

Andrew, Christopher. *Her Majesty's Secret Service: The Making of the British Intelligence Community.* New York: Penguin, 1987. 619p.

The principal focus of this work is on pre–Cold War British intelligence. The emergence of the British military and naval intelligence services is recorded along with the creation of MI-5 and SIS, the two civilian intelligence services that roughly parallel the Federal Bureau of Investigation and the Central Intelligence Agency. For those especially interested in espionage it provides a wealth of information about the development of British counterespionage activities and the evolution of its code breaking capabilities. Relatively little attention is given to British intelligence's post–World War II struggle to cope with the Kim Philby affair.

Bamford, William. *Body of Secrets: Anatomy of the Ultra-Secret National Security Agency*. New York: Anchor, 2002. 763p.

Bamford begins his history of the signals intercepts with the closing days of World War II. He rapidly moves through the 1950s and to the early 1960s and the Cuban missile crisis. From there he begins to recount the National Security Agency's contributions to containing communism by building an electronic wall around the Soviet Union and its allies. Included are detailed accounts of two highly controversial attacks on the American intelligence platforms: the USS *Liberty* by Israel and the USS *Pueblo* by North Korea, as well as the role of signals intelligence in the Vietnam War. Bamford's history of the National Security Agency is especially valuable for its highly readable account of its electronic eavesdropping and computer information processing capabilities. This edition contains an afterword written following the attacks of September 11, 2001. In it Bamford concludes that the National Security Agency must undergo a metamorphosis, changing both its culture and technology to meet the new national security challenges facing the United States.

Barron, John. *Breaking the Ring: The Bizarre Case of the Walker Family Spy Ring*. Boston: Houghton Mifflin, 1987. 244p.

John Walker is described by many as the greatest spy ever recruited by the KGB. This book details the activities of the Walker spy ring, with particular attention being given to the espionage of John Walker and Jerry Whitworth. The account details both the information stolen and the tradecraft used to steal the information and pass it along to the Soviets. The efforts of the FBI to capture the Walker spy ring are also presented in great detail, revealing both the strengths and weaknesses of its counterespionage capabilities. Barron intermixes his historical narrative with commentary concerning the long-term impact of Walker's espionage on U.S. national security.

Barron, John. *KGB: The Secret Work of Soviet Secret Agents.* New York: Bantam, 1974. 623p.

From one perspective the KGB is no different from other intelligence organizations in that it engages in intelligence analysis, covert action, and espionage. Viewed from another perspective the KGB is unique in that it was a key force that the Communist Party relied upon to rule over the Soviet Union. This book provides insight into both sides of the KGB. It contains chapters on espionage and spying as well as an appendix that details how to recruit Americans abroad and a detailed listing of Soviet citizens stationed abroad engaging in clandestine operations. Taken as a whole, Barron's account provides an excellent base from which to understand Cold War Soviet espionage activities against the United States.

Bennett, Richard. *Espionage: An Encyclopedia of Spies and Secrets.* London: Virgin, 2002. 371p.

This book presents an alphabetical listing of spies, spy organizations, and terms. It is historical and comparative in focus. Bennett not only covers espionage but also other aspects of intelligence such as covert action and assassinations. Especially valuable is his coverage of the history and structure of foreign intelligence organizations. More than fifty countries are covered, ranging in size from Switzerland, the Vatican, and Albania to the superpowers. There is a section of photographs in the center of the book. The book also contains an index and brief summary bibliography.

Blitzer, Wolf. *Territory of Lies: The Exclusive Story of Jonathan Jay Pollard: The American Who Spied on His Country for Israel and How He Was Betrayed.* New York: Harper and Row, 1989. 336p.

The author, who works for the *Jerusalem Post* and CNN, bases much of his account on exclusive interviews with Pollard while Pollard was in prison. He presents a straightforward account of Pollard's life as a spy and of his detection and capture. Central to Blitzer's account is the gradual and deliberate corruption of Pollard by his Israeli handlers. One of the strengths of this book is the insight it provides into the workings and outlook of Israeli intelligence. In the concluding chapter the author seeks to answer several of the more troubling questions raised by the Pollard case.

Burrows, William. *Deep Black: Space Espionage and National Security.* New York: Random House, 1986. 401p.

Where many accounts of espionage focus on individual stories, Burrows centers his account of espionage in the Cold War competition between the United States and Soviet Union. Three areas are identified in which space espionage plays an important role in national security: providing details on the enemy's weapons systems, virtually eliminating the possibility of surprise attack, and supporting arms control. The author begins his history with the American Civil War and how artists were sent aloft in tethered balloons to construct pictures of the evolving battlefields. He then moves through World War I and World War II and the development of the SR-71 (Blackbird) and U-2 spy planes. As the title suggests, however, the bulk of his account is with the development and operation of spy satellites. Although most of the book deals with American space espionage, it also presents information on Soviet space espionage.

Calvocoressi, Peter. *Top Secret Ultra.* New York: Ballantine, 1980. 149p.

This slim volume presents an insider's account of how British intelligence was able to break German codes and ciphers during World War II. Enigma was the name the Germans gave to their cipher machine. This machine took every letter of a message and transformed it into another letter. The task facing the British was to determine what the logic or rules were by which this transposition occurred. ULTRA was the code name given to the intelligence the British obtained by breaking Enigma. World War II battles in which ULTRA proved invaluable are chronicled in the book. In the final chapter the author also briefly touches upon some of the cryptoanalytic successes of the Germans during the war.

Dulles, Allen. *The Craft of Intelligence.* New York: Harper and Row, 1963. 277p.

Written by one of the founding figures in American intelligence, this work remains a classic and is still cited in contemporary studies of intelligence. Dulles provides a historical overview of the development of intelligence in the United States and discusses the various dimensions of intelligence work, including espionage and counterintelligence. Dulles also addresses the questions of the role of intelligence in a free society and its place in the Cold War. Particularly valuable is the insight it provides on the day-to-day, on-the-street life of an agent.

Felix, Christopher. *A Short Course in the Secret War.* 4th ed. Lanham, MD: Madison, 2001. 351p.

A widely popular and readable account of intelligence operations written by a former practitioner. The book is divided into two parts. Part I presents an overview of the different aspects of intelligence: analysis, espionage, counterespionage, and covert action. Part II presents an account of the author's personal involvement in intelligence operations in Soviet-occupied Hungary in 1946 and 1947. Together the two parts provide an excellent introduction to espionage and associated intelligence activities. This edition has been updated to include an afterword with the author's reflections on Kim Philby and the fate of Raoul Wallenberg, the Swedish diplomat and businessman who saved some 100,000 Hungarian Jews from death at the hands of Nazi Germany.

Fiakla, John. *War by Other Means: Economic Espionage in America.* New York: Norton, 1997. 242p.

This book is about more than economic espionage, although several of the chapters do address this issue. There are excellent accounts of Russian, Chinese, and French economic espionage against the United States and a chapter on the post–Soviet Union KGB. Much of the book, however, is more accurately described as an account of the shadier side of international economic competition. There are chapters on international money laundering, Japanese and Chinese predatory trade policies designed to acquire American technology, and efforts to keep American firms out of foreign markets. Emerging from these chapters is a theme of unpreparedness and naïveté on the part of American government officials and business leaders. Fiakla concludes by presenting a set of recommendations for fighting back and winning this economic war.

Fishel, Edwin C. *The Secret War for the Union: The Untold Story of Military Intelligence in the Civil War.* Boston: Houghton Mifflin, 1996. 752p.

This is the first major work to examine the American Civil War from the perspective of intelligence. By doing so, Fishel is able to address a number of myths and popular folktales that have grown up around Civil War spies and spy catchers. He is able to restore some people's reputations and call into question the accomplishments of other individuals. Fishel examines all aspects of intelligence, from cavalry reconnaissance to classical spying to interrogating deserters and prisoners of war. He gives special attention to the bureaucratic nature of intelligence work and argues that in this area the North had an advantage over the South.

Gannon, James. *Stealing Secrets, Telling Lies: How Spies and Codebreakers Helped Shape the Twentieth Century.* Washington, DC: Brassey's, 2001. 324p.

Gannon presents eight stories that detail significant code breaking successes and eight classic cases of espionage. Substantively the focus is on World War I, World War II, and the Cold War. The author mixes accounts of famous spies and code breakers with lesser-known cases. For example, the actions of well-known spies Richard Sorge, Donald Maclean, and Klaus Fuchs are chronicled along with the less publicized efforts of Takeo Yoshikawa, a Japanese naval intelligence officer assigned to gather intelligence on Pearl Harbor, and Ryszard Kuklinski, a CIA mole in Poland during the 1970s. Gannon takes similar pains to highlight the contributions of code breakers who are virtually unknown to Americans, such as Maria Rejewski, a Polish mathematician who broke the Enigma system seven years before the more famous Alan Turing did so.

Godson, Roy, ed. *Intelligence Requirements for the 1980s: Counterintelligence.* Washington, DC: National Strategy Information Center, 1980. 339p.

This book is part of a multivolume series published in the 1980s on the state of American intelligence. Other volumes cover such topics as intelligence analysis, clandestine collection, covert action, and domestic intelligence. Each book consists of a series of highly readable papers presented by academics and intelligence professionals, along with the transcripts of discussions of those papers. Topics covered in this volume include terrorism, Soviet intelligence activities in the United States, national technical means of verification, how to build a counterintelligence capability, and legal issues involved in counterintelligence operations.

Havill, Adrian. *The Spy Who Stayed Out in the Cold: The Secret Life of FBI Double Agent Robert Hanssen.* New York: St. Martin's, 2001. 262p.

Described by the author as the first inside account of the Philip (Robert) Hanssen spy case, this book presents an overview of Hanssen's life and attempts to decipher the motivations behind his espionage for the Soviet Union. Considerable attention is given to his conservative Catholic religious beliefs and how they influenced his behavior. A distinguishing feature of the book is the extensive reproduction of Robert Hanssen's letters to his Soviet handlers. It also contains an excellent bibliography of popular works on espionage.

Herman, Michael. *Intelligence Power in Peace and War.* Cambridge, UK: Cambridge University Press, 1996. 414p.

Herman served twenty-five years in British intelligence and then went on to a career in academics. His account is both scholarly and readable. It is directed at a general audience rather than specialists. This is more than a book about espionage, although ample references to espionage, human intelligence gathering, and counterespionage are found here. In this book Herman combines a review of the literature on intelligence with personal experience and reflection. Topics covered include the evolution of intelligence; its component parts; and the effects of intelligence, accuracy, evaluation, and management. Distinguishing features include a discussion of intelligence in the 1990s and attention to the structure and operation of foreign intelligence organizations. It contains an excellent bibliographic guide to the scholarly literature on intelligence.

Kahn, David. *The Codebreakers: The Story of Secret Writing.* Rev. ed. New York: Macmillan, 1996. 1182p.

The author asserts that code breaking is the most important form of secret intelligence because it produces more trustworthy information than do spies. This book presents a comprehensive historical overview of espionage, beginning with hieroglyphics and ending with computers. Kahn's account is particularly valuable because of his ability to introduce the basic elements of cryptology in a clear and concise fashion. This information is presented both in stand-alone chapters and interspersed in the historical narrative. In addition to shedding light on the American experience with cryptology, attention is also given to the code breaking efforts of the British and Russians. This volume is an updating of the original 1967 edition.

Kalugin, Oleg. *The First Directorate.* New York: St. Martin's, 1994. 375p.

For thirty-two years, Oleg Kalugin served in the KGB, rising to the rank of major general and the position of chief of counterintelligence. His unit was responsible for recruiting spies within the CIA and penetrating the Italian and French intelligence services. His career in espionage began in New York in 1959 and ended in 1990 when, after several years in bureaucratic exile and now disenchanted with communism, Kalugin publicly exposed the inner workings of the KGB. He has excellent chapters on Kim Philby and on the structure, operation, and internal politics of the Soviet counterespionage bureaucracy. Kalugin is not a defector in the classic sense of the term, because he has spoken out after his retirement. He has been tried and convicted in absentia in Russia for his public revelations.

Knightly, Phillip. *The Second Oldest Profession: Spies and Spying in the Twentieth Century.* New York: Penguin, 1988. 436p.

The author presents a historical and interpretive overview of espionage activities in the twentieth century. Much of the attention is given to the Kim Philby affair and to presenting the author's interpretation of the motivations of such Soviet defectors as Oleg Penkovsky and Anatoliy Golitsyn. The treatment is more in depth on the British experience than it is on the American experience. The book contains information on the evolution and activities of the KGB as well as on CIA covert action. The concluding chapter takes up the issue of intelligence reform in the United States during the Carter administration.

Mahoney, M. H. *Women in Espionage: A Biographical Directory.* Santa Barbara, CA: ABC-CLIO, 1993. 253p.

This encyclopedia presents a survey of the most important women spies. The author consulted experts in clandestine operations in compiling the volume. Selections were based on the extent to which these women made major contributions to some aspect of the spy game. The contributions made by women to the study of intelligence has historically been undervalued, and these biographies provide an important corrective effort to this situation. Selections are presented from across time periods and across countries. A bibliography and index are included.

Martin, David. *Wilderness of Mirrors.* New York: Ballantine, 1980. 233p.

This book chronicles the careers of the two most prominent spy catchers in the American national security establishment: James Angleton and William Harvey. The phrase "wilderness of mirrors" refers to the distorting effect that the constant obsession with deception and misinformation can have on one's ability to construct a coherent view of the world one lives in. With everything suspect, there is little left to believe in, and conspiracy theories proliferate. Martin's account of their efforts to catch Soviet spies during the Cold War provides a detailed account of their personalities and the internal workings of the Central Intelligence Agency.

Melton, H. Keith. *The Ultimate Spy Book.* New York: DK Publishers, 1996. 176p.

A coffee table–type reference volume, this book presents a brief, engaging, and illustrated overview of espionage throughout history. Detailed coverage begins with the period surrounding World War I. The treatment of topics is extensive but brief; each topic is discussed in about two pages. There is an emphasis on photographs of key individuals and the tradecraft of intelligence. Vignettes are presented in boxed sections. Attention is given both to human and technological espionage.

Odom, William. *Fixing Intelligence: For a More Secure America.* New Haven, CT: Yale University Press, 2003. 230p.

The author is a former director of the National Security Agency. In this book he updates and expands upon the findings and conclusions of a study group he chaired in the late 1990s that produced a volume on intelligence reform for the National Institute for Public Policy in light of the events of September 11, 2001. Odom has separate chapters covering military intelligence, signals intelligence, imagery intelligence, human intelligence, and counterintelligence. He is particularly interested in managerial and structural problems. Odom notes in this regard that the major problem confronting discussions of intelligence reform is the lack of a commonly understood and accepted doctrine for intelligence organization and management. For example, he notes that counterintelligence is the most arcane, organizationally fragmented, and politically sensitive intelligence activity. Odom's conclusions are clearly stated and provide a solid perspective from which to address the contemporary debate over intelligence reform. He includes references to important intelligence reform studies and a helpful appendix on organizational organizations and processes.

O'Toole, G. T. A. *The Encyclopedia of American Intelligence and Espionage.* New York: Facts on File, 1988. 539p.

This volume provides an excellent source of information about individuals and organizations involved in intelligence throughout American history. A particular strength of the book is its attention to what might be described as second-order individuals within the contemporary period, individuals who appear in treatments of intelligence during the Cold War and Vietnam but whose biographies are not found elsewhere. The coverage extends beyond espionage to other aspects of intelligence. It contains an index and an extensive bibliography.

Peebles, Curtis. *The Corona Project: America's First Spy Satellites.* Annapolis, MD: Naval Institute Press, 1997. 351p.

The author, an internationally known aerospace historian, has written a readable and thorough account of the *Corona* reconnaissance satellite program. *Corona 1* was launched February 28, 1959; *Corona 145* was launched on May 25, 1972. Initially marked by a series of failures, *Corona* revolutionized U.S. national security policy. Its photos allowed American officials to accurately count the number of Soviet nuclear forces, thereby reducing fears of a surprise attack and permitting the United States to enter into arms control negotiations. Viewed in a broader context, Peebles asserts that the *Corona* project serves as a study in government-military-industry relations. The book contains an excellent appendix that lists significant data from all 145 *Corona* flights.

Petersen, Neal. *American Intelligence, 1775–1990: A Bibliographic Guide.* Claremont, CA: Regena, 1992. 406p.

A volume that advanced students of intelligence will find useful. It is a thorough bibliographic guide organized by subject matter but containing no commentary regarding the nature of the works. The first chapter presents an overview of intelligence, The next ten chapters cover the history of American intelligence in chronological fashion. The last two chapters deal with technology issues and the emerging agenda of intelligence. No specific entries are listed under espionage or spying, but relevant material can be found here.

Raviv, Dan, and Yossi Melman. *Every Spy a Prince: The Complete History of Israel's Intelligence Community.* Boston: Houghton Mifflin, 1990. 466p.

Widely considered one of the most authoritative accounts written on the inner workings of Israel's intelligence community, this book provides information on all three major branches of Israeli intelligence: the Mossad, which is responsible for foreign operations; AMAN, which is responsible for gathering military intelligence; and Shin Beth, which is responsible for internal security. Written in the aftermath of the Pollard affair, the book puts forward a generally supportive and positive history of Israeli intelligence while acknowledging the existence of problems.

Richelson, Jeffrey. *Foreign Intelligence Organizations.* Cambridge, MA: Ballinger, 1988. 330p.

Richelson is a prolific writer on intelligence; he has written several accounts of the U.S. intelligence community. His strength as an author is in presenting detailed organizational histories and discussing technology-related issues. This book is one of the few that examine non-U.S. intelligence organizations in detail. For each country Richelson discusses the origins of the intelligence organizations, reviews their structure and operation, and provides highlights. Where it is relevant he also include a discussion of liaisons with U.S. and other intelligence organizations. The countries covered are Great Britain, Canada, Italy, West Germany, France, Israel, Japan, and China.

Riebling, Mark. *Wedge: From Pearl Harbor to 9/11: How the Secret War between the FBI and CIA Has Endangered National Security.* New York: Simon and Schuster, 2002. 592p.

This is a reprint and updating of the book Riebling published in 1995. In it he examines what he sees as he pattern of cooperation, or more accurately noncooperation, between the FBI and CIA on intelligence matters. Riebling examines the Ames and Hanssen cases and shows how this lack of trust and information sharing slowed down the efforts to apprehend these spies. In this edition he extends his analysis to the events leading up to 9/11. Riebling's concern for the rivalry and competitive nature of the relationship between the members of the intelligence community is also frequently commented upon in studies of intelligence analysis and estimates.

Romerstein, Herbert, and Eric Breindel. *The VENONA Secrets: Exposing Soviet Espionage and America's Traitors.* Washington, DC: Regnery, 2000. 608p.

Written by two former staff members of the House Permanent Select Committee on Intelligence, the goal of this book is to correct what the authors describe as the conventional wisdom that members of the American Communist Party were left-wing heretics rather than disloyal conspirators engaged in espionage for the Soviet Union. Particular attention is given to the Rosenberg, Bentley, Chambers, and Soble spy rings. In the course of presenting this information the book seeks to establish that Soviet espionage activities in the United States were far more extensive than the public realizes. VENONA was the code name given to the program begun in 1943 that broke Soviet codes and allowed American officials to read Soviet communications. The cables intercepted were sent between 1940 and 1948. It is believed that the Soviets were informed by spies in 1944 that their codes had been broken. The United States began releasing VENONA intercepts in 1995.

Seth, Ronald. *Encyclopedia of Espionage.* Garden City, NY: Doubleday, 1972. 718p.

This volume presents an extensive discussion of espionage-related topics presented in alphabetical order by a prolific writer on intelligence matters. Each entry is followed by one or two bibliographic entries. The coverage of topics is global in scope and addresses both historical eras and the contemporary period. The coverage of topics is uneven, however. Some entries are brief and provide an overview of the subject, but others are quite lengthy and tend to focus on one episode in a spy's life or on one event. The discussion is detailed but needs to be supplemented by contextual material for the novice reader to understand its significance.

Shannon, Elaine, and Ann Blackman. *The Spy Next Door: The Extraordinary Secret Life of Robert Philip Hanssen, the Most Damaging FBI Agent in U.S. History.* Boston: Little, Brown, 2002. 247p.

The authors conducted more than 150 interviews in piecing together this history of Hanssen's career as a spy. Neither Hanssen, who is not permitted to give interviews until his debriefing by the government is complete, his lawyers, nor family members granted interviews to the authors. In their view only the espionage activities engaged in by Aldrich Ames and John Walker caused more damage to American national security. The account stresses Hanssen's actions more than the belated effort by the FBI to identify him as a spy. Shannon and Blackman attribute Hanssen's spying in large part to emotional wounds suffered much earlier in his life and not simply to money.

Shaw, Mark. *Miscarriage of Justice: The Jonathan Pollard Story.* St. Paul, MN: Paragon, 2001. 265p.

The Jonathan Jay Pollard spy case has generated more commentary than any recent case of espionage against the United States. In part this is because he spied for an ally (Israel) and because Israel seemed to abandon him once he was captured. It is also because of the severe sentence Pollard received. The book examines Pollard's activities as a spy as well as the domestic and international politics surrounding efforts to secure a pardon for him. This sympathetic account argues that Pollard has been treated improperly by the U.S. legal system and that his Fifth Amendment rights were violated. In presenting his argument Shaw draws comparisons with the case of Alfred Dreyfus, a Jewish French military official convicted of spying in the late 1800s, and the case of Theodore Hall, a scientist at Los Alamos, who gave information about the atomic bomb to the Soviet Union.

Smith, Richard. *OSS: The Secret History of America's First Intelligence Agency.* Berkeley: University of California Press, 1972. 458p.

Relying heavily upon interviews with OSS (Office of Strategic Services) veterans, Smith has authored a compelling history of this first American intelligence agency. The book was written at the height of public suspicions of the CIA, and one of Smith's goals is to help readers address the paradox inherent in intelligence work that requires it to serve the national interest yet engage in actions that are morally and ethically questionable. Of particular concern to Smith are loosely made claims condemning the CIA or championing it as the defender of the national interest. OSS exploits against Germany and Japan are recorded in the book, and attention is given to William Donovan, the founder of the OSS.

Stafford, David. *The Silent Game: The Real World of Imaginary Spies.* Rev. ed. Athens: University of Georgia Press, 1991. 257p.

This unique book explores the world of imaginary spies and spy writers. It is a history of spy fiction. The author presents a compelling narrative that links the lives of these writers to the spies they create. Among those whose works receive attention are John Buchan, Compton Mackenzie, Somerset Maugham, Ian Fleming, and Graham Greene. All of these individuals had real-life careers in intelligence. A central theme of Stafford's work is that although these spies wrote about spying, their primary purpose was not to document the world of intelligence. Instead, these authors used intelligence as a vehicle for addressing broader themes such as war, international crises, and imperial decline.

Stevenson, William. *A Man Called Intrepid.* New York: Ballantine, 1976. 541p.

One of the most successful espionage and intelligence operations run during World War II was conducted by the British in the United States. Sir William Stephenson was Intrepid. Working out of New York City under the cover of British Security Coordination, Stephenson was the primary channel by which British intelligence was given to the United States. Stephenson also served as a key confidant of William Donovan, who headed the Office of Strategic Services (OSS), and he used his influence to help shape American thinking on what type of intelligence organization the United States needed.

Stober, Dan, and Ian Hoffman. *Convenient Spy: Wen Ho Lee and the Politics of Nuclear Espionage.* New York: Simon and Schuster, 2001. 384p.

Wen Ho Lee was a Chinese-American working at the Los Alamos labs who was arrested for spying. Plea bargains resulted in virtually all charges against him being dropped, as the government's case was riddled with problems. This book is as much about the attempt to prosecute Lee as it is about his alleged spying. The authors conclude that Lee's explanations for his activities, "backing up his computer files on tape," is undercut by critical facts. At the same time they acknowledge that all of the alternative theories, including the suggestion that he was spying for China or Taiwan, are inadequate. With regard to the overall politics of the Lee case, the authors conclude that it demonstrated too much of a willingness on the part of the government to sacrifice freedoms in the futile search for a spy.

Vise, David A. *The Bureau and the Mole: The Unmasking of Robert Philip Hanssen, the Most Dangerous Double Agent in FBI History.* New York: Grove Press, 2002. 285p.

Vise's account of the Hanssen spy case is notable for its inclusion of many pieces of original correspondence between Hanssen and his Russian handlers, e-mails, and other correspondence authored by Hanssen. Vise attributes Hanssen's espionage both to the pursuit of money and an emotional response to his treatment by the FBI, which he viewed as a corrupt father figure. In the epilogue he notes that every time he was passed over for promotion, Hanssen responded by "attempting grand, daring feats of espionage." Vise's account of the Hanssen case also gives considerable attention to the actions of FBI Director Louis Freeh and his clashes with President Bill Clinton's White House over how to proceed on the Hanssen case.

Wise, David. *Nightmover: How Aldrich Ames Sold the CIA to the KGB for $4.6 Million.* New York: HarperCollins, 1995. 356p.

Wise, a prolific author of works on intelligence, details the espionage activities of Aldrich Ames and his arrest. The book begins with Ames's capture and then traces his career backward. Wise also gives attention to the CIA and FBI efforts to find the mole in its midst. This account provides vivid insight into the highly bureaucratic and compartmentalized nature of intelligence organizations and the impact this has on counterintelligence work. In presenting Ames's story, the author provides detailed information about the process by which potential spies are identified and recruited, along with the techniques used to pass information along.

Wise, David. *Spy: The Inside Story of How the FBI's Robert Hanssen Betrayed America*. New York: Random House, 2002. 320p.

Wise has written widely on intelligence matters over his career, including the *Invisible Government* (1964) and the *Politics of Lying* (1973). What distinguishes Wise's account of the Hanssen spy affair is this placement of the case within a more historical context. Wise notes that the FBI's problems with foreign spies in their midst can be traced as far back as 1962. The flawed efforts to uncover these spies are recounted. Of particular merit is Wise's discussion of how a CIA agent was wrongly identified as the spy in this case. In his account of Hanssen's behavior, Wise shares with other authors an emphasis on Hanssen's unstable personality.

Wright, Peter. *Spy Catcher: The Candid Autobiography of a Senior Intelligence Officer*. New York: Viking, 1987. 392p.

Peter Wright retired in 1976 after working for two decades in British intelligence. He was an officer in MI-5, which is roughly equivalent to the FBI and is charged with counterespionage in the name of protecting British state secrets from foreign spies and preventing domestic subversion and sabotage. His account provides insight into the sharing of information between Western intelligence organizations. It also provides a firsthand account of British efforts to deal with Soviet penetrations of its intelligence organizations.

## Journal Articles

Berkowitz, Bruce, and Allan E. Goodman. "Why Spy—And How—In the 1990s?" *Orbis* 36 (1992): 269–281.

Written shortly after the fall of the Berlin Wall in 1989, this article is important because it makes an early post–Cold War case for the continued importance of intelligence and intelligence agencies. Where later accounts would stress the growing importance of economic espionage to national security, Berkowitz and Goodman make the case for the continued need for military-oriented intelligence. They also present an agenda for intelligence reform that includes liberating the intelligence budget from the Defense Department, enhancing the power of the Director of Central Intelligence, and improving relations between the users and producers of intelligence. This article does not directly address espionage in the post–Cold War era but does provide an important reference point for understanding the larger debate over intelligence reform of which the future of espionage is a major part.

Clarke, Duncan. **"Israel's Economic Espionage in the United States."** *Journal of Palestine Studies* 27 (1998) 4: 20–36.

Relying heavily upon American government documents and newspaper accounts, Clarke describes the scope of Israeli economic espionage in the United States. He attributes four motives to Israel in this matter: strengthening its industrial base, selling information for profit, trading information with other states, and confidence that it will not be punished and that its espionage efforts will not affect U.S.-Israel strategic relations. Although Israel is not the only state to engage in economic espionage in the United States, it is seen as being the most effective. Examples given include espionage directed at gaining state-of-the-art optical equipment for aerial surveillance, blueprints for the F-16 fighter, and nuclear-grade weapons uranium. The article concludes with a discussion of the reasons for the lax response to evidence of Israeli economic espionage. Again, although the circumstances are unique, that tepid U.S. response is seen as being commonplace.

Demarest, Geoffrey. **"Espionage in International Law."** *Denver Journal of International Law and Policy* 24 (1996): 321–348.

The author notes that intelligence gathering, including espionage, is a well-established and accepted practice in world politics. At the same time it is widely acknowledged that spying as an activity is illegal, and spies can be punished. In this work Demarest explores the dual nature of espionage. He correctly notes that to the extent that international law has addressed espionage, it has done so in a wartime context. The conventional approach is to treat peacetime espionage as an issue of domestic law. Going back to the writing of Hugo Grotius and moving forward to the 1977 Geneva Protocols, Demarest traces the manner in which spying and spies are treated in international law. The Francis Gary Powers U-2 incident is discussed in some depth as an example of peacetime spying. Of particular concern to Demarest is the peacetime tendency to focus on trying to control the target of espionage or the cover used rather than the act of espionage.

Fraumann, Edwin. **"Economic Espionage: Security Missions Redefined."** *Public Administration Review* 57 (1997): 303–309.

Increasingly, espionage organizations are directing their energies to obtaining economic, scientific, and technological intelligence. The author notes that the United States is particularly vulnerable to economic espionage because American firms and research centers rely heavily upon computer systems and electronic networks to process and store information. Asserting that more than fifty states engage in economic espionage, Fraumann presents an overview of intrusive and nonintrusive methods used to obtain economic intelligence. After giving thumbnail sketches of economic espionage activities by various states, he divides states into three categories of threat depending upon their technical capabilities and their level of expertise. The greatest danger is posed by those possessing both: France, Japan, Germany, China, and Israel. The second half of the article presents an overview of the intelligence organizations attempting to stop economic espionage in the United States and of the federal statutes relating to economic espionage.

Hitz, Frederick. **"Unleashing the Rogue Elephant: September 11 and Letting the CIA Be the CIA."** *Harvard Journal of Law and Public Policy* 25 (2002): 756–781.

Hitz served as inspector general of the CIA from 1990 to 1998. His well-reasoned and balanced article examines the question of whether or not the CIA and other intelligence agencies have been unwisely constrained from pursuing terrorist targets by Cold War–era reforms. Of particular importance to the conduct of espionage today are calls for loosening restraints on employing "dirty assets" for intelligence gathering and covert action purposes and removing impediments to using journalists, academics, and clergy as covers for intelligence gathering operations. Hitz examines these issues along with the prohibition on assassination and giving the CIA domestic law enforcement powers. With regard to the first issue he notes that to some degree the issue is misleading because by definition spies are liars, lawbreakers, and traitors. This work is especially valuable because it presents a discussion of key congressional actions, including the USA PATRIOT Act, and executive branch proclamations that govern the actions of the intelligence community.

Johnson, Loch. **"Spies, September/October 2000."** *Foreign Policy* 120 (2002): 18–28.

In this article Johnson examines a series of questions that are pertinent to making a judgment about the relevance of espionage to national security in the post–Cold War era. He asks whether spying is a Cold War anachronism and concludes that believing it to be so is just wishful thinking. He then notes that with the end of the Cold War we Americans need to look more closely at the points of convergence and divergence in national interest between intelligence agencies. No longer can we assume that an enemy of our enemy is a friend. Johnson examines the issue of economic espionage and finds that although it is of increased importance today, it may be premature to see it as more important than traditional military intelligence concerns. He finds that technology has made spying both easier and harder and that although open intelligence has become more plentiful, there is still a need for the classic spy. Finally, Johnson concludes that democracy and espionage are not incompatible.

King, Robert. **"Treason and Traitors: Ethical Implications of Espionage."** *Society* 35 (1998): 329–339.

This article begins with the provocative observation that where once espionage was universally treated as the most despicable crime, in some quarters it has come to be seen as a "forgivable" offense and one made understandable by circumstances. King rightly notes that treason is one of the most fascinating intellectual and ethical issues ever debated. What is treason? Why do people betray their country? When is treason justified? King observes that there never has been a clear answer as to when treason is wrong and when it is not. In developing his argument the author examines fictional and real-world cases of espionage and treason ranging from Aldrich Ames, who spied for the Soviet Union against the United States, to Count Claus von Stauffenberg, who tried to kill Adolph Hitler. The bulk of his account focuses on the actions of Donald Maclean, Guy Burgess, and Kim Philby, who spied for the Soviet Union against Great Britain. King concludes that they should be viewed with scorn and not pity.

# Government Documents

United States House of Representatives, Permanent Select Committee on Intelligence. November 30, 1994. **Report of Investigation: The Aldrich Ames Espionage Case.** Washington, DC: U.S. Government Printing Office. 33p.

This is the unclassified summary of the CIA inspector general's report. It contains an executive summary and organizes information according to a series of questions. They include the following. "What was Ames's career history?" "What were the strengths and weaknesses of Ames's strategy?" "Was the counterespionage investigation coordinated properly with the FBI?" "Was the mole hunt properly managed?"

United States Senate, Select Committee on Intelligence. November 1, 1994. **An Assessment of the Aldrich Ames Espionage Case and Its Implications for U.S. Intelligence.** Washington, DC: U.S. Government Printing Office. 136p.

This report is broken down into three parts. Part One presents a factual summary of the Ames case. It is organized around a chronology of his career prior to engaging in espionage and after beginning to do so. Part Two contains the conclusions and recommendations of the Senate Intelligence Committee. Part Three is an appendix that contains CIA documents and the transcript of an interview Chairman Dennis DeConcini had with Ames. Their conversation is particularly revealing of Ames's thinking, the conduct of espionage operations, and the day-to-day workings of the intelligence community.

# Electronic Sources

**Canadian Security Intelligence Service**
http://www.csis-scrs.gc.ca

This is the site of the Canadian Security Intelligence Service. Every year since 1991 it has issued a public report regarding its activities. Counterintelligence is a frequent topic of these reports. The 2001 report contains a discussion on economic intelligence, transnational criminal activity, proliferation, and information operations. The Canadian site is valuable for those interested in comparative espionage and provides an interesting counterexample to the United States's experience and practice of intelligence work.

**Center for the Study of Intelligence, Central Intelligence Agency**
http://www.odci.gov/csi/studies.html

The Center for the Study of Intelligence publishes a declassified journal, *Studies in Intelligence.* This site gives electronic access to the journal. There is an index of declassified articles going back to 1992. Several of the articles deal with espionage.

**Center for the Study of Intelligence, Central Intelligence Agency**
http://www.cia.gov/csi/

This site also links to the Center for the Study of Intelligence. It provides a listing of publications on various intelligence topics. Among those involving espionage are one on VENONA that details Soviet espionage in the United States from 1939 to 1957 and one on CORONA that provides a historical overview of the United States's first satellite program.

**Federal Bureau of Investigation**
http://www.fbi.gov/libref.htm

This links to the library and reference page of the FBI. One of the links is to famous espionage cases. Included are case studies of Robert Hanssen, Aldrich Ames, the atomic spies, Nazi spying in the United States, and espionage in the defense industry.

**Federation of Atomic Scientists**
http://www.fas.org/siteindx.html

This links to the Intelligence Resource Program of the Federation of Atomic Scientists. It is a selection of official and unofficial resources on the structure, operation, and functions of intelligence organizations. Specific links include terrorism, worldwide intelligence agencies, imagery, intelligence operations, and official documents.

**International Spy Museum**
http://www.spymuseum.org/index.asp

This links to the International Spy Museum, located at 800 F Street NW in Washington, D.C. Its mission is to educate the public about spying in such a way as to foster an understanding of the contribution that espionage has made to current and past events. The focus is on human espionage. In addition to providing engaging and interactive exhibits, the International Spy Museum is developing an extensive outreach program that will help schoolteachers develop lesson plans and acquire resources that can be used to enhance their classroom teaching.

**National Security Agency**
http://www.nsa.gov

This is the homepage of the National Security Agency. It provides links to several topics related to espionage. There are links to the National Cryptologic Museum, the history of cryptology, and World War II cryptology.

**National Security Archive**
http://www.gwu.edu/~nsarchiv

The National Security Archive is maintained at George Washington University. It is an independent nongovernmental research institute and library that collects and publishes declassified documents acquired through the Freedom of Information Act. One of its efforts is a U.S. Intelligence Policy Document Project under the direction of Jeffrey Richelson. This site contains information on the National Reconnaissance Office, the National Security Agency, and U.S. satellite imagery.

**United States Central Intelligence Agency**
http://www.cia.gov/cia/publications/pubs.html

This site contains links to a number of useful CIA publications on intelligence and espionage. In particular there are links to articles on intelligence in the War of Independence, African-American contributions to Union intelligence during the Civil War, the Office of Strategic Services, and a lengthy listing of books and articles on intelligence.

# Glossary

**agent**   This term has two different meanings. When used to refer to the FBI, an agent is a professional law enforcement official. When it is used in the context of CIA clandestine operations, an agent is the person recruited by the CIA to engage in spying; it does not refer to the CIA official.

**analytical intelligence**   Analyzed information becomes intelligence only after it has been analyzed, subjected to systematic examination, and evaluated. Analytical intelligence may take several forms including basic intelligence, current intelligence, and estimative intelligence.

**basic intelligence**   Factual and fundamental intelligence about another state. It is relatively unchanging and constitutes a type of encyclopedic background picture that can be built upon by intelligence analysts.

**cipher**   A system of secret writing that utilizes a prearranged scheme to prevent its detection and comprehension by the uninitiated.

**clandestine collection**   The secret collection of intelligence. It is contrasted with the overt collection of intelligence, whereby intelligence is collected through publicly available means.

**codes**   Symbols that have a predetermined meaning and are used for secrecy in transmitting a message.

**collection**   The acquisition of information in any manner. Information may be collected through direct observation, through liaison with official agencies, through public sources, or through clandestine means.

**counterespionage**   More broadly, this is often referred to as counterintelligence. Two tasks are involved: first, the protection of one's own secrets; second, the neutralization and apprehension of spies who are employed by foreign powers.

**counterintelligence**   This is an overarching category of activity that includes counterespionage. Counterintelligence is intelligence gathered to thwart espionage, other intelligence activities, sabotage, or assassination conducted by a hostile foreign power or group.

**covert action** Clandestine activity designed to effect a situation in another country. The key to success is that the identity of the sponsoring country or organization is not revealed. Covert action is different from clandestine collection, which seeks to acquire information but not to influence events in the target state.

**cryptanalysis** The science of translating secret messages into plain text. It may operate either deductively or inductively. In the former type the analysis hinges on the detection of patterns that allow analysts to move from recurring combinations to more unique ones. Inductive analysis is based on hunches to possible words in the message that produce leads to the meaning of the message. Cryptanalysis generally is treated as an applied science, whereas cryptography is abstract and theoretical in nature.

**cryptography** The abstract science of secret writing. Mathematical equations are often used for establishing its basic parameters and translation rules.

**current intelligence** A category of analytical intelligence that stresses up-to-date information that is of immediate interest to policymakers.

**damage assessment** An evaluation of the impact of a compromise in security that results in the loss of secret information. The assessment includes both a judgment regarding the benefits gained by an adversary and the impact on one's own collection capabilities, and ways to prevent its recurrence.

**dead drops** A method of exchanging intelligence, instructions, and money between a spy and his or her handler. Dead drops are exchanges that do not involve actual physical contact between the two persons involved. Rather, a location is chosen for the exchange and a signal used to indicate that material has been put in place to be picked up. Dead drops are seen as the safest way of making an exchange.

**defector** An individual in the employ of a foreign government who is either induced to come over to one's own side or does so voluntarily.

**dirty tricks** A catchall phrase used to describe activities undertaken as part of a covert action plan. Dirty tricks are designed to disrupt a target's ability to perform some important function. Espionage is important in the use of dirty tricks because it may provide information about a target's vulnerabilities.

**disinformation** False information that is deliberately provided to an adversary in order to confuse him or her. This is different from noise, which is random information that the adversary picks up and which makes analysis difficult. Once a spy has been discovered, intelligence organizations may use the spy to transmit disinformation back to the adversary. One of the major challenges facing intelligence organizations is to determine what pieces of information provided to them by defectors are valid and which ones constitute disinformation.

**economic espionage**   Espionage directed at acquiring foreign economic intelligence. It targets both governments and private businesses. Of interest are such items as production methods, financial and taxation systems, research and development projects, dual use technologies, and government contracts.

**espionage**   Also referred to as spying, this is the secret collection of information. Often referred to today under the heading of clandestine collection. It may be carried out either through technical means or by agents who infiltrate key organizations in order to acquire documents, photographs, or other material of value.

**handler**   This refers to the intelligence official who manages a spy. The handler is the spy's point of contact with the intelligence organization he or she is working for.

**information**   Also referred to as raw intelligence. It is unanalyzed data that have been collected but have not yet been evaluated for their reliability, validity, and meaning.

**intelligence**   Evaluated information. Until information has been assessed for its reliability and validity and then evaluated for its significance it remains raw data. One of the major fallacies of intelligence is that facts are self-interpreting or that they "speak for themselves."

**intelligence community**   Those national security bureaucracies in the United States that are involved in the collection, analysis, and dissemination of intelligence. The most prominent members of the intelligence community include the CIA, National Security Agency, Defense Intelligence Agency, FBI, and Bureau of Intelligence and Research within the State Department. One of the major problems facing the U.S. intelligence community is the effective coordination of action by two or more agencies; each of these organizations has its own bureaucratic culture and set of values as well as a unique sense of mission and purpose.

**intelligence cycle**   The functional stages by which information is acquired, turned into intelligence, and made available to policymakers. Typically the steps involved are described as tasking, collection, processing and evaluation, reporting, and feedback.

**mole**   A spy who has been secretly placed within an adversary's intelligence service or other important national security organization. The mole may be quiet or inactive for a long period of time before becoming active and providing intelligence.

**noise**   In gathering information, intelligence agencies must distinguish between signals and noise. Signals are valid indicators of an adversary's intentions or capabilities. Noise is the clutter of irrelevant background information that surrounds any activity. It can be seen as similar to the static one encounters in trying to tune in a distant radio station.

**open source information**   Information may be collected from a variety of sources. Open source information refers to information that is obtained from public sources. Its collection requires no deception or espionage. Open sources include the Internet, newspapers, journals, speeches, and government documents. Clandestine collection is the other broadly defined means of collecting information.

**polygraph test**   This is commonly referred to as a lie detector test. It is used to establish the truthfulness, loyalty, and reliability of an individual. Polygraph tests are not used uniformly throughout the national security bureaucracies, and when they are used, successful spies are known to have passed polygraph tests. Many consider the most useful way to look at a polygraph is as a deterrent to spying rather than a device than can catch spies.

**secret information**   A security designation given to information, which, if disclosed, could reasonably be expected to cause serious harm to national security.

**signals intelligence**   Often referred to as SIGINT. Signals intelligence is intelligence derived from signals intercepts coming from communications intelligence, electronic intelligence, and foreign instrumentation signals intelligence, regardless of how it is transmitted.

**spy ring**   A group of spies who are organized around a central individual or who work closely with one another in obtaining secret information.

**strategic intelligence**   A category of analytical intelligence that focuses on information related to an adversary's strategic forces. Typically, this involves forces with a nuclear capability. Strategic intelligence encompasses information about both weapons systems and military doctrine.

**surveillance**   The process of shadowing, observing, and monitoring the actions of an individual who is suspected of being engaged in espionage. Surveillance may take place through human or technical means.

**tasking**   The first stage in the intelligence cycle. Tasking is the process by which intelligence needs are identified.

**technological espionage**   This form of espionage involves the collection of information through scientific and technical means such as by monitoring or intercepting foreign commercial or military communications, satellite transmissions, and weapons telemetry. It is contrasted with human espionage or spying.

**walk-in**   A spy who volunteers his or her services to an adversary's intelligence organization. This is the opposite of a spy who is singled out and recruited by an intelligence organization.

# Index

# About the Author

**Glenn Hastedt** received his Ph.D. in political science from Indiana University. He is professor of political science and head of the Department of Political Science at James Madison University. He conducts research on U.S. foreign policy with an emphasis on intelligence policy issues. Among his publications are *American Foreign Policy: Past, Present, Future,* (fifth edition; 2003); *Controlling Intelligence* (1991); and, with Kay Knickrehm, *International Politics in a Changing World* (2003).

LaVergne, TN USA
12 January 2010
169759LV00003B/80/P